IMAGES
of America

LAKE COUNTY
1871–1960

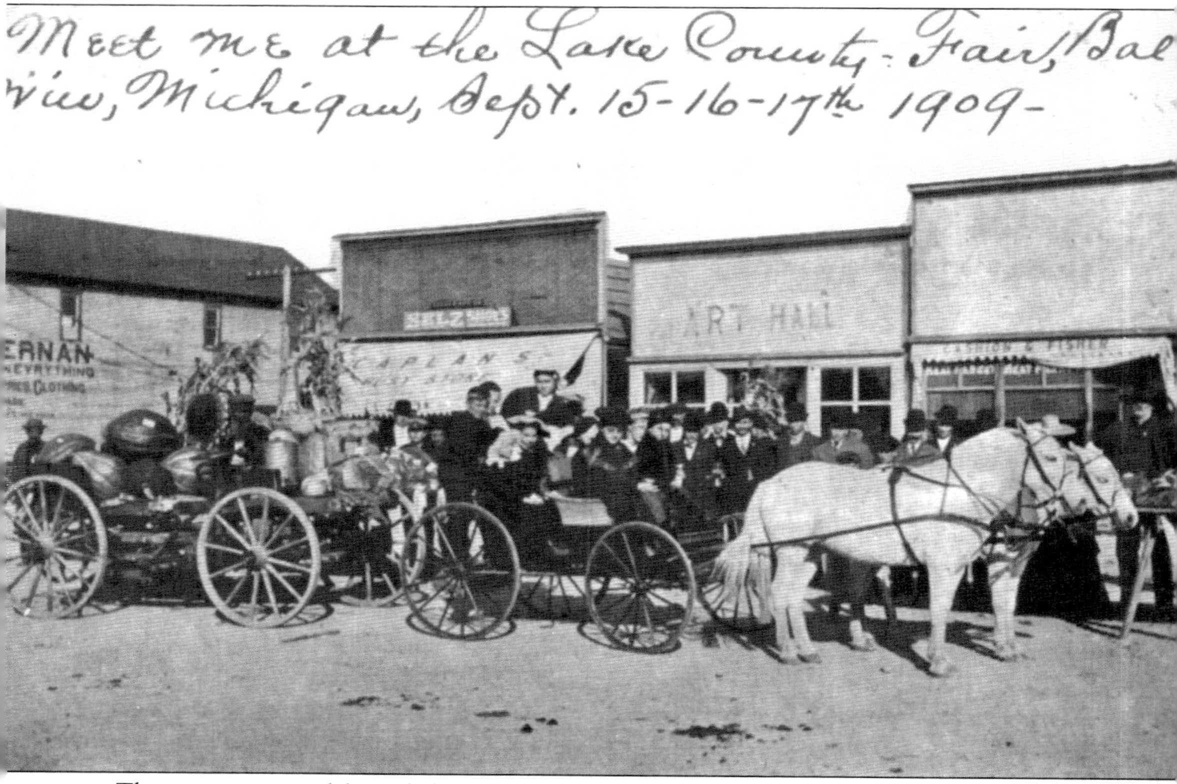

The community celebrated the culmination of the harvest with the Lake County Fair. This postcard illustrates the bounty grown by area farmers. In addition to the displays of vegetables submitted for judging, there were baseball games, horse races, free street vaudeville, dancing, and variety shows. Moving pictures were a special highlight of the 1912 fair. People from all around Lake County came for three days of fun and entertainment. (Courtesy of Bruce Micinski.)

On the cover: Andrew Bradford, born in 1842, moved to Lake County in 1889. A Civil War veteran, an early operator of the Arlington Hotel, a construction supervisor, and a fishing guide, he later served as president for the village of Baldwin as well as justice of the peace. Earning the nickname of "Old Brad," his photograph was used for posters advertising fine fishing on the Pere Marquette River. (Courtesy of Michael Oostmeyer.)

IMAGES
of America

LAKE COUNTY
1871–1960

Lake County Historical Society

ARCADIA
PUBLISHING

ISBN 978-0-7385-6017-5

Published by Arcadia Publishing
Charleston, South Carolina

Printed in the United States of America

Library of Congress Control Number: 2009925350

For all general information contact Arcadia Publishing at:
Telephone 843-853-2070
Fax 843-853-0044
E-mail sales@arcadiapublishing.com
For customer service and orders:
Toll-Free 1-888-313-2665

Visit us on the Internet at www.arcadiapublishing.com

The Lake County Historical Society dedicates this book to all those who recorded bits of history and thus preserved them for future historians.

Contents

ACKNOWLEDGMENTS

A comprehensive pictorial history book of Lake County has been on the Lake County Historical Society's list of things to do for many years. When approached by Arcadia Publishing, we saw the opportunity to fulfill this dream. A core team of authors was formed by the group. This team was led by Bruce T. Micinski, president of the society and lead author. Coauthors were Paul Bigford, Jill Engelman, Darci Maldonado, and Susan Bradford Tripp. This team gathered, scanned, and researched many treasured photographs and postcards of Lake County.

We would like to acknowledge the many people who helped make this book come true. First, we thank past society members who are no longer here, yet contributed so much—Marie Moore, Paul Rudbeck, and Harold Allison among others. Marie Moore collected countless stories of Lake County and had them typed for *Lake County: A Collection of Historical Writings Book I* and *Lake County: A Collection of Historical Writings Book II*. Paul Rudbeck did extensive research on Marlborough (Marlboro) and brought this ghost town to life. And last, Harold Allison printed his own booklets containing fascinating stories of Lake County. Our history could not have been written without their research.

Also, we thank local authors. Ann Chase helped with writing and advice. Charles Johnson wrote numerous booklets on early settlements, schools, and logging towns. Special thanks go to Donald Baut, vice president of the society, for his expert advice, many years of collecting and recording newspaper articles, and birth and death records; to the *Lake County Star* for recording history since 1873; to Jane Miller, who is a walking encyclopedia of Baldwin history and enabled the authors to tell the county's story with accuracy; and to Maude Bigford and Kathy Oostmeyer for their proofreading. We express our gratitude to all the individuals and organizations that allowed us to archive their treasured photographs for this project and to all society members who supported our efforts. Finally, we thank all the settlers who had the dream of making Lake County their home, for they are the ones who made our history.

INTRODUCTION

For thousands of years, the Potawatomi, Chippewa, and Ottawa tribes occupied the lands known as northwestern lower Michigan. They called themselves Anishinabek, the "first people." Their footprints were light ones. In 1763–1764, Alexander Henry, English colonist, fur trader, and explorer, traveled through west Michigan and crossed what is now Lake County. The Homestead Act of 1862, enacted during the Civil War, provided that an adult citizen who had never borne arms against the United States could claim 160 acres of surveyed government land. In 1863, Lorenzo Conklin settled in section 34 of Chase Township in Lake County and became the first pioneer to start a new life here. Union soldiers were some of the earliest to come. In the southwest corner of the county, 12 families of Union soldiers, including Charles Carr and Benjamin Barnett, staked their claims. More veterans settled in Chase and Luther on the east side of the county.

In Europe dreams of religious freedom, new job opportunities, and a climate in northern Michigan that reminded them of their homeland drew more families to this pristine land. In 1877, immigrants such as Jesse and Sarah Bradford moved from England and settled in Baldwin with their 11 offspring. They stayed to raise 15 children to adulthood.

Lake County, first named Aischum County in honor of a Potawatomi chief, was formally organized in 1871. Early surveyors recorded that Lake County had vast tracts of virgin white pine. As a result, logging and railroad companies crisscrossed the land making a checkerboard of the county. For three decades the timber industry boomed. Lumber camps were small villages with the sawmill, stores, horse barns, woodworking shops, and a blacksmith. After the lumber companies cut the pine forests and moved on, new centers of commerce and industry blossomed. Not all of them were destined to endure. Following the discovery of marl deposits in North Lake, south of Baldwin, Fredrick Farnsworth, a Detroit banker and investor, dreamed of building a metropolis to rival any in the state of Michigan. By 1905, there were 400 settlers in Marlborough (Marlboro), 200 of them employed in the cement plant built on the west shore of North Lake. The village boomed. Marlborough became a town of class with an opera house, streetlights, school, post office, mercantile, and an 88-room hotel. Just as loggers ran out of white pine to cut, Marlborough ran out of marl. By 1910, Marlborough was bankrupt, its buildings torn down, and the cement plant in rubble. The immigrants left to find their fortunes elsewhere. Haunting ruins still remain in this ghost town covered by moss and scrub trees.

A dream of a different nature was born in 1912. Four white couples, Erastus and Adelbert Branch, and their wives Flora and Isabelle, along with Wilbur and Mayme Lemon, and Alvin and Modolin Wright, purchased 2,700 acres around Idlewild Lake. They developed it as a resort community without prejudice toward African Americans in a time when segregation was the norm. The Idlewild Resort Company featured desirable lakefront properties, hotels, and a clubhouse. The resort became a safe and tranquil place for blacks. Chicago surgeon Dr. Daniel Williams built a cottage there. In later years, celebrity performers came and a vibrant nightlife grew and prospered. The popularity of the area reached a peak in the 1950s. Famous singers Della Reese and Ella Fitzgerald appeared in the Flamingo and Paradise Clubs. Heavyweight boxer Joe Louis had a training camp in Idlewild. Today a new cultural center showcases the resurgence of Idlewild, as it prepares for its 100th anniversary.

Other businesses, such as the Lake-Osceola State Bank, remain deeply rooted in the community. Founded in 1908 as the Lake County Bank, partners Curtis W. MacPhail and Elias L. Cole hired a young man named Robert J. Smith as their first bank employee in Baldwin. Today Smith's descendants still manage this fine establishment.

In 1889, a Christian visionary named Martin Gustave Johnson constructed a simple log cabin on Big Bass Lake. Living the life of a recluse, he farmed the land, painted landscapes, celebrated nature, and photographed it all with his hand-built large-format camera. In thanks to the Chicago Hyde Park YMCA for providing him shelter in prior years, he donated his land in northern Lake County to the YMCA to build a summer camp for boys. His home is now a museum located at Skinner Park in Irons.

Another artist named Raymond Overholzer came to Lake County from Ohio and built a hunter's cabin on the Pere Marquette River. He filled this cabin with white pine stumps and roots salvaged from fields and rivers. He crafted them into tables, chairs, and beds unlike anything ever seen. Today the Shrine of the Pines sits on the bank of the Pere Marquette River as a rustic furniture museum.

These are but a few of the stories embedded in our history. Many thousands of men, women, and children have contributed their hard labor, their visions, and their talents to a county that took in people from all walks of life. More than 60 settlements have been identified by members of the Lake County Historical Society over the years. Although many of the towns have vanished, the county seat of Baldwin remains. Named for Michigan's governor Henry Baldwin in 1872, today Baldwin is home to a variety of stores, gas stations, churches, schools, a bank, and a remodeled courthouse.

By 1950, Lake County had earned a well-deserved reputation as both a premier residential and vacation spot. A total of 156 lakes and 46 trout streams, along with the resurgent forests planted by the Civilian Conservation Corp in the 1930s, enhance the scenic beauty of the area. Frequent encounters with wildlife delight the naturalist. Numerous private clubs, resorts, motels, restaurants, and sport shops cater to tourists and sportsmen.

Since 1983, the Lake County Historical Society has collected historical documents, stories, photographs, and other memorabilia. Using it as a base of information, the authors have endeavored to accurately relate the history of Lake County. Stories change as time passes and memories fade. To the best of our knowledge, the historical information and personal recollections related in this book have been faithfully represented.

With a copy of the book in hand, prepare to relax and enjoy the journey through Lake County's history as illustrated and described in the following chapters.

One

EARLY DAYS

In 1840, when the county was named Aischum County, Henry David Thoreau's Concord, Massachusetts, had been an incorporated village for over two centuries. History does not tell the name of the first European to walk through the majestic white pine that sheltered the clear and free-flowing rivers of the county. Archaeologists have dated county Native American arrowheads to 6,000 years ago, and undoubtedly there are older objects to be found. Certain areas of the county are rich in these artifacts and serve as testimony to the hunting-based communities that were the original settlements.

The county was first surveyed in 1839. Originally named after a Native American chief (Aischum), by March 18, 1843, the county was renamed Lake County. While one can assume trappers and early traders passed through the county for many decades, the first recorded settler was Lorenzo Conklin in 1863, settling in the Chase Township area. John Nelson arrived in the Luther area, and other settlers arrived soon thereafter in the Carr Settlement area on the western side of the county. By 1870, the population of Lake County had swollen to 548 people.

White pine was the early attraction. Logging camps, followed later by logging railroads, sprang up like morels after a May rain. Towns like Edgetts, Summittville, Foxville, Renoe, Haaks, Lions Crossing, Ruggles, and Canfields were established around mills and along railroads. Early chroniclers noted that the population of Chase would routinely swell to 5,000 on weekends as the logging camps emptied for a brief respite from long days of strenuous labor in the deep woods. Vanished mill towns like Stearns Siding had as many as 2,700 residents at their peak. Hundreds of millions of board feet of lumber were dragged, hauled, or floated down rivers to distant mills, and on to market. Many midwestern and western towns were built with Michigan pine. It is believed that local lumber was used to help rebuild Chicago after it burned.

After the supposedly inexhaustible white pine was logged off, the county was barren of most trees. Due to the logging, streams were torn up by log drives and their banks were eroded. There was a loss of shade trees, and efforts were made to straighten the rivers by blasting through some bends. As the mills closed down some of the workers elected to stay on and farm. Others worked for the railroads or opened businesses in towns and villages.

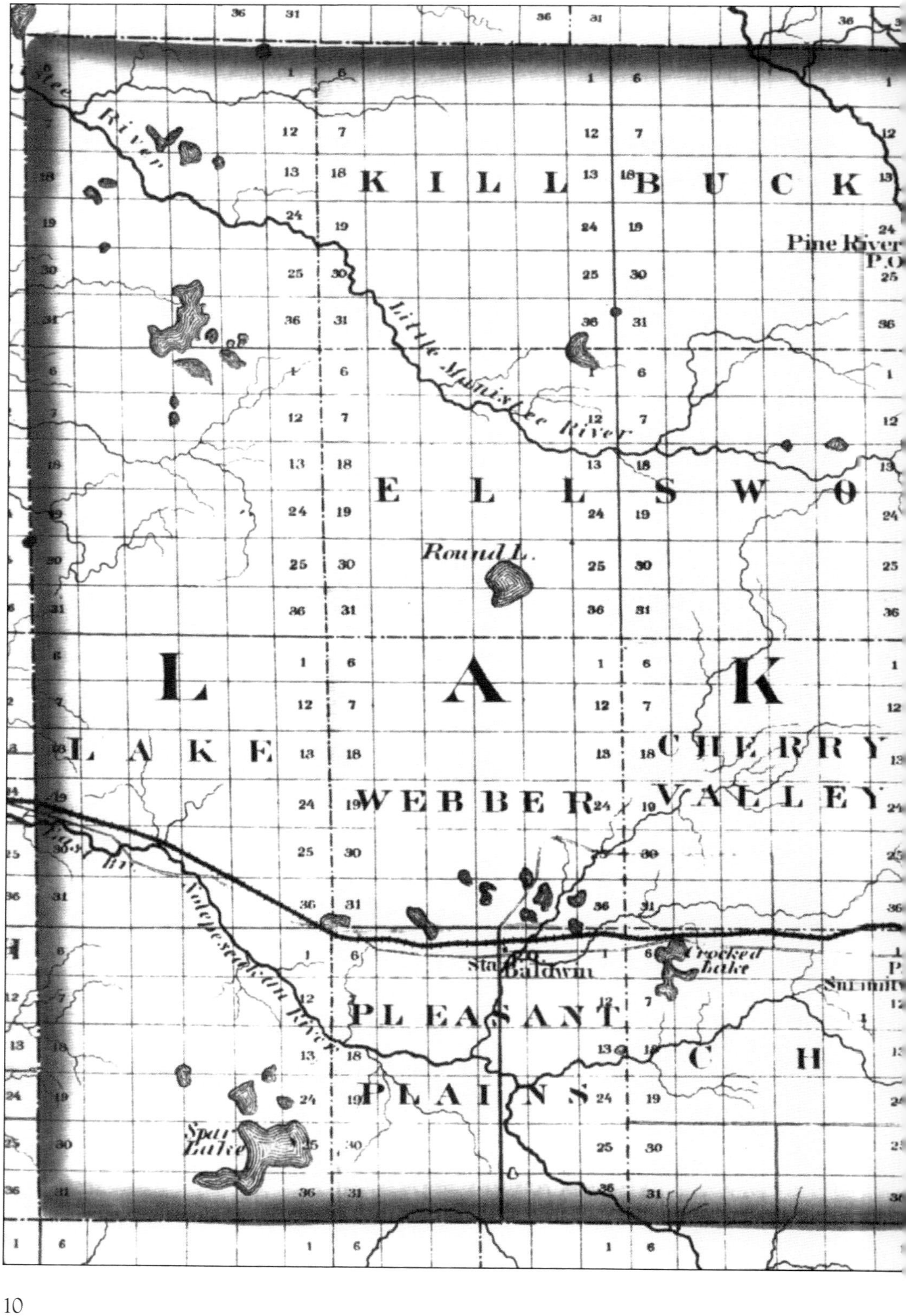
KILL BUCK
Pine River P.O.
Little Manistee River
ELLSWO
Round L.
LAK
LAKE
WEBBER
CHERRY VALLEY
Sta.
Baldwin
Crooked Lake
PLEASANT PLAINS
Spar Lake
CH

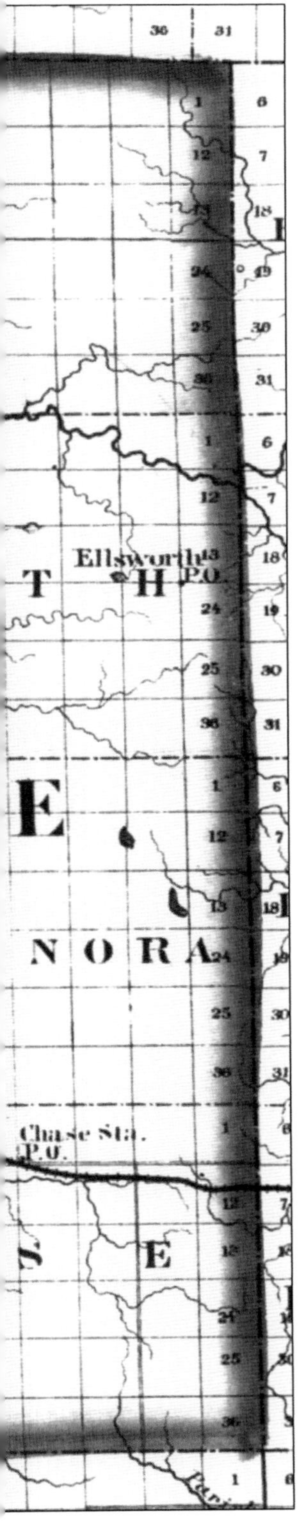

Lake County's initial survey occurred in 1837. The first atlas of Michigan was the 1873 Tackabury atlas, published in Detroit and drawn by H. F. Walling. The page illustrating Lake County is shown here. Note the bygone township name of Killbuck and the double, triple, and quadruple size of townships. The Pere Marquette River was labeled as the Notepeseukun River, meaning "river with heads on stakes." One can see that many changes have transpired over the years. (Courtesy of Paul Bigford.)

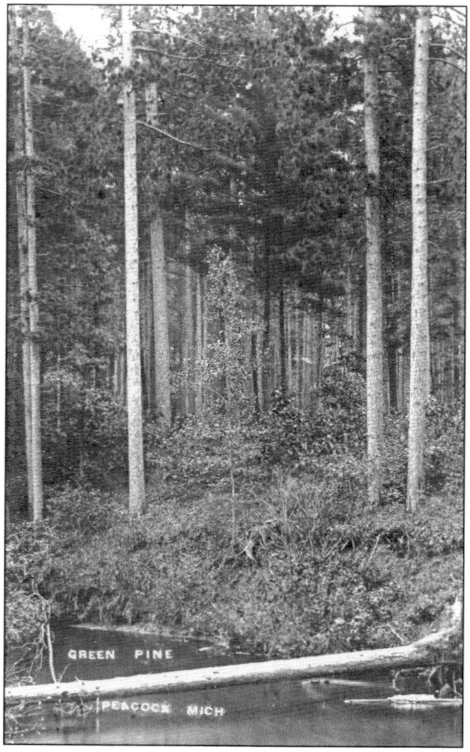

Portions of Lake County were well forested with red and white pine prior to the advent of logging. This stand of red pines, called green pines in this postcard, was located near Peacock. Early inventories of the forests also included hardwoods, hemlock, cedar, tamarack (larch), and limited prairies. (Courtesy of the Martin Johnson Heritage Museum.)

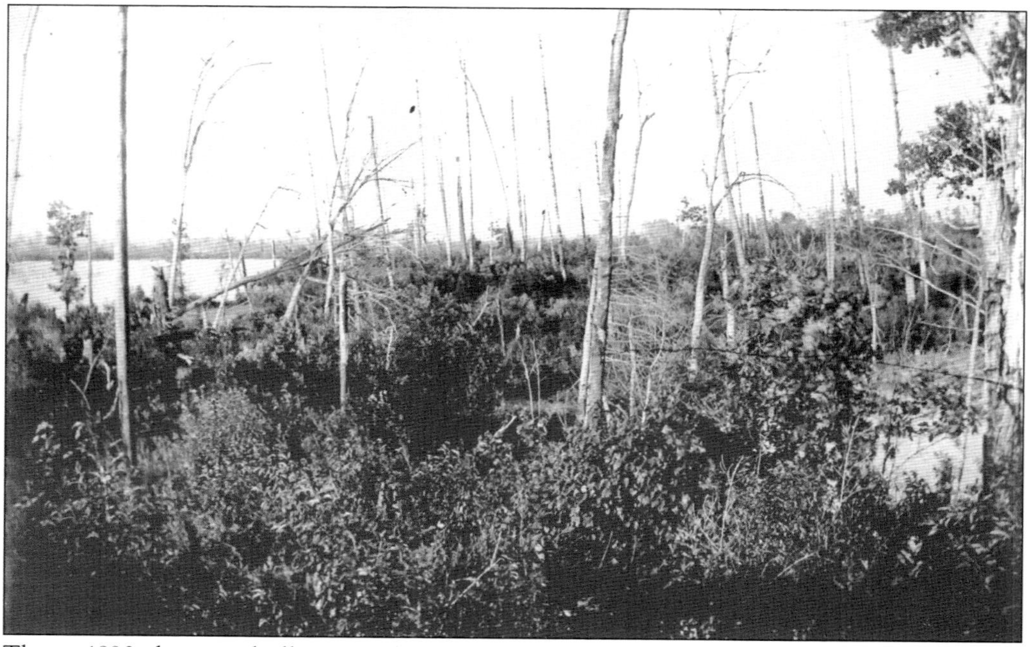

This *c.* 1890 photograph illustrates the general landscape after the removal of large marketable timber; in this case the scene is Big Bass Lake in the northwestern portion of Lake County. Areas with better soil were converted to small farms while much of the county reverted to forestland. (Photograph by Martin Johnson, courtesy of the Martin Johnson Heritage Museum.)

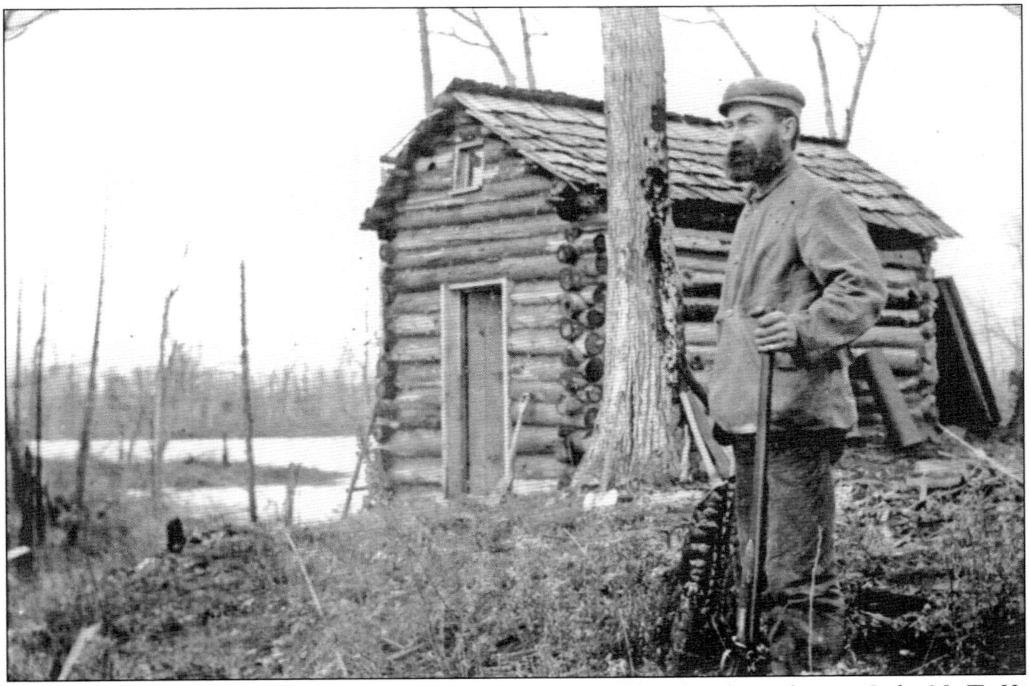

Swedish immigrant Martin Gustave Johnson constructed his first log cabin on Lake Na-Ta-Ki (Big Bass Lake) in 1889. The scarred land left after the logging industry moved on was harsh, but Johnson saw the beauty that would come in future years. This early pioneer was a farmer, artist, taxidermist, and photographer living off the land and celebrating its splendor. (Photograph by Martin Johnson, courtesy of the Martin Johnson Heritage Museum.)

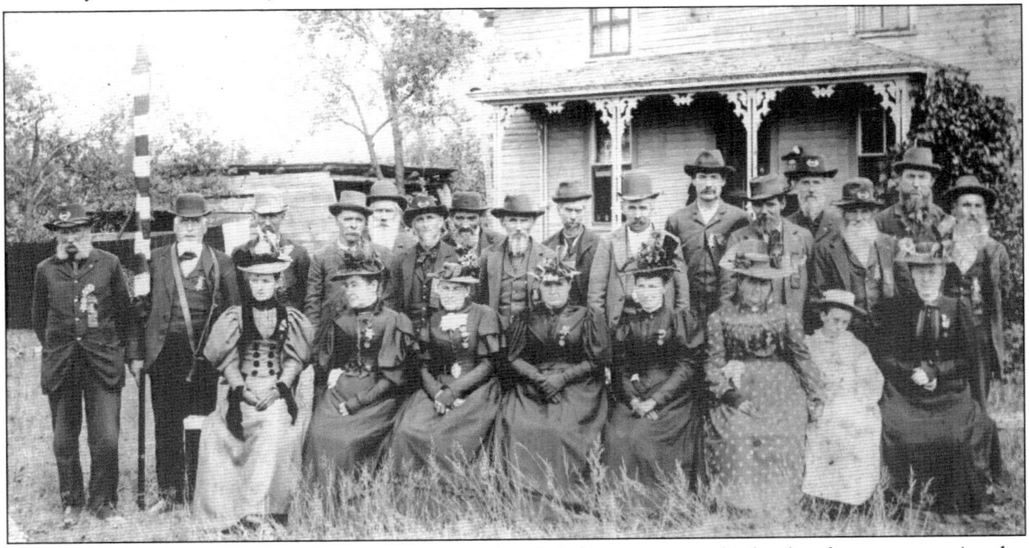

After the Civil War, many veterans migrated to Michigan to work the lumber camps. As the sawmills shut down in the 1890s, some married and settled permanently in Lake County. The Chase Grand Army of the Republic (GAR) Post 272 was active from 1884 until 1908. The six-foot-square flag of Chase GAR Post 272 resides in the Chase Library, one of only two post flags known to have survived in Michigan. (Courtesy of Joyce Ackerman.)

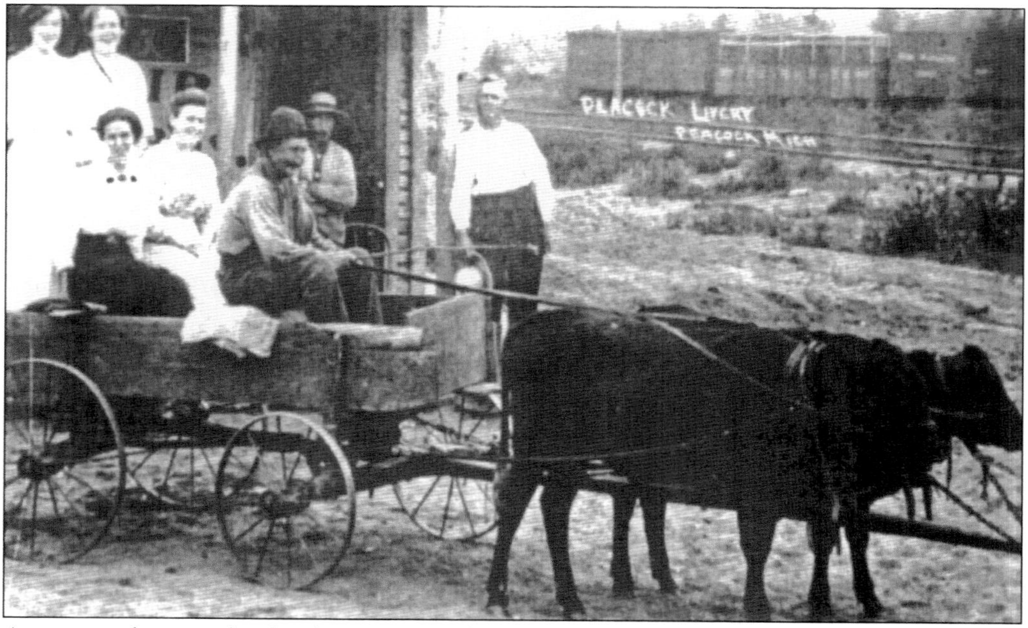

A teamster driving a four-hitch oxen wagon from the Peacock Livery poses with his young women passengers near the Peacock Depot. The boxcar in the background is identified as property of the Pere Marquette Railroad. The photograph was taken in the 1890s. (Courtesy of the Martin Johnson Heritage Museum.)

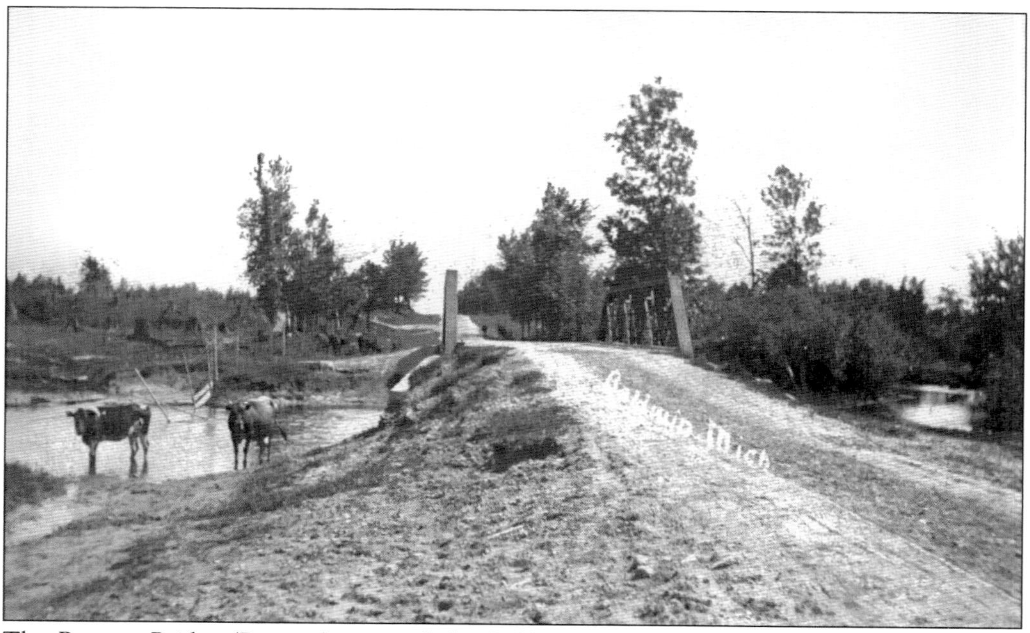

The Bonnye Bridge (Bonney) spanned the Baldwin River just south of Baldwin on what is known today as M-37. This image was postmarked in 1908. Today's farming practices would not allow cattle to enter the river. The cattle appear to be contained by the fence on the roadway instead of off the roadway. (Courtesy of Paul Bigford.)

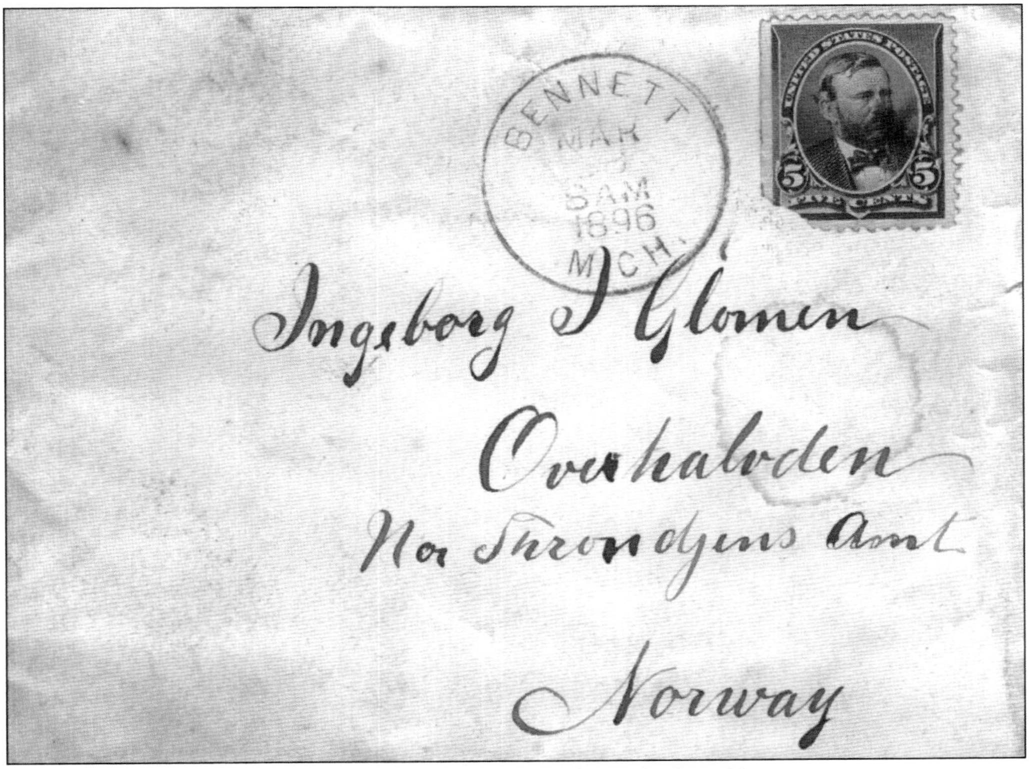

Many towns and post offices have disappeared since the early days. Historians are not even sure where Bennett was; most evidence points to the Bennett Post Office being at Stearns Siding, west of Baldwin, but it could have been south of there near Big Star Lake. Bennett Post Office operated from 1887 to 1890. The author of this letter was writing to his future bride in Norway. Wingleton was closer to Baldwin along the Pere Marquette Railroad. Wingleton was a mill town and later became the site of a large fishing and hunting club. The Wingleton depot, a former boxcar, is preserved today in private hands. Lake County had 28 post offices throughout the years. (Courtesy of Paul Bigford.)

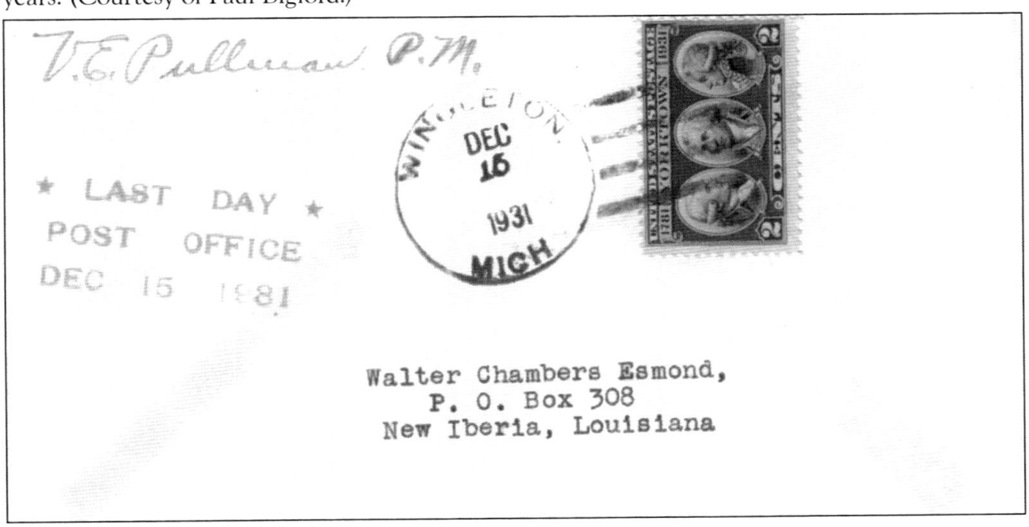

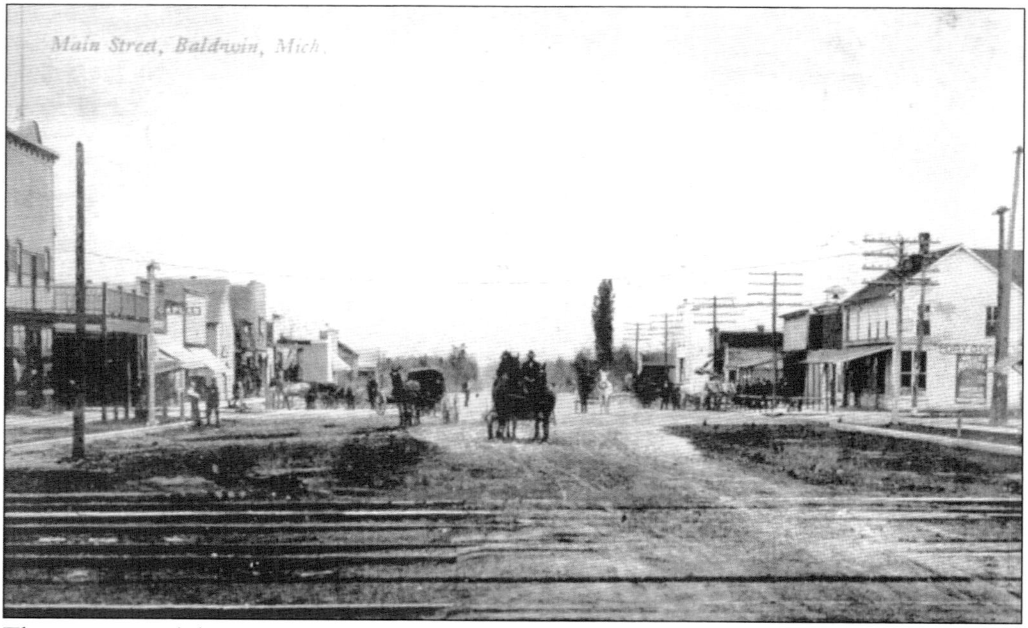

This preautomobile image of downtown Baldwin is looking south from the railroad crossing over what is known today as M-37. The first building on the left is the opera house and is the oldest standing building in Baldwin today. This c. 1890 postcard was still being sold in Drillings Hardware during the 1930s. (Courtesy of Jill Engelman.)

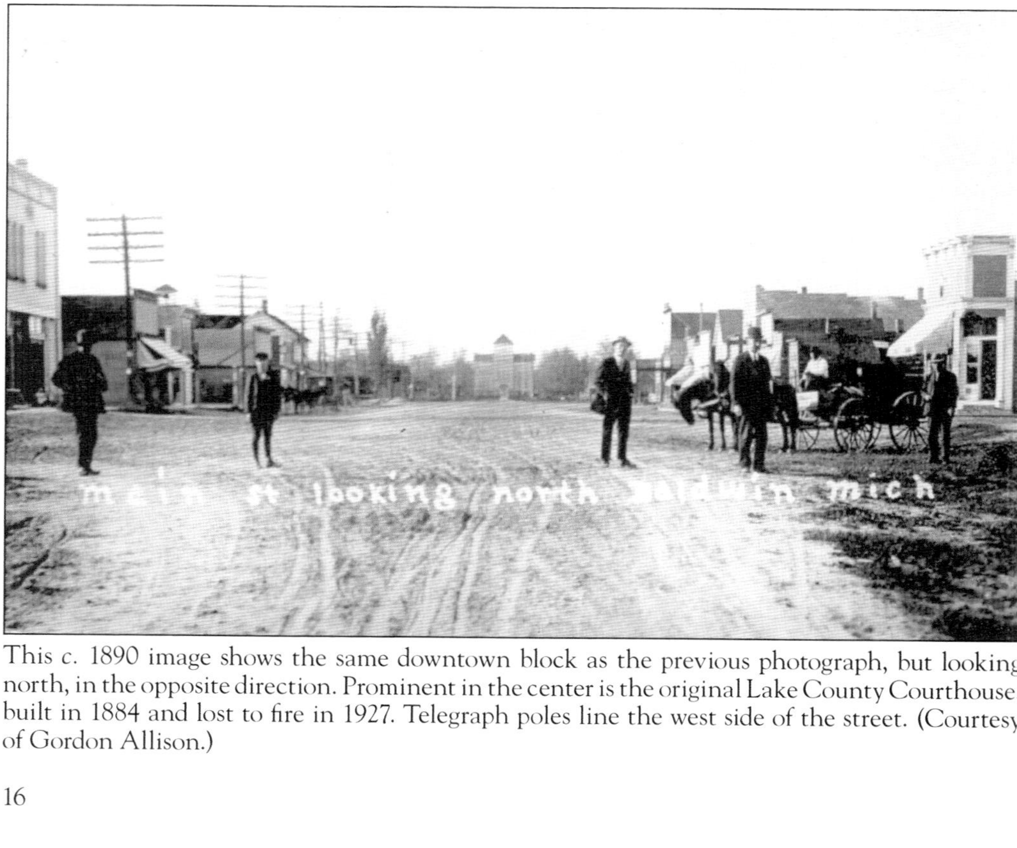

This c. 1890 image shows the same downtown block as the previous photograph, but looking north, in the opposite direction. Prominent in the center is the original Lake County Courthouse, built in 1884 and lost to fire in 1927. Telegraph poles line the west side of the street. (Courtesy of Gordon Allison.)

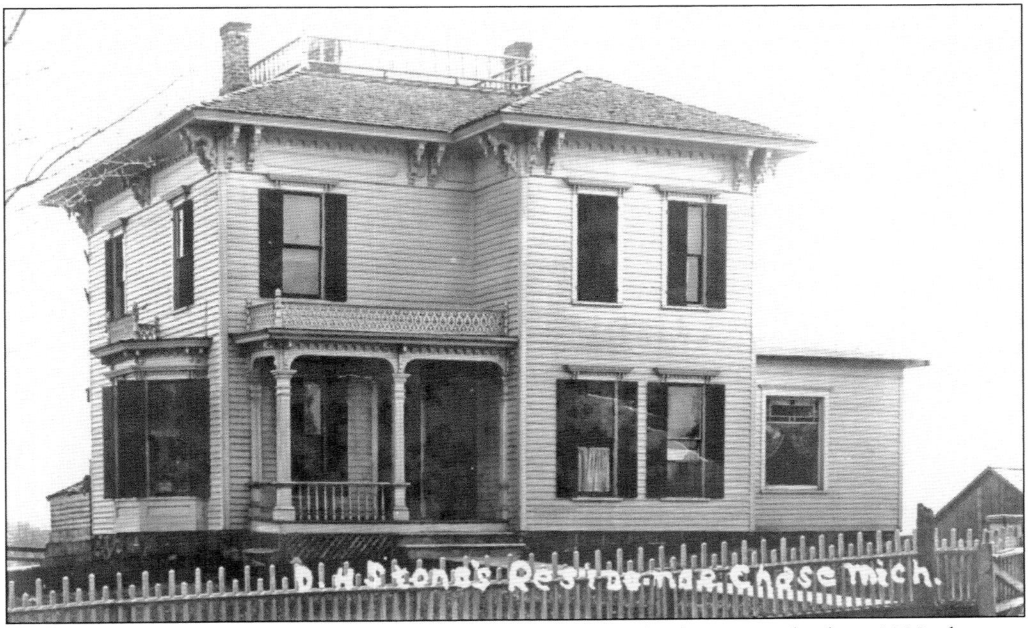

Settled in 1867, Chase is the oldest town in Lake County. This home was built in 1882, the year Chase was incorporated. The original owner of the home was Charles Joiner, who had a sawmill nearby. Darius H. Stone had purchased the home by the time this photograph was taken. In 1892, a devastating fire destroyed 67 buildings. As a result, very few photographs were preserved from early years. (Courtesy of Dennis Ellison.)

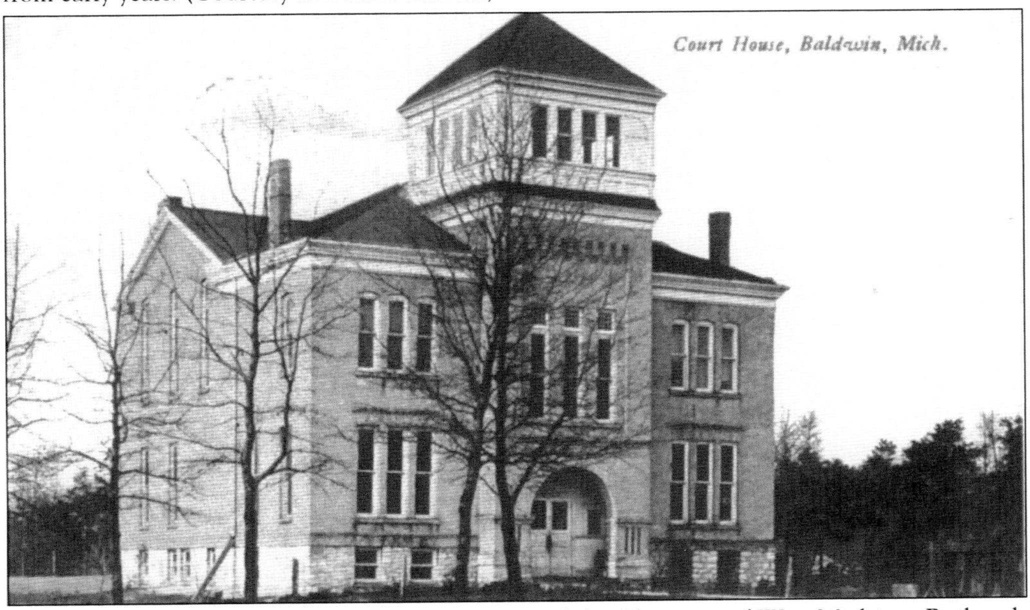

The intersection of the Flint and Pere Marquette and the Chicago and West Michigan Railroads in Baldwin was a major factor in the town becoming the county seat in 1875. The first permanent courthouse was built in 1886. The $6,000 structure was constructed of local materials including beige colored bricks made from marl and clay found along the banks of the Pere Marquette River. (Courtesy of Gordon Allison.)

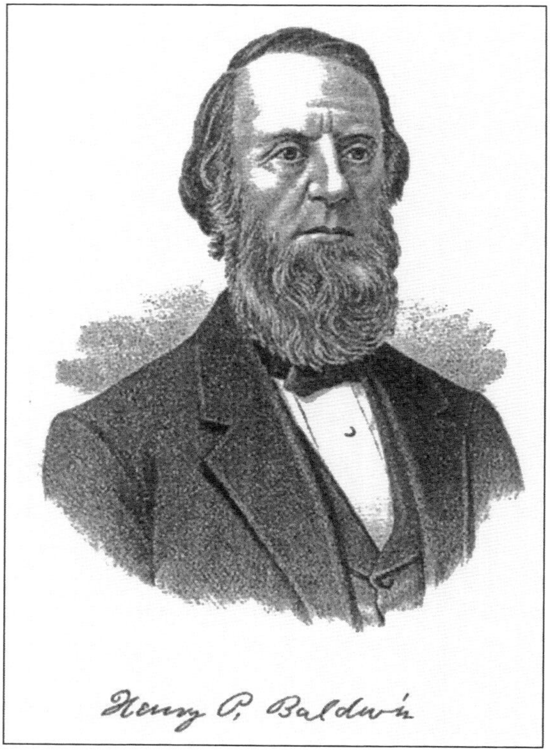

In 1872, the village of Baldwin was incorporated and named in honor of Michigan governor Henry P. Baldwin. Serving from 1869 to 1873, Governor Baldwin was so honored that he presented the village with a large American flag. Baldwin also served as a state senator in 1861–1862 and as a United States senator from 1879 to 1881. He also organized the Republican Party in Jackson in 1854. (Courtesy of the Lake County Historical Society.)

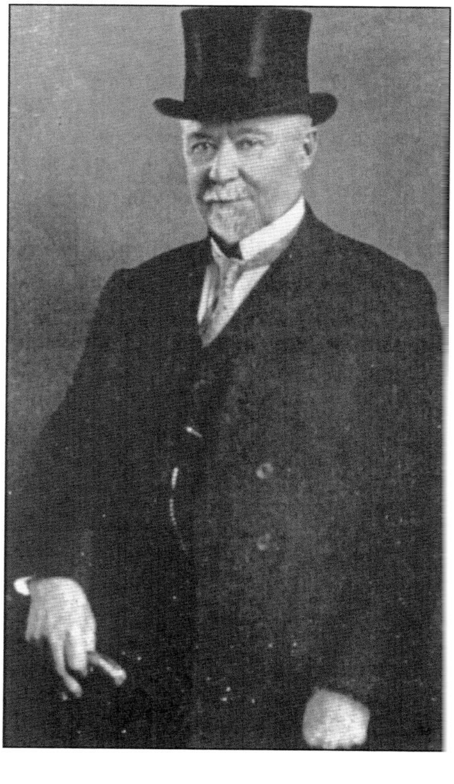

Born in 1855, Dr. George Field served as a physician for over 60 years, working in the lumber camps and for the Pere Marquette Railroad in the Chase area. In 1918, he attended to 500 cases of influenza but did not lose a single patient. He served on the Chase village council at the time of the great fire that burned the majority of the town in 1892. (Courtesy of the Lake County Historical Society.)

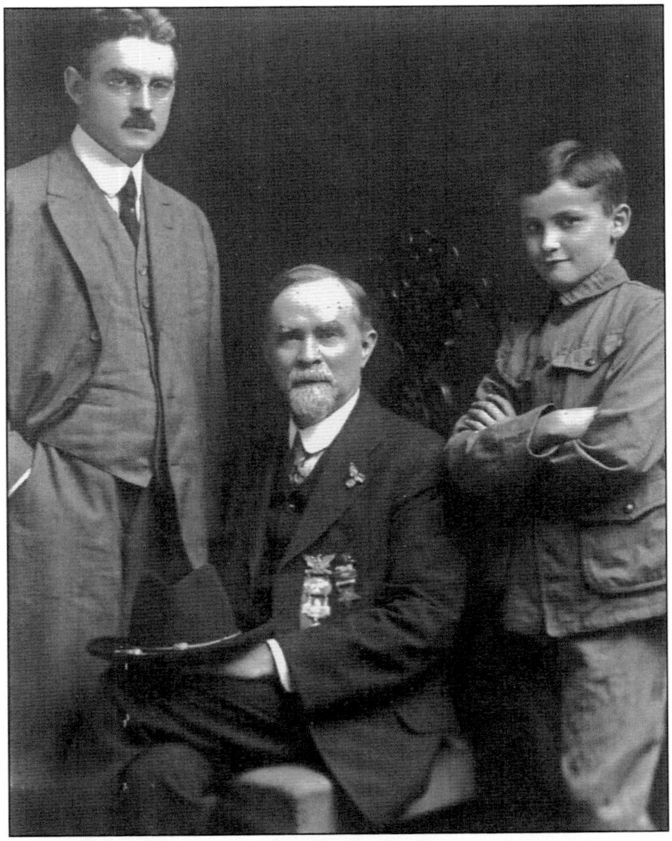

The *Lake County Star* was first published on May 10, 1873, by Charles Kelly Radcliffe, a Civil War veteran. In the photograph at right, Radcliffe, center, is shown with his son William Radcliffe, left, and his grandson Ellis Radcliffe, right. Herbert Davis was the fifth and longest-serving (47 years) editor of the newspaper. In the image below, Davis (and his wife with her back to the camera) is standing by a printing press in an early Star office. Trays of type can be seen on the table in the foreground. The *Lake County Star* is the longest continuously operating business in Lake County and is published today by the Pioneer Group. (Courtesy of the Lake County Historical Society.)

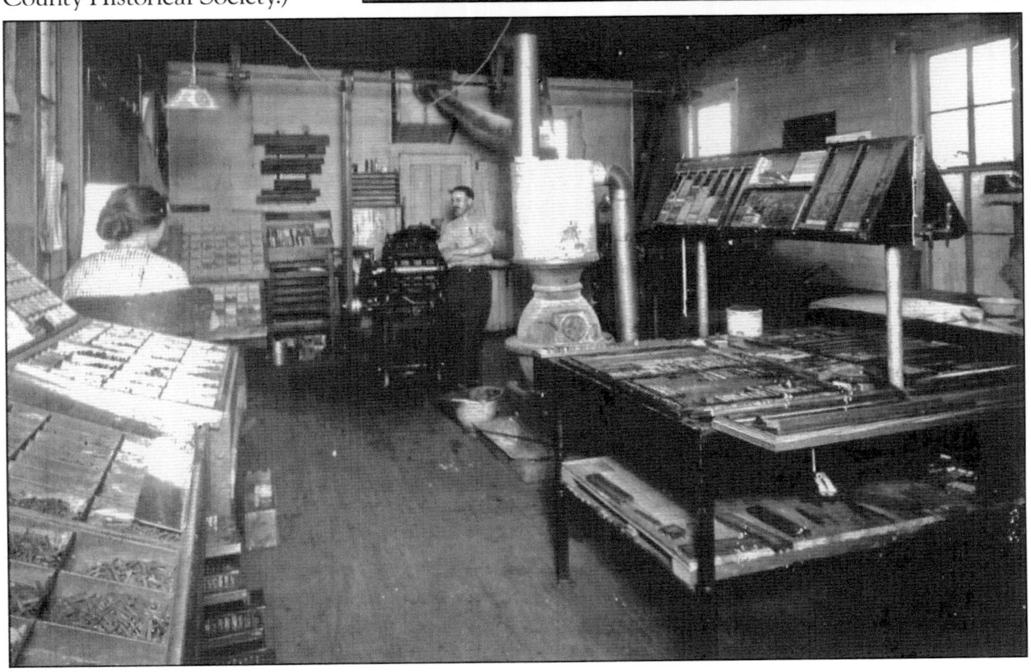

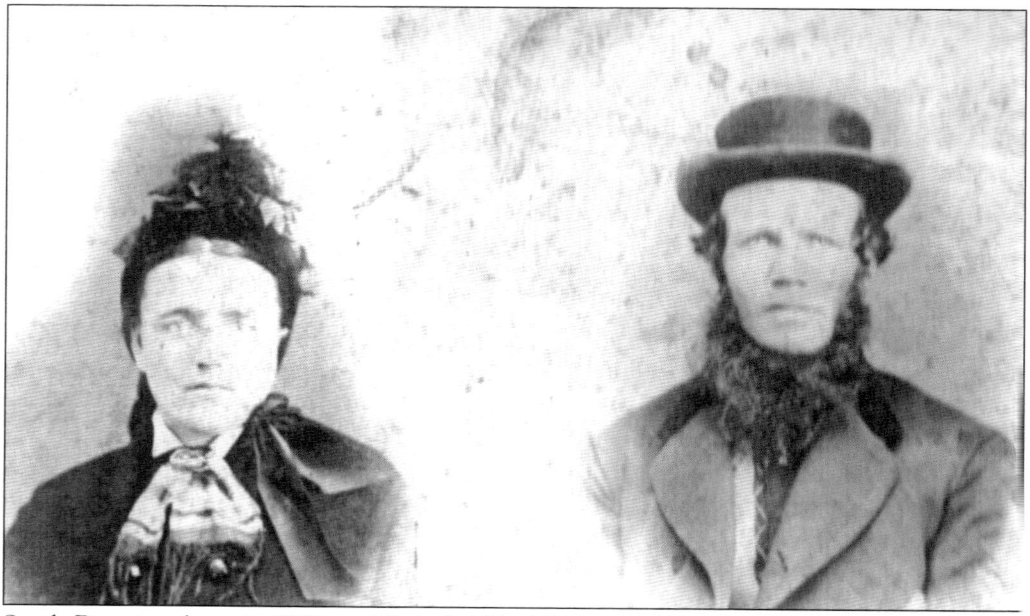

Sarah Denning, born in 1833, and Jesse Bradford, born in 1825, of Lyme Regis, England, were married on the island of Aldernay, England, on June 29, 1849. The couple immigrated to Lake County by 1877. The Bradfords had 18 children with many descendents living in Lake County today. The Bradford farm was located two miles east of Baldwin. Bradford also had a milk route to Marlborough (Marlboro). (Courtesy of Susan Bradford Tripp.)

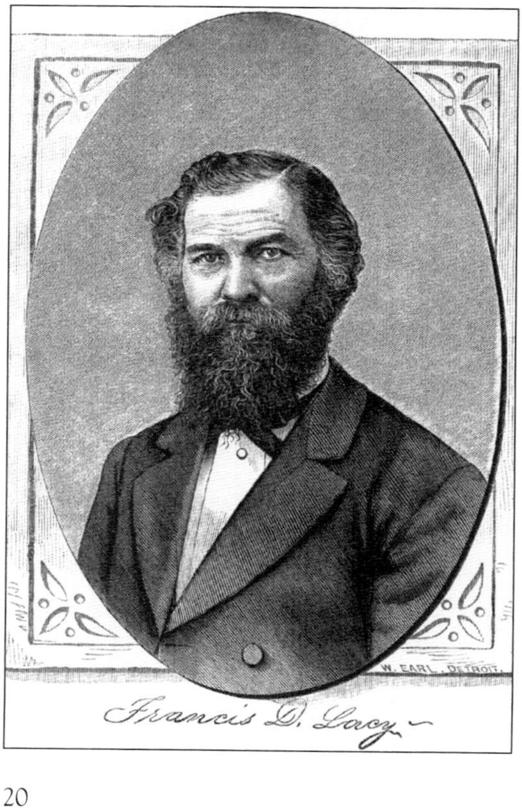

Francis Daniel Lacy, born in Nirvana in 1876, was an author, teacher, and photographer. The Lacys operated one of 12 lumber mills that were in Nirvana at the same time. Francis authored several romance novels. His son, Arthur Jay Lacy, ran for governor in 1934 and also ran for state representative and state senator. Arthur Lacy married one of Dr. George Field's daughters. (Courtesy of the Lake County Historical Society.)

Two

TRAINS AND TIMBER

The history of Lake County's trains and timber is tightly woven. Anyone who contemplates or actually fells a large tree, and is faced with transporting it as 16-foot-long logs, can appreciate the challenges to the early loggers. The giant pine and hardwood logs weighed many hundreds of pounds. Roads did not exist, nor did any convenient way of moving logs. Today there are tractors, skidders, crane-equipped logging trucks, and wonderful roads. The early lumberjacks not only lacked these modern tools, they also lacked the chainsaws to harvest the mighty trees.

The earliest loggers used draft animals, including oxen, to drag logs out of the woods. Soon it was discovered that this task was easier in the winter when snow and frozen ground made the logs slide more easily. Next came sleds and iced trails used to deliver the logs to the sawmills. Trees were cut year-round, skidded in the winter, and sawn year-round.

Some logs were taken to rivers to be stockpiled for the spring floods. When the water reached its highest point, the logs were pushed down the "rollaways" and into the streams for the trip to the mouth of the river and sorting for the various mills. Loggers, called rivermen or river rats, were given the job of busting up logjams and keeping the logs moving—even if it meant using dynamite.

Inventions like the "big wheel" helped ease the work. A single large log, or a bundle of lesser logs, was hung under the axle of a pair of 10-foot-high wheels and hauled out of the woods by draft animals; but it was the development of the logging railroad that really mechanized timber production. Work crews, speaking many languages, built railroads through the woods to bring logs great distances to the mills. Traces of these railroads are evident today.

Railroad junctions and sawmills along the lines provided the basis for early settlements. Many of the present towns, as well as many ghost towns, were thus established. As the timber disappeared, some of these early settlements vanished, literally taken apart to construct new buildings, while others became business centers that persist to this day.

The railroads, like the mills before them, employed many early citizens of Lake County. Today's single remaining railroad passes through many unmarked but not forgotten settlements, tying the past and future together.

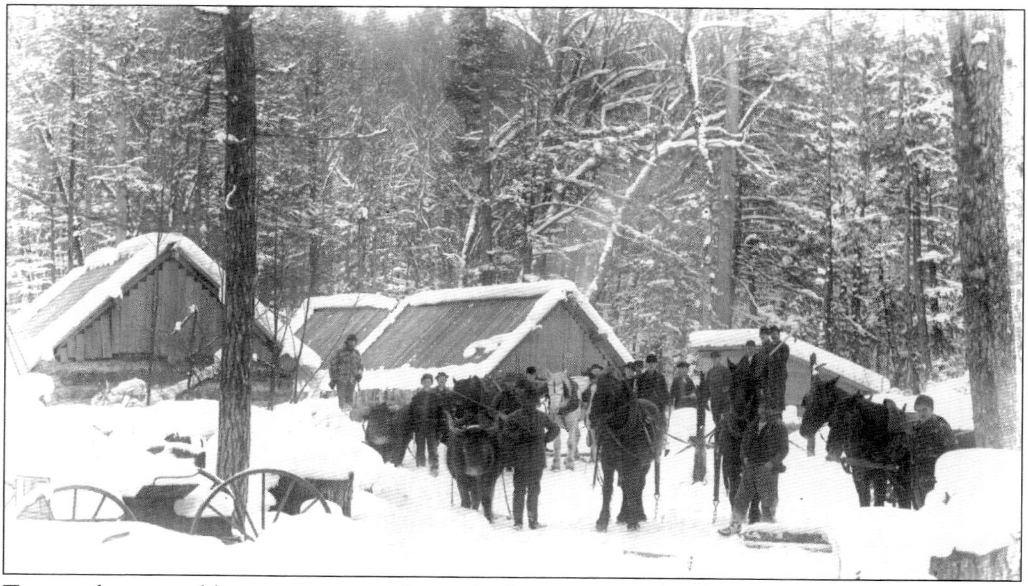

Teams of oxen and horses prepare to leave the logging camp for the woods. The buildings with no snow on the roofs are uninsulated bunkhouses. Much of the timber in the early days was moved in the winter, when snow and ice made dragging the logs much easier. Logs were dragged to a mill, to a streamside roll away to float down the river, or, later, to a railroad flatcar. (Courtesy of Orville Mund.)

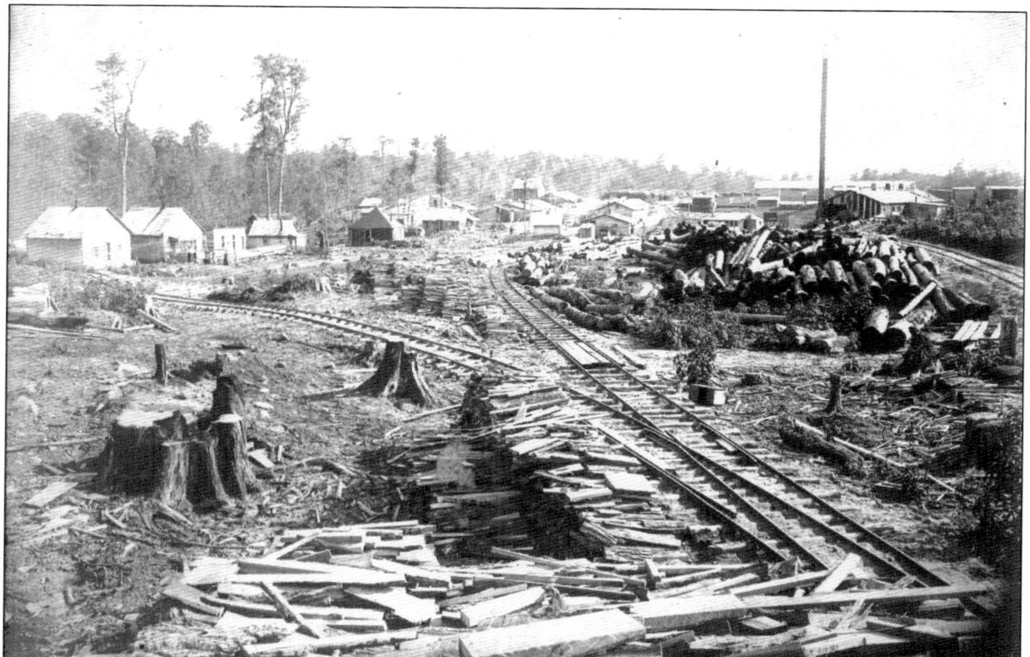

This Chase area sawmill site was probably typical. A tall chimney pinpoints the mill, with four water barrels on the roof for fire protection. The other buildings are workshops and dwellings for the workers. Slabwood, the pieces removed when a log is squared off to make a square cant, has been cut up into firewood, possibly to fuel a locomotive. (Courtesy of Orville Mund.)

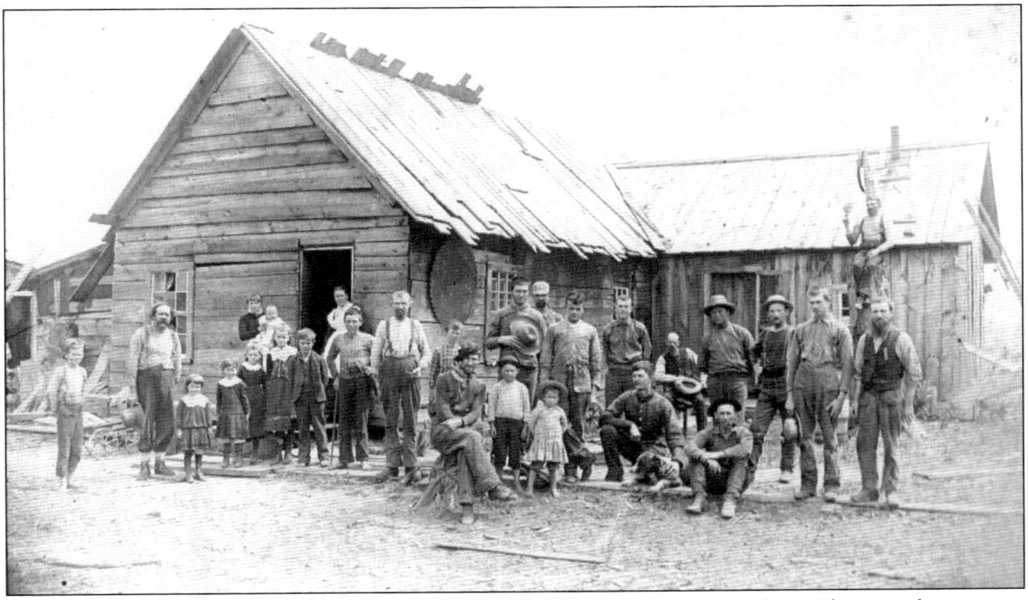

This photograph was taken around 1900 near Olivers in Chase Township. The circular saw on the building wall tells that the structure is most likely a saw shop or sawmill. Note the woman and girls dressed in their Sunday best. One can only imagine the photographer's instructions: "Take those hats off or push them back!" (Courtesy of Orville Mund.)

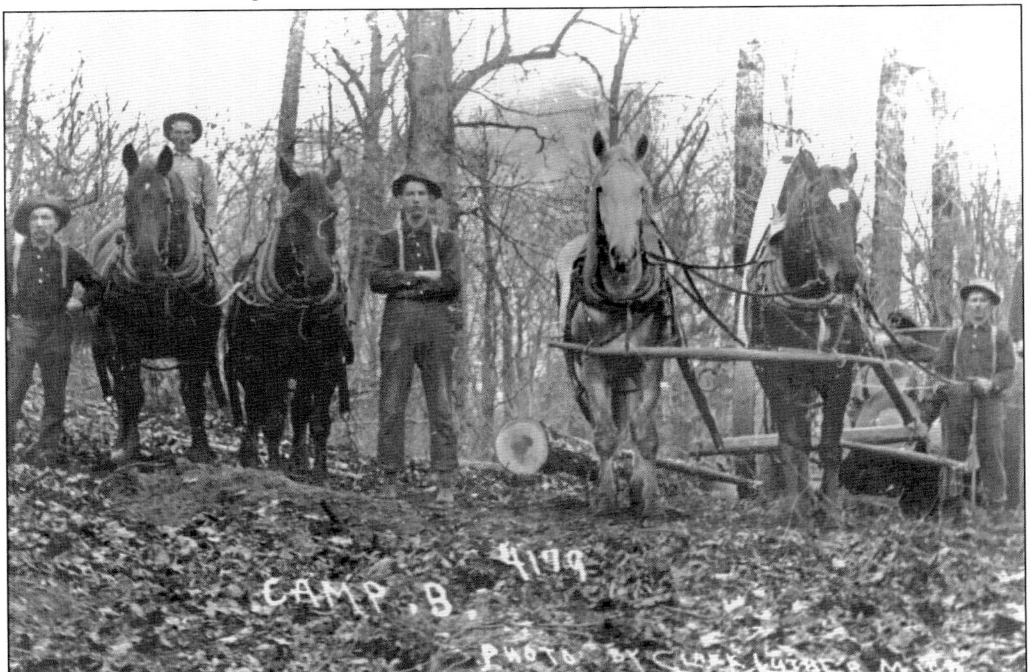

The location of this timber cut is near Luther. The team on the left is pulling a single log while the team on the right is using a big wheel. The big wheel was used by positioning it over a clutch of logs, winching them partially off the ground (to reduce friction), and then hauling them away. (Courtesy of Tennis Trucks.)

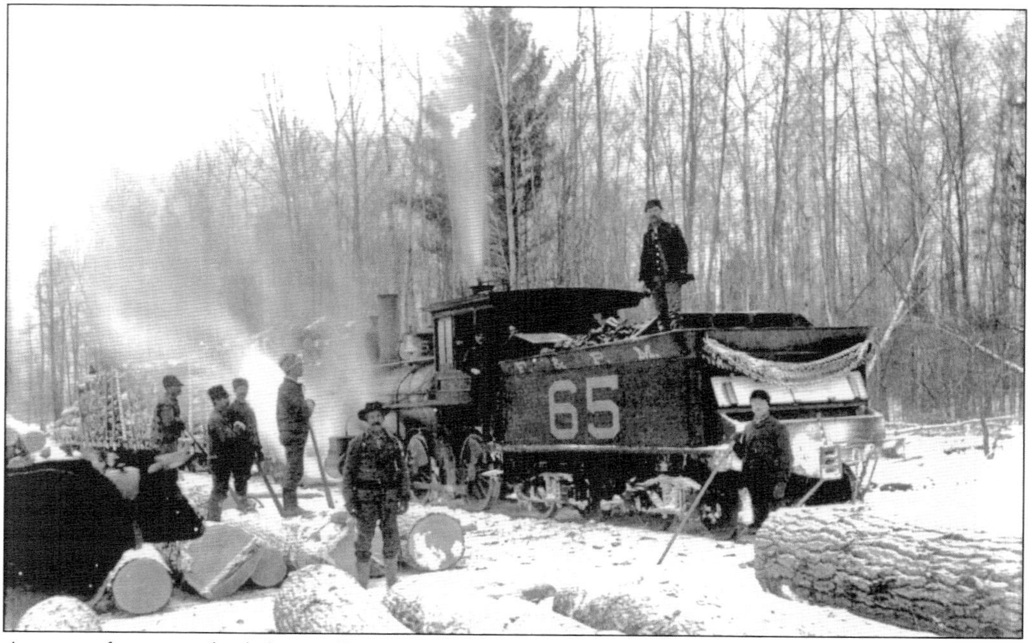

A team of oxen at the left is pulling up pine sawlogs to be loaded on flatcars. This scene shows a steam engine on the Lake County Rail Road (LCRR) in western Lake County about 1895. The coal tender is marked Flint and Pere Marquette Railroad, a larger line that intersected the LCRR in what is today Sweetwater Township. (Courtesy of Roger Jones.)

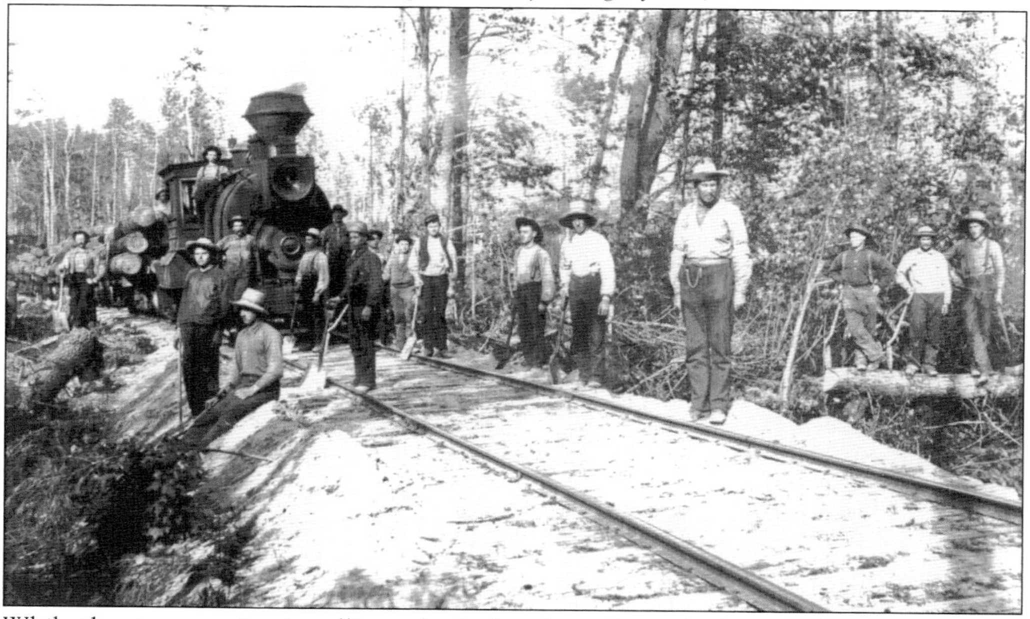

While the steam engine is pulling a load of sawlogs, the tools these workmen are wielding indicate they are part of the crew that built and maintained the line. Crews would dig a series of "Swede Holes" along the intended railroad bed and throw the soil up to the bed. The larger trees in the background were probably spared because they are double-trunked trees with smaller diameters. (Courtesy of Roger Jones.)

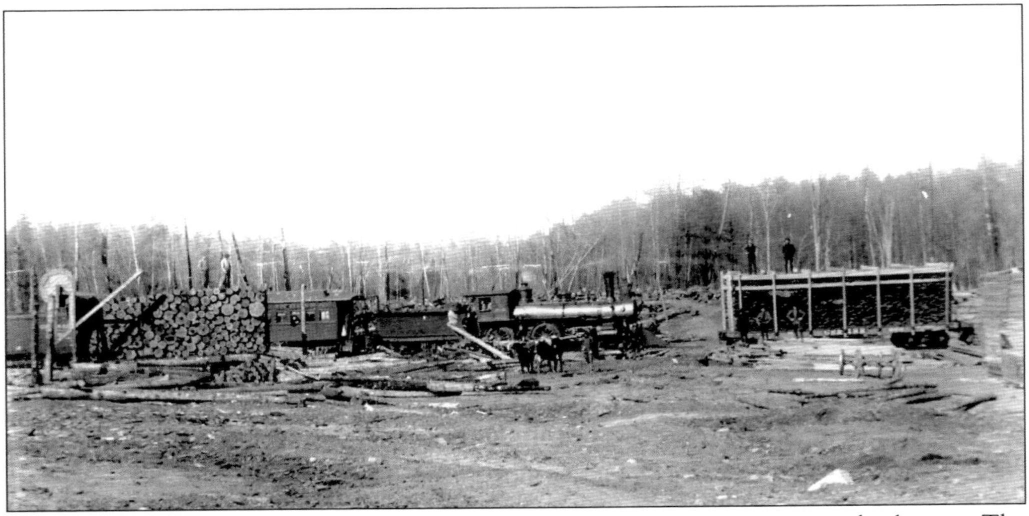

In this Chase photograph the engine is pulling a tender, a passenger car, and a boxcar. The flatcar on the closer track appears to have bolts on the left and perhaps bark (used for tanning hides) or firewood on the right. The round object appears to be a circular saw crate that may have been pressed into service as part of a site-built crane to load the railcars. (Courtesy of Orville Mund.)

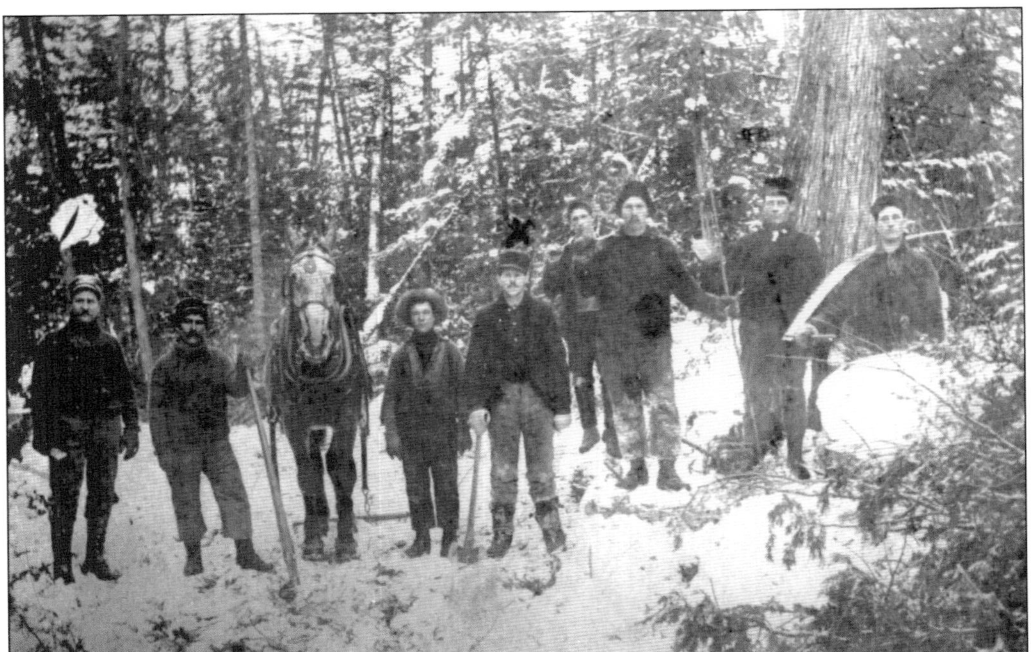

Trees were typically notched with an axe and then felled by cutting with a two-man saw on the side of the trunk opposite of the intended direction of fall. The tree was then bucked into logs by sawing, and then hauled away by a team of horses or oxen. George Matson, standing with an axe, is identified with the X in this 1905 photograph. (Courtesy of Don and Barbara Hart.)

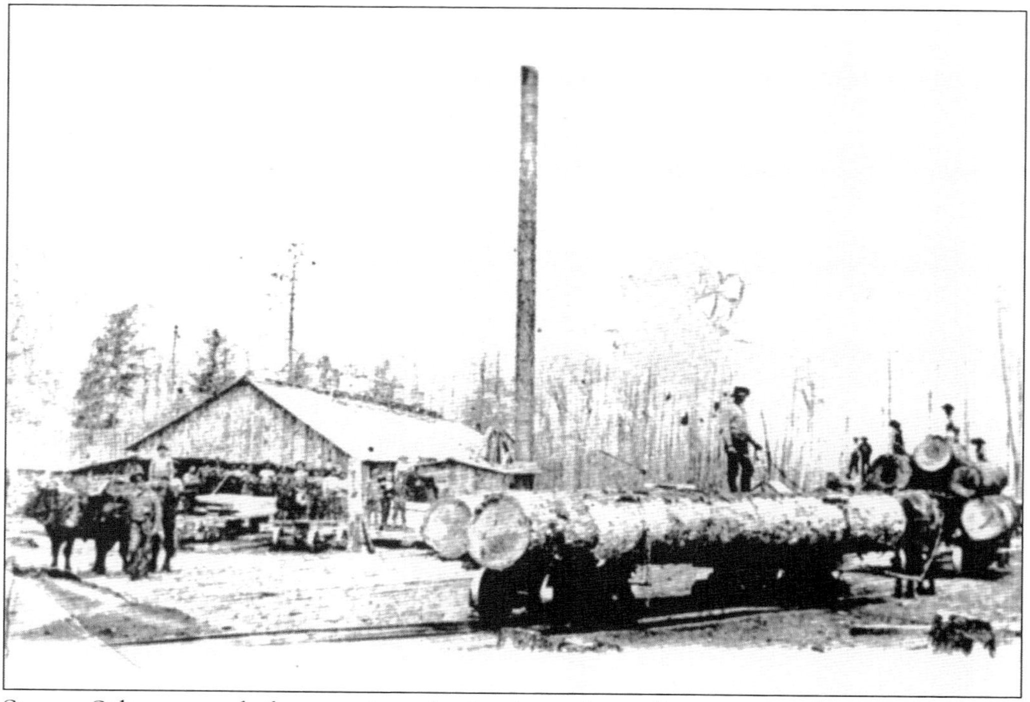

Stearns Siding, named after prominent lumber baron Justus Stearns, was a logging community between Baldwin and Branch on the Pere Marquette Railroad. This photograph may have been taken to showcase the exceptional logs shown in the foreground. Note the roof-top water barrels for fire suppression. (Courtesy of Paul Bigford.)

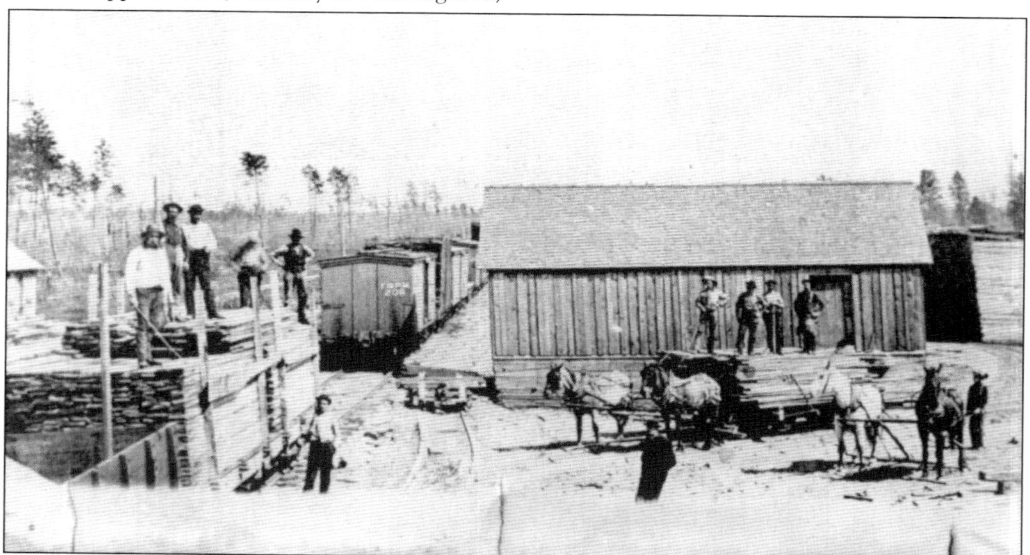

Workers are stacking dried lumber on a flatcar for transport to market, probably on a rail line through Ludington. Both sawn lumber and shingles were produced and shipped from Stearns Siding. Justus Stearns was one of the wealthiest men in Michigan at the time, and although the town was named for its founder, it was called Bennett by the post office. (Courtesy of Al George.)

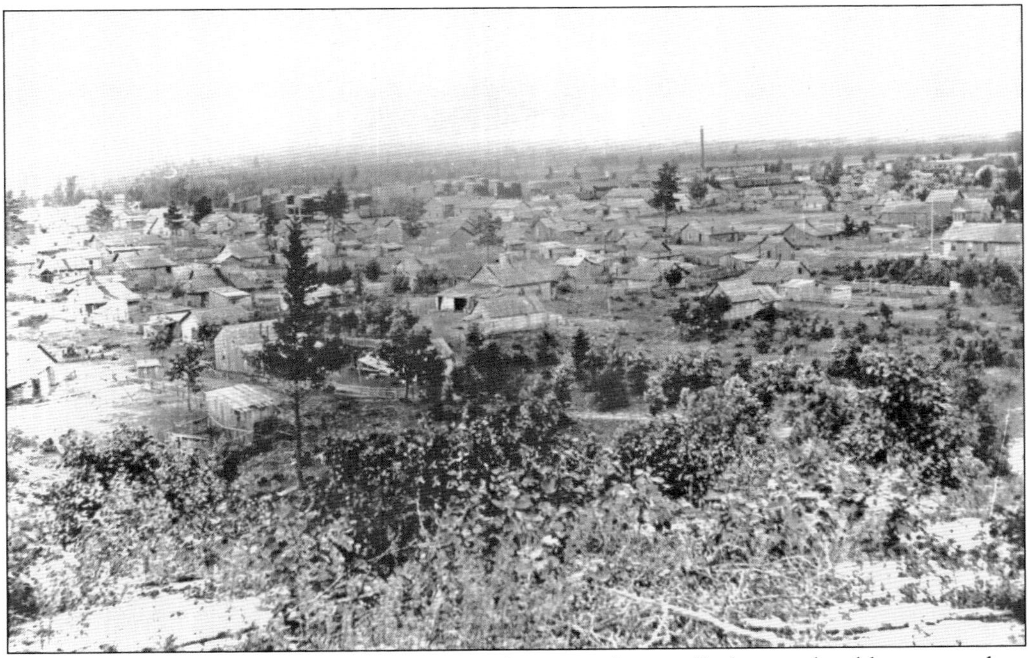

In 1890, Stearns Siding was a large community boasting three mills, houses, bunkhouses, and, to the right, a school. This photograph shows many stacks of lumber and a mill chimney. The town had nearly 2,700 residents, burned Halloween night in 1899, and was never rebuilt. (Courtesy of Al George.)

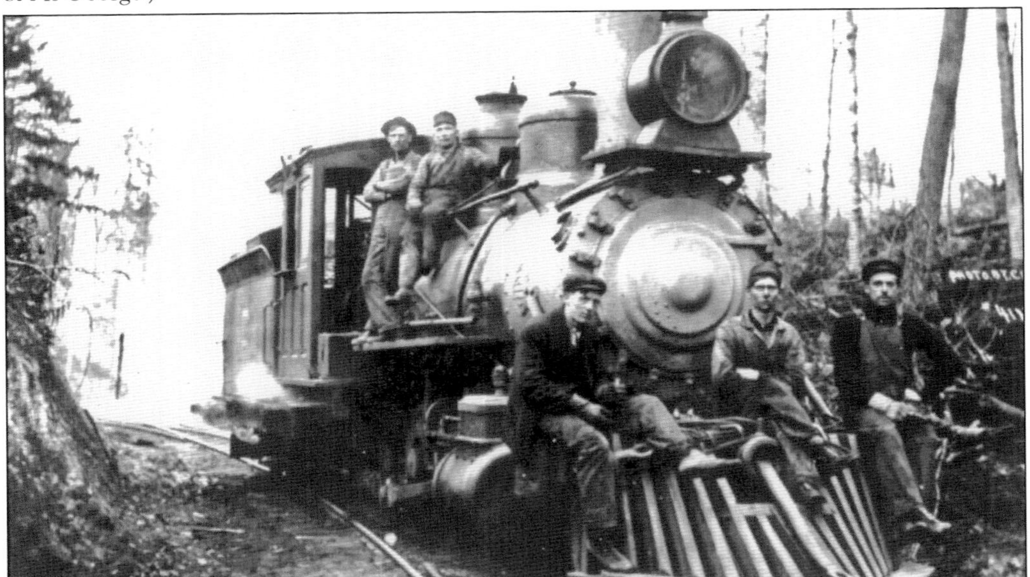

This engine was built by the Baldwin Locomotive Company, which is not associated with the village of Baldwin. The Manistee and Luther Railroad (M&L) was organized in 1889 with capital stock of $1 million. It operated originally as a logging railroad but evolved into a freight-hauling line. In 1898, the M&L had 100 flatcars, 4 boxcars, 2 passenger/baggage cars, and 3 locomotives. (Courtesy of Al George.)

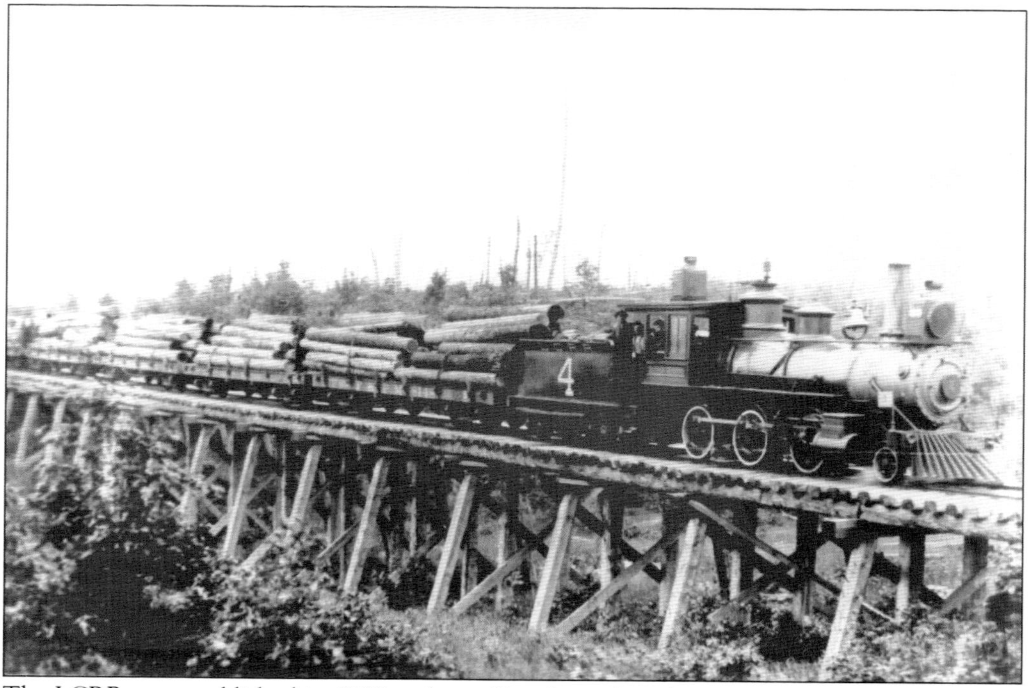

The LCRR was established in 1880 and was 11 miles in length, running north from the ghost town of Elk (also called Renoe) near the Pere Marquette River. The railroad started with 3 engines and 40 cars with initial authorized stock of $60,000. They hauled 10,771,122 board feet of logs in the first six months of 1893, the year the railroad was abandoned. Below is another photograph of the Brooks 2-6-0 engine. The builder's number 1290 denotes it as being built in November 1887. The LCRR was a 56.5-inch-gauge railroad. This photograph shows the LCRR crossing either the Flint and Pere Marquette in Sweetwater Township or the Manistee and Grand Rapids Railroad or the Danaher and Melendy Railroad in Sauble Township. (Courtesy of Paul Bigford.)

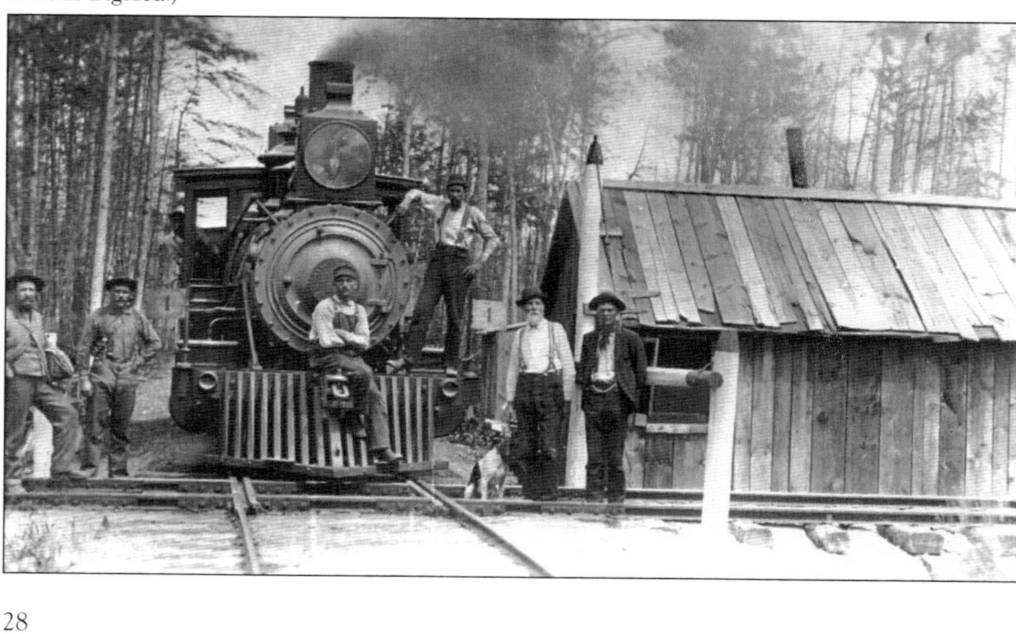

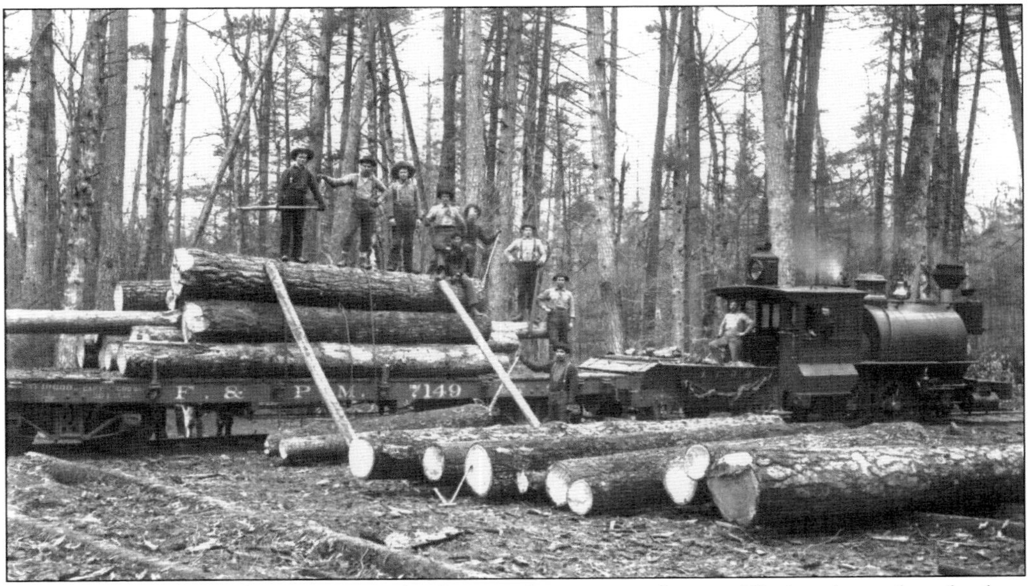

Workers equipped with peaveys are loading sawlogs onto a flatcar. Chains, looped under logs and then back over the flatcar, were hitched to the waiting draft animals seen on the other side of the flatcar. As the team walked away from the tracks, the logs were rolled up the poles and into position on the stack. Each row of logs was chained to the car for transport to the sawmill. (Courtesy of Roger Jones.)

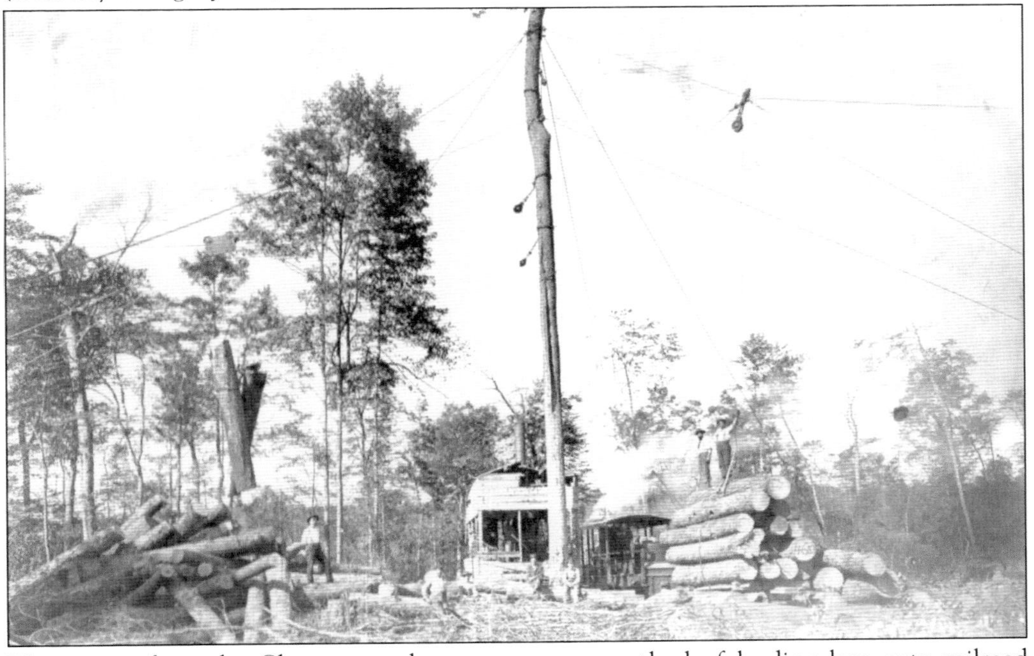

This scene, from the Chase area, demonstrates one method of loading logs onto railroad flatcars. A steam-powered winch is located in the small building behind the tall pine, while a steam locomotive can be seen between the winch house and the loaded logs. The number drawn on the logs may refer to the number of board feet contained in the load. (Courtesy of Orville Mund.)

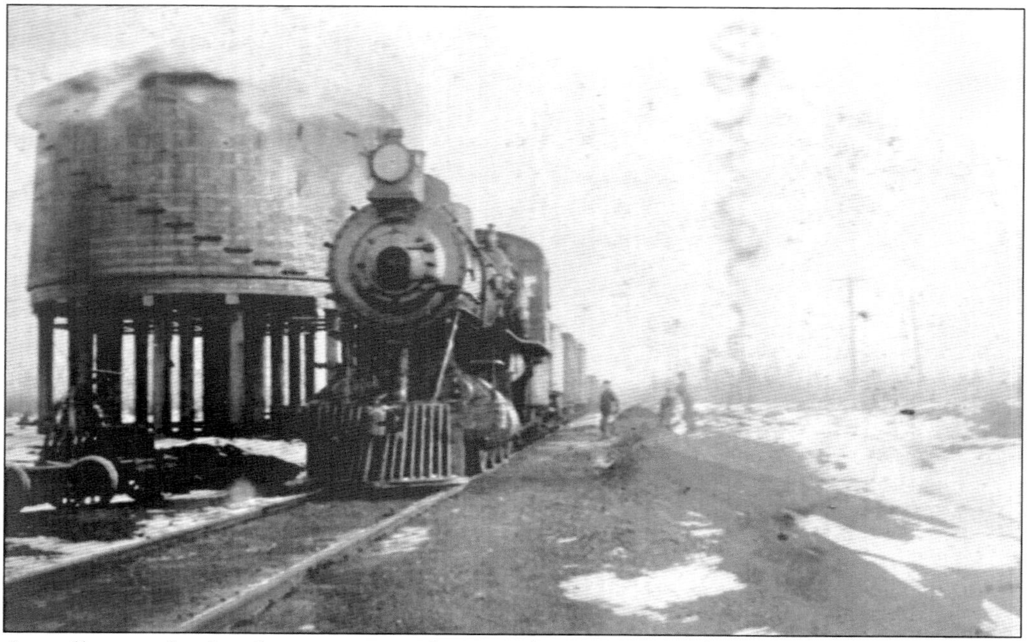

A small waterwheel and pump in a creek pumped water up into this elevated water tank. From there, the water flowed by gravity to replenish steam engines such as the one shown here. Engine No. 348 was a Brooks 2-8-0 in service from 1901 to 1935. This site was called Sweetwater Tank with the view looking toward the east. The foundation is still visible today. (Courtesy of Paul Bigford.)

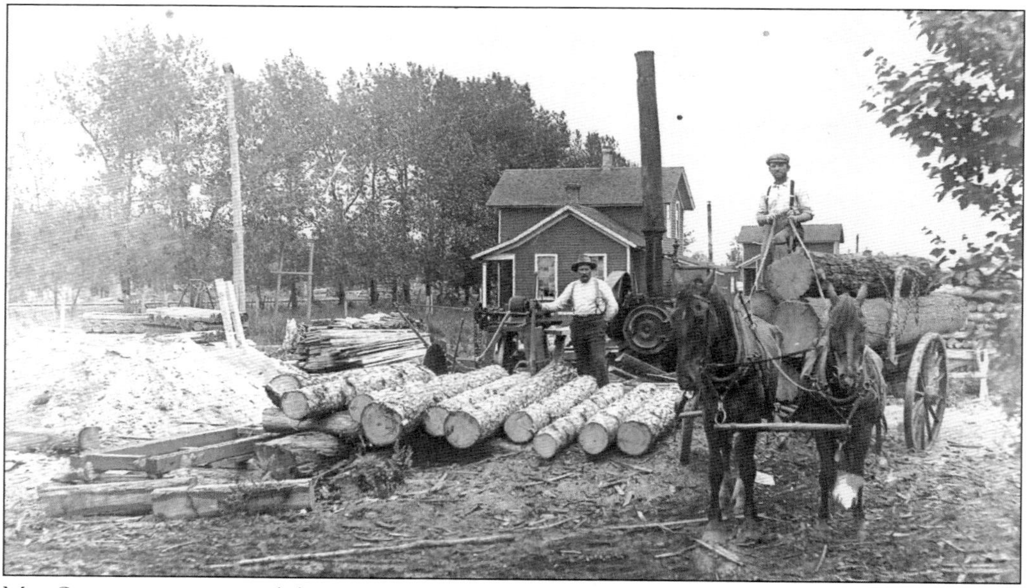

Mat Stevensen emigrated from Norway in 1888, followed by Ingebord, whom he married in 1898. They settled in Swede Settlement, north of present-day Branch. Stevensen is seen here operating his sawmill, using a steam tractor for power, while Benjamin Barnett brings up another load of logs on his wagon. The mill was located near Branch, just south of the Pere Marquette Railroad visible in the background. (Courtesy of Bruce Bosley.)

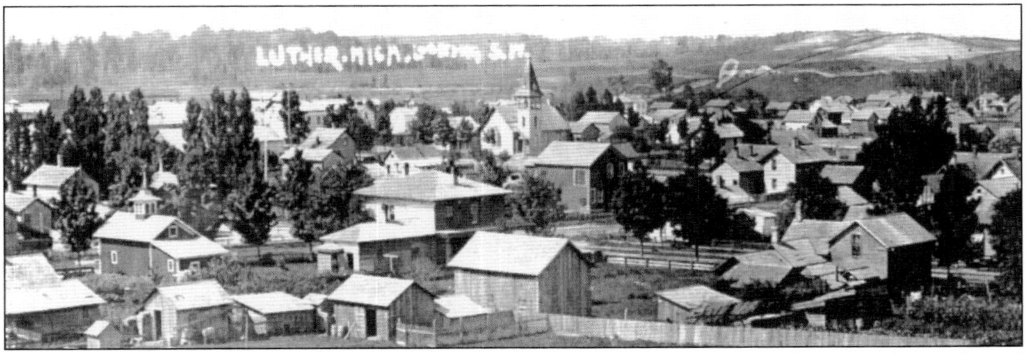

The building visible between the row of Lombardy poplars on the left is the Grand Rapids and Indiana Railroad depot in Luther. The view is to the southwest. The area's church, schoolhouse, homes, barns, sheds, and the cutover landscape can be seen in the distance. (Courtesy of Paul Bigford.)

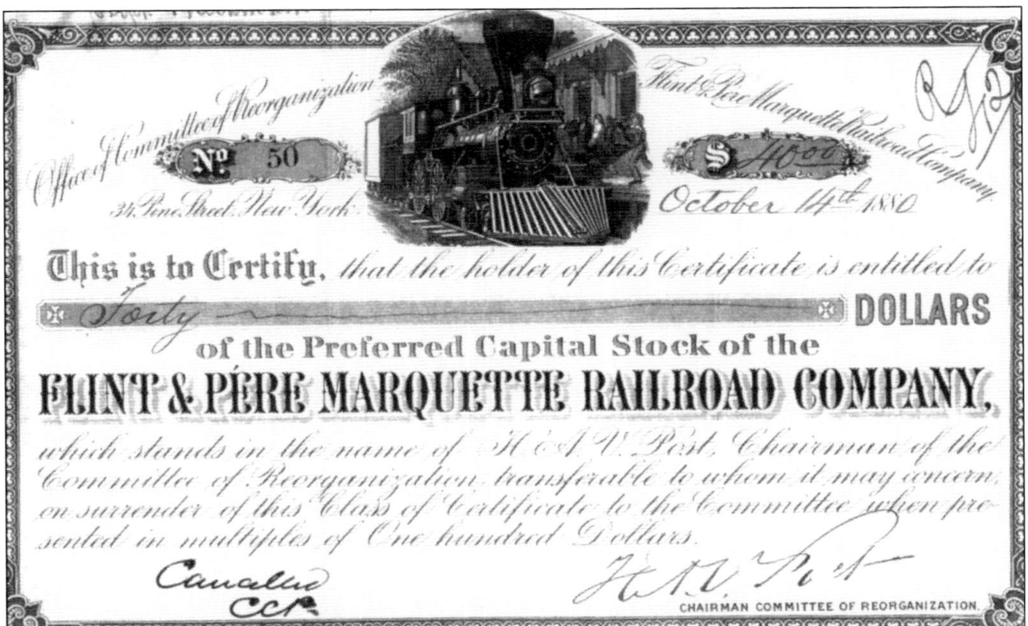

Office of Committee of Reorganization
Flint & Pere Marquette Railroad Company
No. 50
$40.00
34 Pine Street, New York
October 14th 1880

This is to Certify, that the holder of this Certificate is entitled to
Forty DOLLARS
of the Preferred Capital Stock of the
FLINT & PÉRE MARQUETTE RAILROAD COMPANY,
which stands in the name of H. & A. V. Post, Chairman of the Committee of Reorganization, transferable to whom it may concern, on surrender of this Class of Certificate to the Committee when presented in multiples of One hundred Dollars.

Cancelled
CCP

CHAIRMAN COMMITTEE OF REORGANIZATION.

The Flint and Pere Marquette Railroad was chartered in 1857. In 1867, company secretary Henry Potter declared that completing a line to Ludington was crucial to capitalizing on the lumber industry. Building westward from Saginaw, the railroad would reach Reed City in 1871 and Ludington by 1874. The railroad reorganized in 1879, and this certificate was issued a year later. (Courtesy of Paul Bigford.)

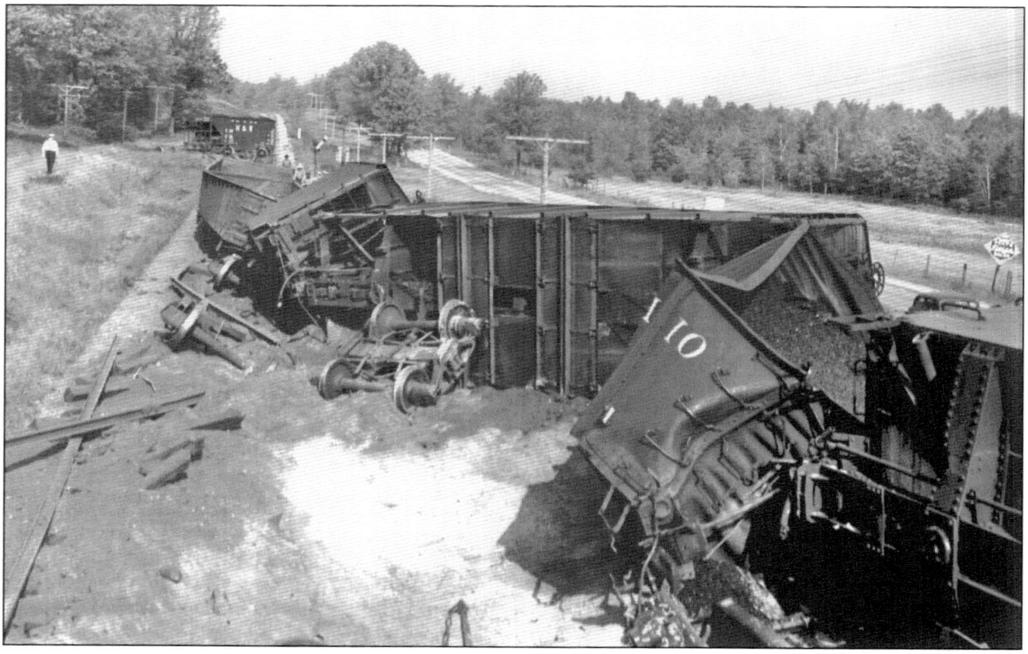

This westbound freight with a load of coal was passing through Nirvana at about 60 miles per hour when it jumped the tracks. The accident occurred in 1957. Early railroad history is rich in dramatic crashes and personal injuries, which led to better communication and safety rules. US-10 is visible in the background. (Courtesy of Al George.)

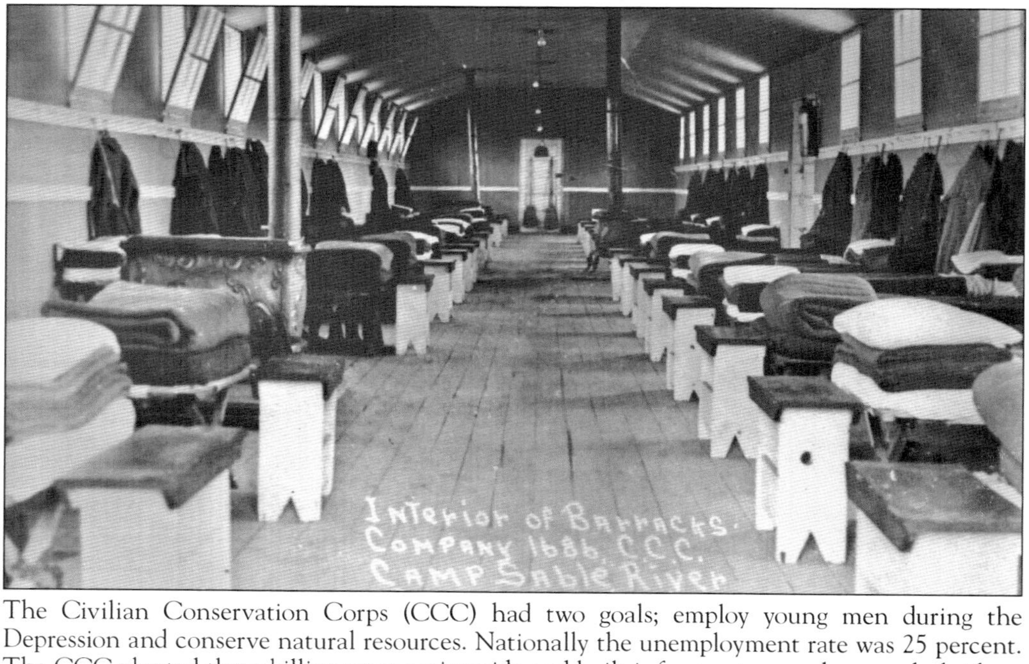

The Civilian Conservation Corps (CCC) had two goals; employ young men during the Depression and conserve natural resources. Nationally the unemployment rate was 25 percent. The CCC planted three billion trees nationwide and built infrastructure such as roads, bridges, and parks. The men at Camp Sauble (Sable), near Loon Lake, as well as other area camps, replanted thousands of white pine throughout Lake County. (Courtesy of Tennis Trucks.)

Three

PLANTING THE SEED

Permanent settlement of northern Michigan was brought about by two important factors. First, returning Civil War veterans were awarded 80-to-160-acre homesteads by the government for service to their country. Second, in the late 1800s most of the land in the county was owned by the railroads that then leased it to the timber companies. Following the cutting of the timber, the railroads had no further use for most of the acreage, so they began advertising and selling it off. Other private loggers, who had personally purchased land, made their fortune and moved on, letting the land revert to the State of Michigan, where it was available for repurchase.

The Pere Marquette Railroad reserved some parcels for parks, school sites, and courthouse squares, but much of its acreage was sold by its land promoters. Northern Michigan was advertised as the land of opportunity for farming, as the trees had already been cut, leaving only stumps to be removed. Farmers coming from the east saw this as a welcome sign, eliminating one of the largest hardships they faced in preparing the soil for planting.

Many of these farmers were immigrants from Europe. The French and Canadians had been here since the fur-trapping days and were now joined by the British, Swedes, Finns, Germans, Poles, Irish, Dutch, Scots, Welsh, and Italians. Each group brought its own heritage and unique character to the homesteads, represented in the style of barns they built, the methods of farming they used, and the fruits and vegetables they planted.

Unfortunately, it was a struggle for most. After logging, much of the topsoil had washed into the rivers, leaving only sand. Game was scarce, as the habitat for fish, fowl, and wild animals had vanished with the loggers. But the farmers in Lake County were stoic. Many stayed and found ways to succeed. Generations later, some of these same families are still farming the land their ancestors plowed and sowed at the dawn of the 20th century.

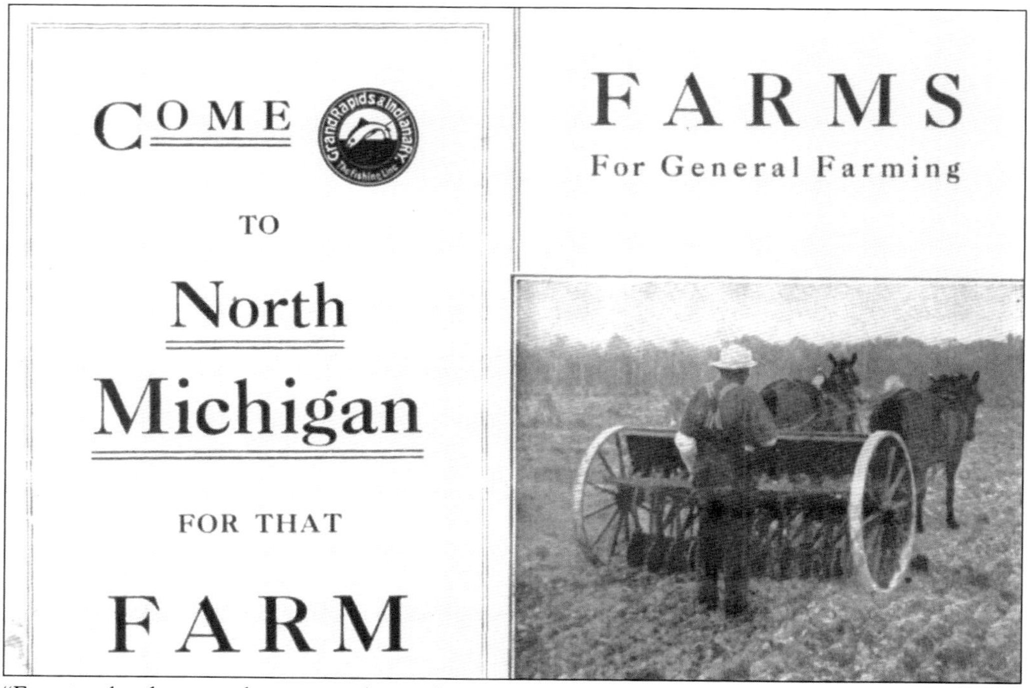

"Farming lands as good as any in the world are to be found in abundance" so advertised the Flint and Pere Marquette Railroad. This 1913 advertisement was posted in depots in Detroit, Chicago, Pittsburgh, and other large cities. It lured new immigrants and enticed factory workers from eastern states to the land of pure air, sparkling streams swarming with fish, and "rich farming soil." (Courtesy of Jerry Poprawski.)

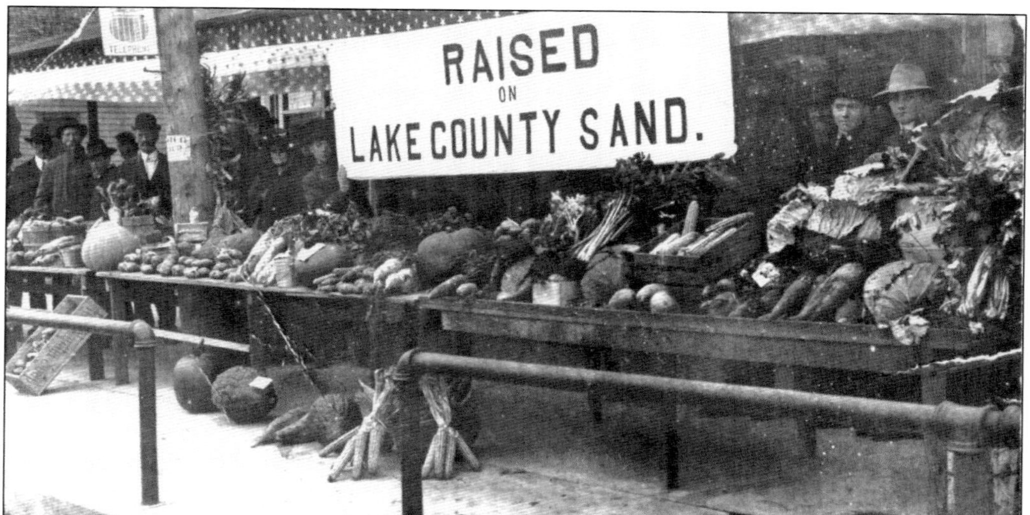

The farmers' market sign depicts the sad sentiment of the ability to farm on Lake County soil. Once the thin layer of topsoil was exhausted, usually within a few years, all that remained was blowing sand. This photograph, taken during the September 1909 Lake County Fair, illustrates that the farmer's efforts though often did end in success. (Courtesy of the Lake County Historical Society.)

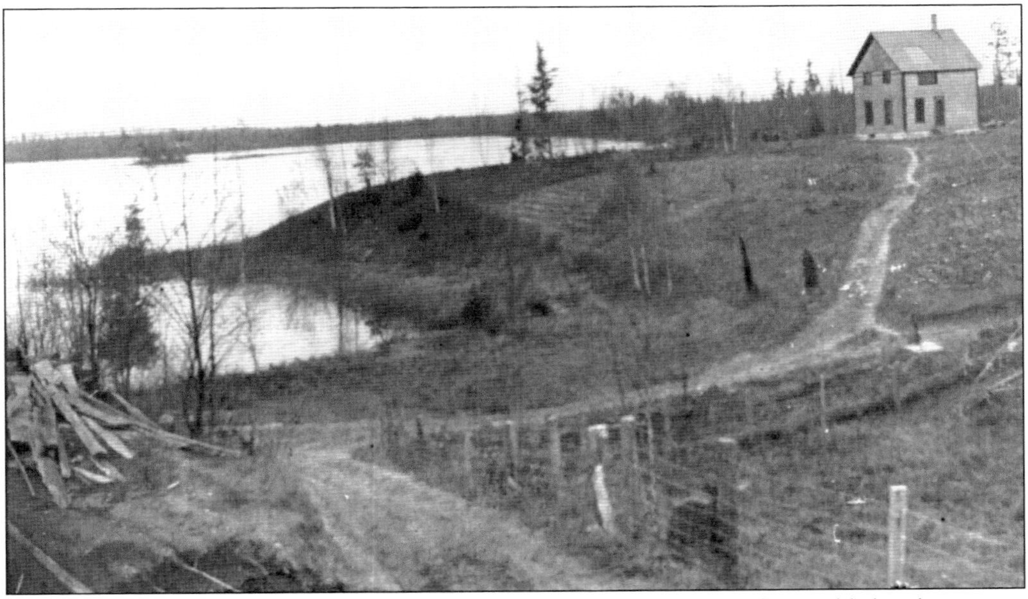

When the first settlers arrived, they were faced with an ocean of highly flammable brush, massive pine stumps, and poor soil. This 1910 photograph of Martin Gustave Johnson's cabin on Big Bass Lake shows what most settlers found on their arrival. Gradually Johnson cleared his land of the stumps and planted fields and orchards. (Photograph by Martin Johnson, courtesy of the Martin Johnson Heritage Museum.)

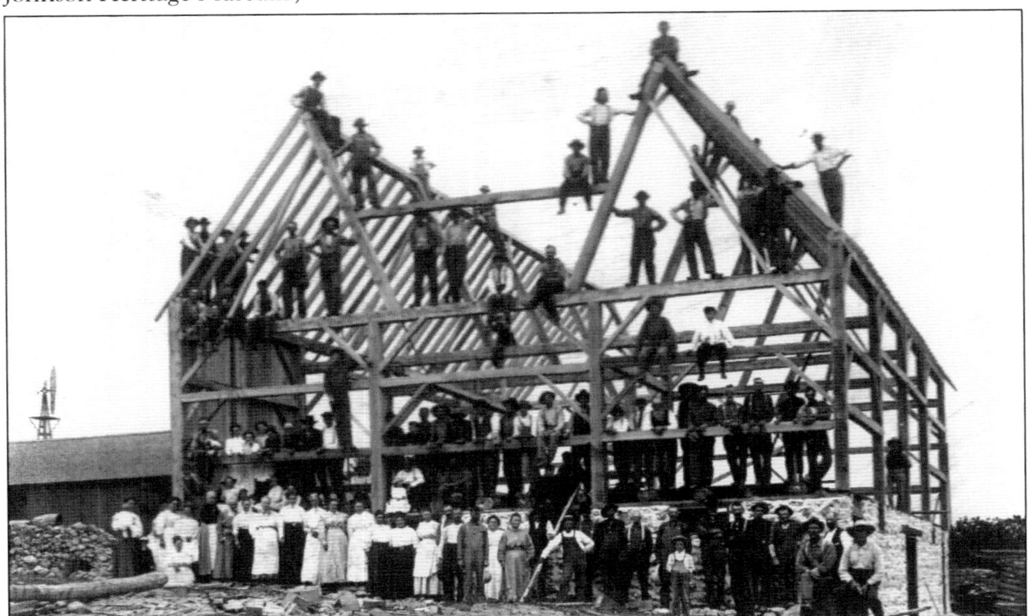

Neighbors, 75 men and 25 women strong, came to lend kind and generous hands in raising the Spears' new barn on July 8, 1910. This large structure would be home to John F. Spears and his wife's 100 head of cattle and their winter feed. Emigrating from Canada 30 years earlier and seeking a new home for his young family, Spears settled on Saddler Road in Pinora Township. (Courtesy of the James Woods family.)

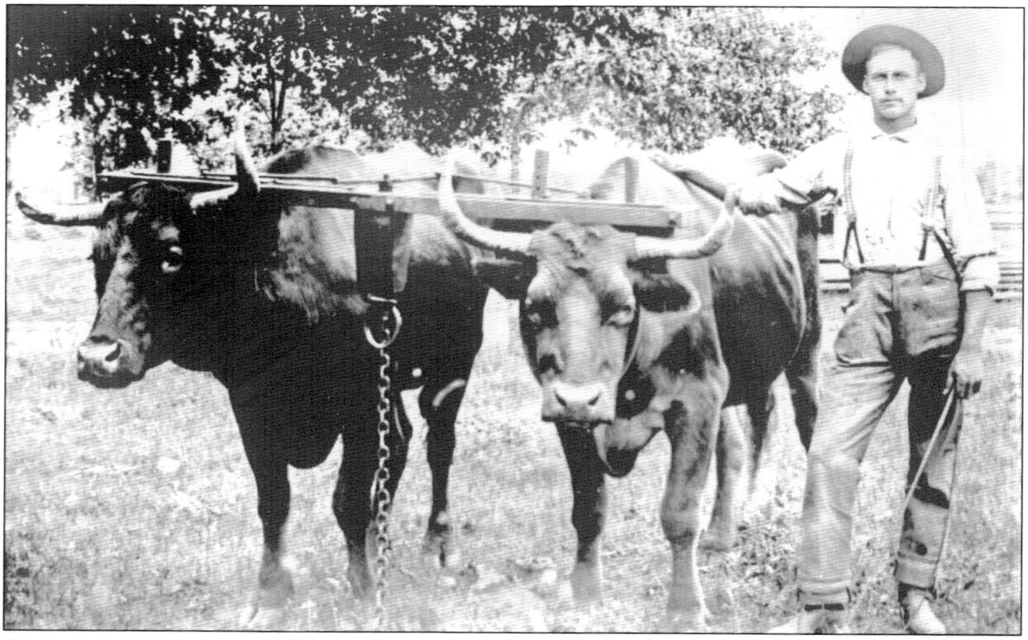

Oxen, being stronger, sturdier, and more suited to pulling plow equipment than horses, were a great asset to George Bradford on the farm his parents, Jesse and Sarah Bradford, established in 1877. Located on Sanborn Creek in Pleasant Plains Township, the farm also included a buttery. Bradford sold his dairy products to the local market and to residents in Baldwin. (Courtesy of Tennis Trucks.)

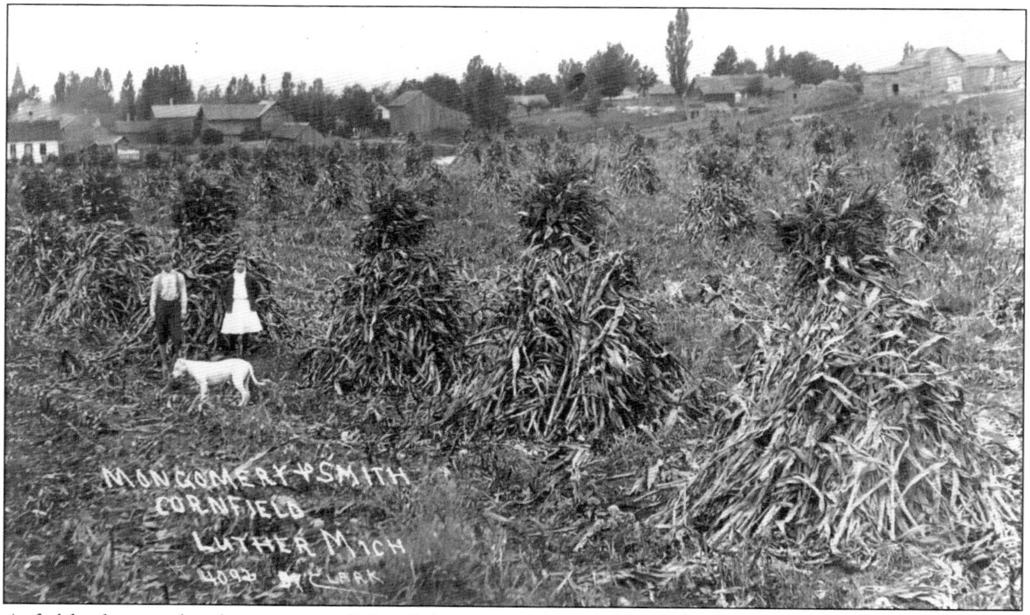

A field of corn shocks was proof that Montgomery and Smith had a successful year. This field lies just on the outskirts of Luther. A booming town in Lake County, Luther consisted of about 750 homes and businesses in 1910, when this photograph was taken. (Photograph by Allan Clark, courtesy of Jerry Poprawski.)

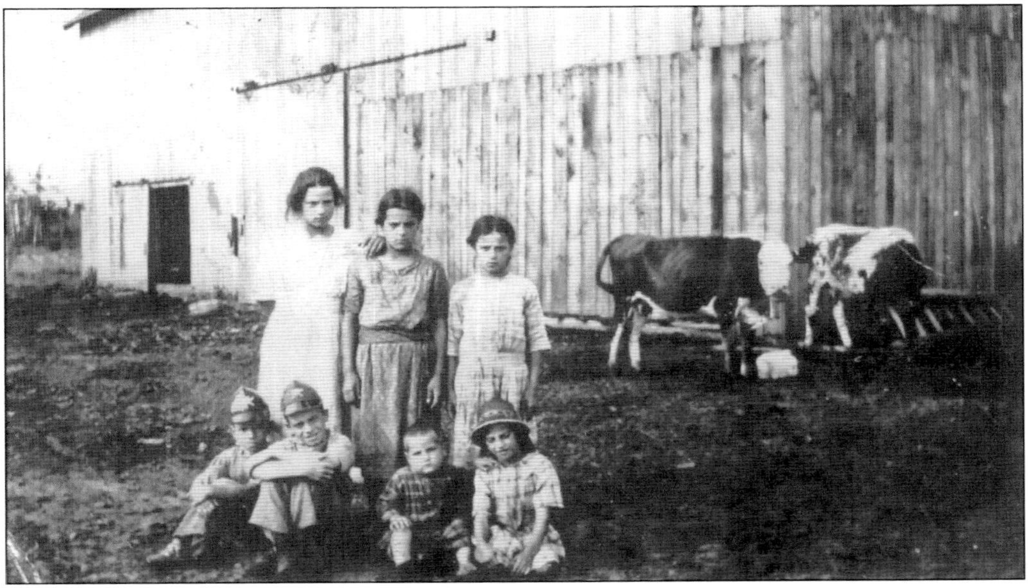

In 1907, the Italian Giammalva family bought 40 acres and another 40 acres in 1909 for a total of 80 acres in Cherry Valley Township. Joe Giammalva cleared the land with an ax and his team of horses. The family survived on venison, home-grown vegetables, and by raising pigs, chickens, and cattle. They made cheese that was taken by train to be sold in Chicago. Above, the Giammalva children, from left to right, (first row) Sam, Tony, Kay, and Rose; (second row) Mary, Emily, and Edith are posing in 1920 in front of the family's 60-by-100-foot barn. Modern-day farming was slow to come. In 1940, the family was still using horses to bring the hay in from the fields to be stored in the barn's haymow. Father Joe, atop the hay, and grown-up Kay, left, and Mary are standing with the horses. (Courtesy of Darci Maldonado.)

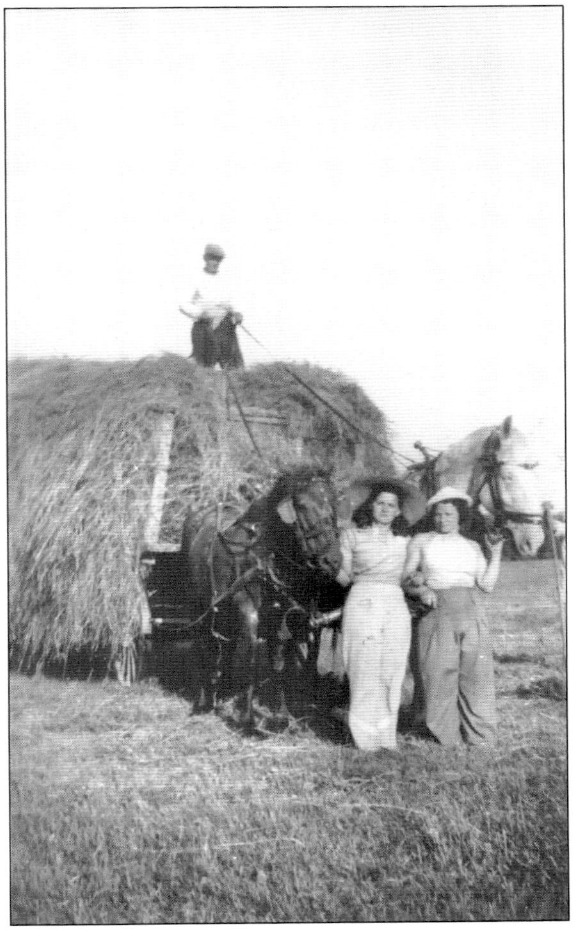

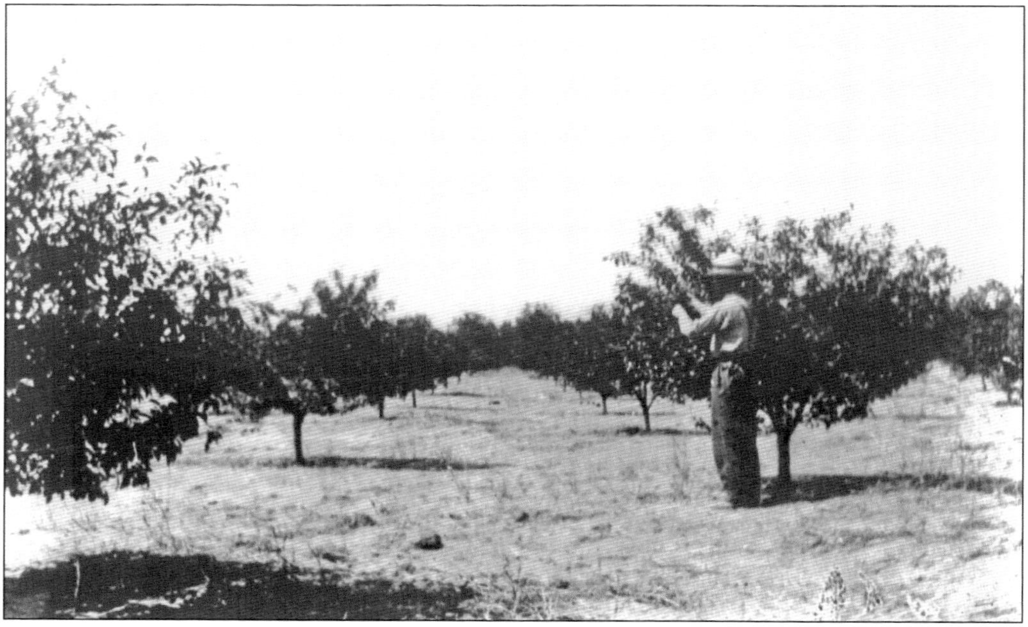

A total of 1,400 new apple tree seedlings were planted in 1910 in the orchard of the Lake View Fruit Farm northwest of Big Star Lake for a total of 2,000 trees. The next year, another 2,000 seedlings were added. This made the Pruitt farm one of the finest orchards in Michigan. Claude Patterson (manager) looks over the apple crop in this 1915 photograph. (Courtesy of the Lake County Historical Society.)

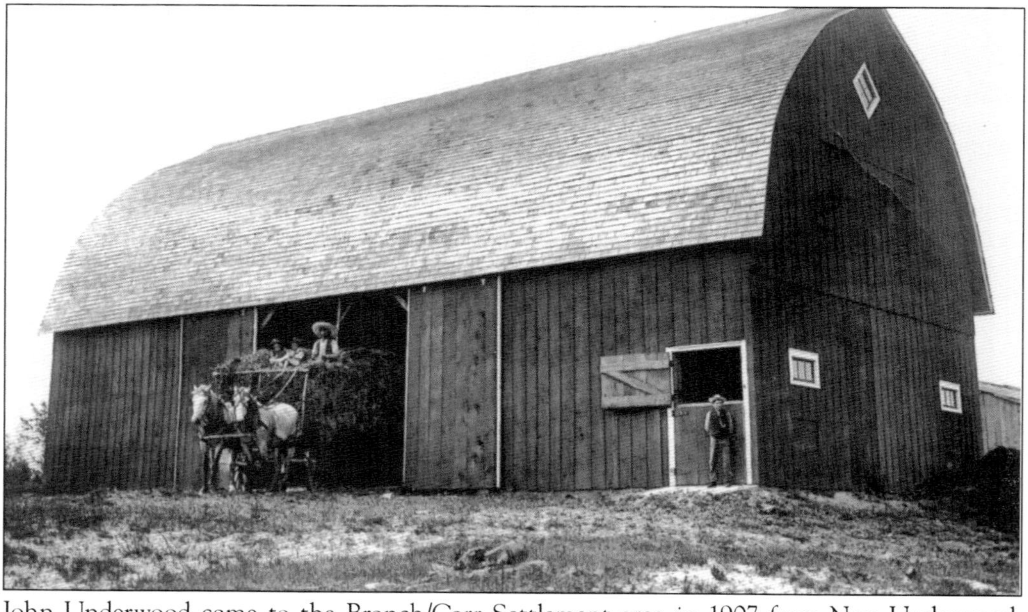

John Underwood came to the Branch/Carr Settlement area in 1907 from New Underwood, South Dakota. The photograph shows his farm after the large dairy barn was constructed. Underwood, sitting on top of the mounded hay with his daughters, is driving the wagon. Daughter Kathryn Underwood later married Leo LaPointe, and they took over the farm, now celebrating its centennial. (Courtesy of LaPointe Farms.)

Four

TOWN LIFE

For the purpose of simplicity, the term *town* in Lake County could easily be interchangeable with the words village, place, community, or settlement. Towns were an identifiable place within a township where a number of people lived, with or without local amenities such as businesses, a school, a church, or a post office. In all, over 60 towns in Lake County have been documented by researchers.

Some have truly vanished and are referred to as ghost towns such as Stearns Siding, west of Baldwin. In 1899, Stearns Siding served over 2,000 immigrants from Norway and Sweden, and today is only found by depressions in the ground that remain from where Michigan basements were dug. Others such as Marlborough (Marlboro), south of Baldwin, still have homes that can be traced back to the early 1900s, when marl was being processed into cement, but the town itself has vanished.

Every town has its own story. Chase boasts of having the original county seat. This designation was "stolen" by ruffians from Baldwin in 1875. With this, Baldwin became the new county seat and constructed a courthouse on the curve in the road for all to view.

Early photographs of Luther show life in a logging town. In a unique event, local photographer Allen Clark captured a tragic moment in 1910 when the dam at the millpond broke.

The town of Peacock sat at the crossroads of two railroad lines and became a boarding town for the steel gang workers who kept the rails repaired. The Peacock baseball team was known for the skills of the Medacco brothers, who were from a Chippewa Indian family living in this settlement.

For many rural families, going to town meant visiting the general store, the butcher, the post office, or the bank. Towns were also the place to have fun, such as playing pool, going to the theater, or eating hand-dipped ice cream. The Baldwin Photo Shop, owned by the Kahl family, as well as local residents, helped document community life through its many years of photographing events. Experience town life in Lake County through these images, as earlier generations did first hand.

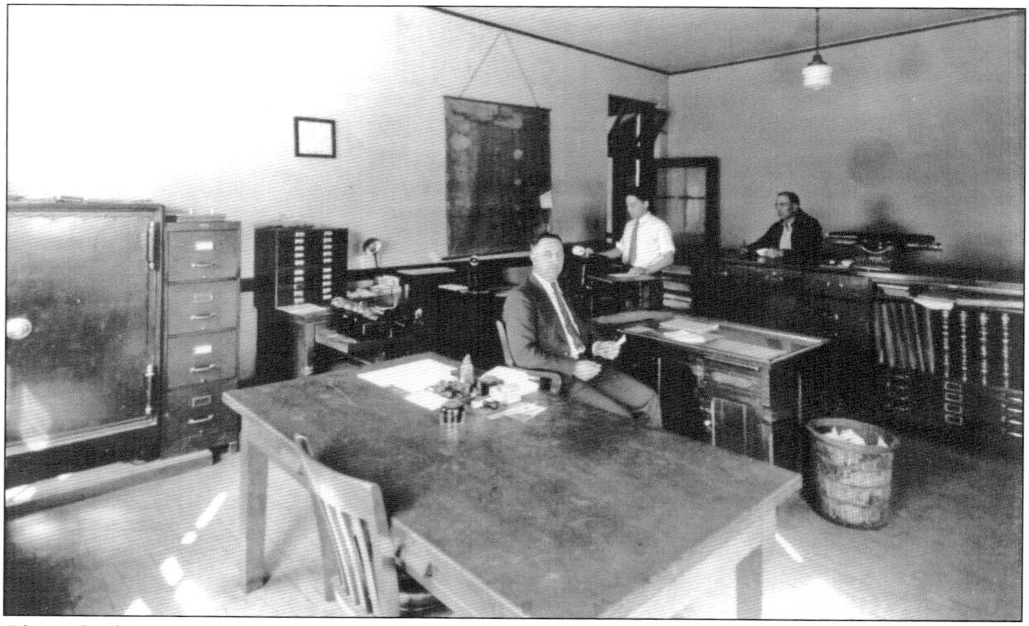

Chase had claimed rights to the county seat and in 1873 purchased a safe from Mosler and Bahmann Company of Cincinnati for $1,000. An angry mob from Baldwin armed with crowbars, peaveys, hand spikes, and broom handles stole the safe on April 30, 1875, in the "Great Battle of Chase," successfully relocating the county seat to Baldwin. The famous safe is shown here in the treasurer's office in the courthouse. (Courtesy of the Dorrell Bradford family.)

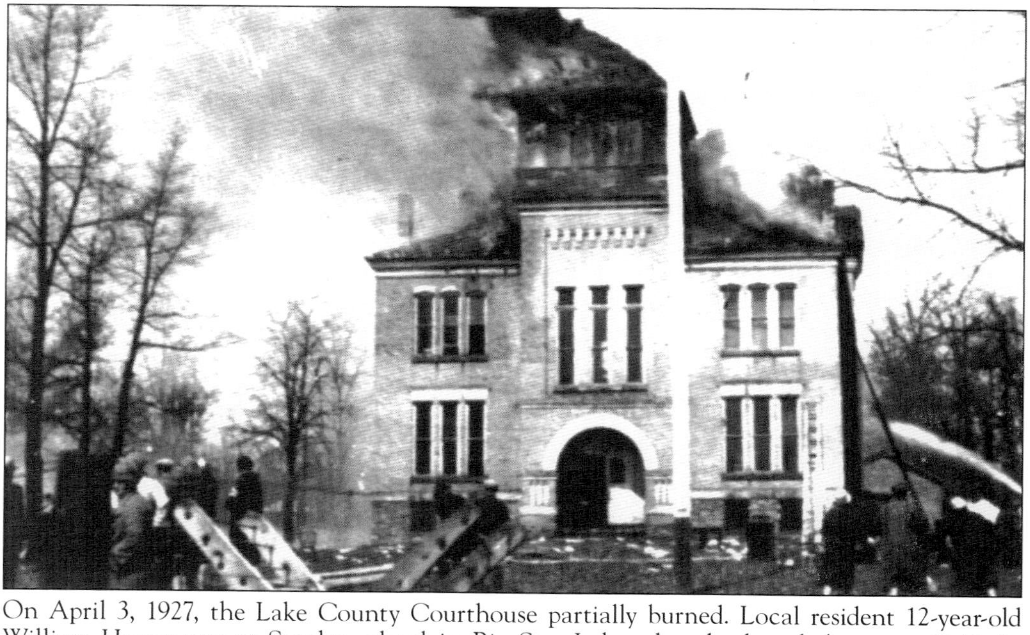

On April 3, 1927, the Lake County Courthouse partially burned. Local resident 12-year-old William Homer was at Sunday school in Big Star Lake when he heard the news. Baldwin firefighters, with two-wheeled hose carts, battled the fire for seven hours. The roof and cupola were burnt, but no county records were lost. The American flag flying that day was saved by young William. (Courtesy of the Lake County Historical Society.)

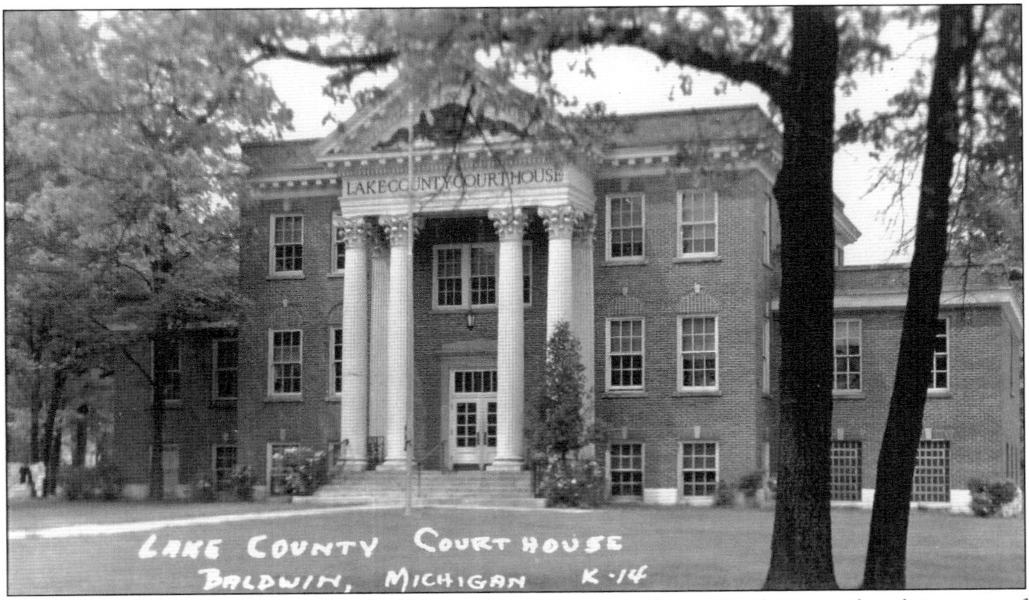

Pictured is the 1927 remodeled Lake County Courthouse with its Greek Revival architecture of red brick, Corinthian fluted columns, and classical pediment. The renovation cost was $50,000. The jail was located on the far right where the bottom two windows are. The sheriff and his family lived in the basement next door. It appears the sheriff's laundry is hanging out to dry at the left side of the building. (Courtesy of Gordon Allison.)

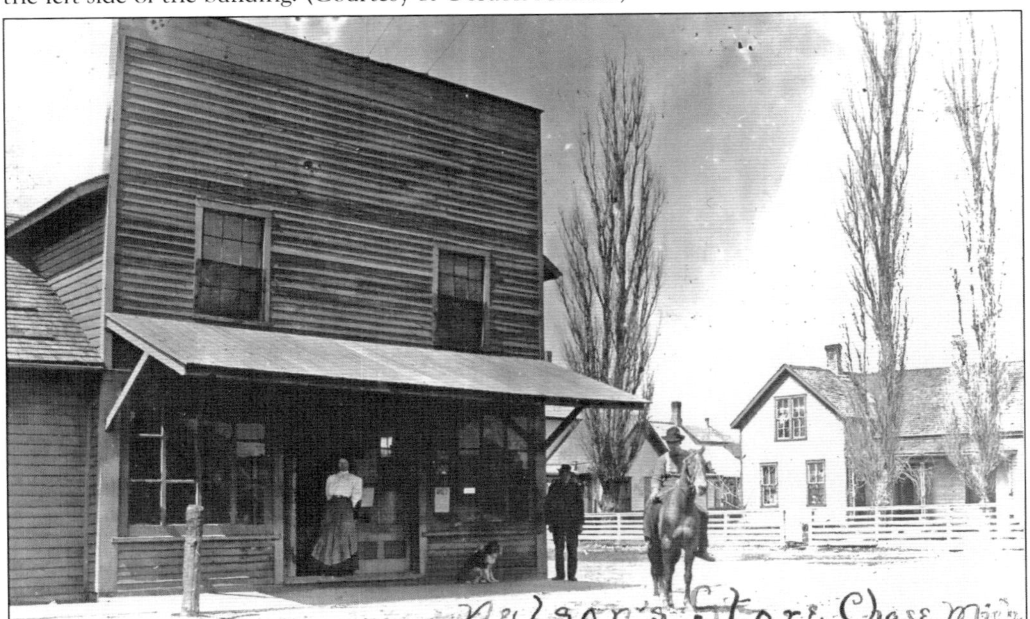

After the logging companies stripped the area of white pine, the Pere Marquette Railroad continued service from Saginaw to Ludington and began shipping supplies. Chase remained a key railroad stop along the way with the 1908 Nelson's Store benefiting from this new venture. The Lombardy poplar trees seen here were planted by settlers. The species grew quickly, providing necessary shade. (Courtesy of Dennis Ellison.)

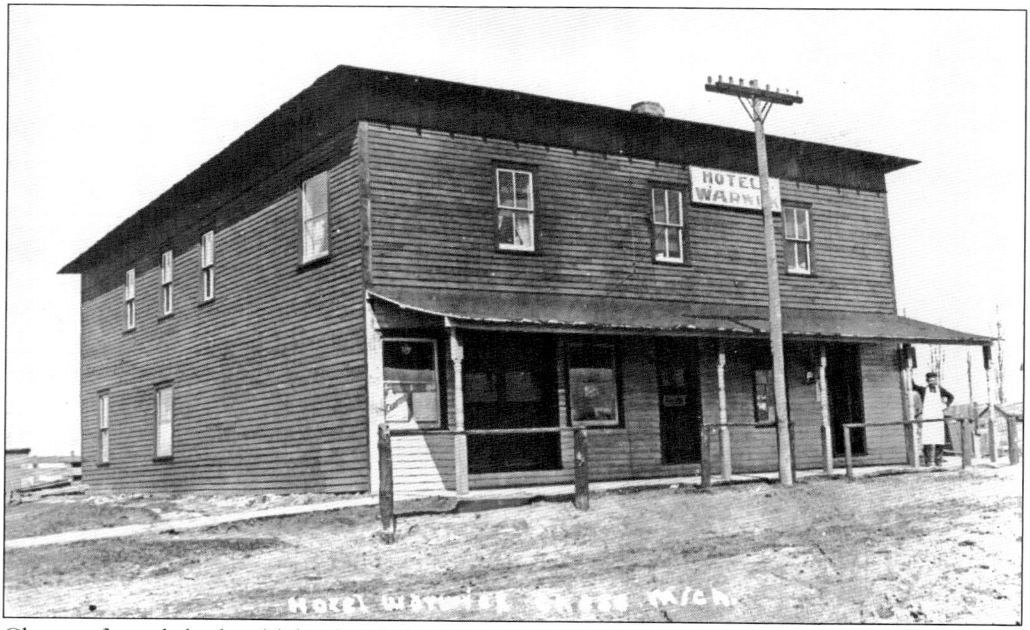

Chase reflected the hard life of early logging and railroad towns. This gray weathered building was the Warwick Hotel from the 1900s, built by longtime resident Dr. George Field to meet the demand for lodging. Located on Depot Street and U.S. 10 in Chase, it was convenient to travelers. (Courtesy of Dennis Ellison.)

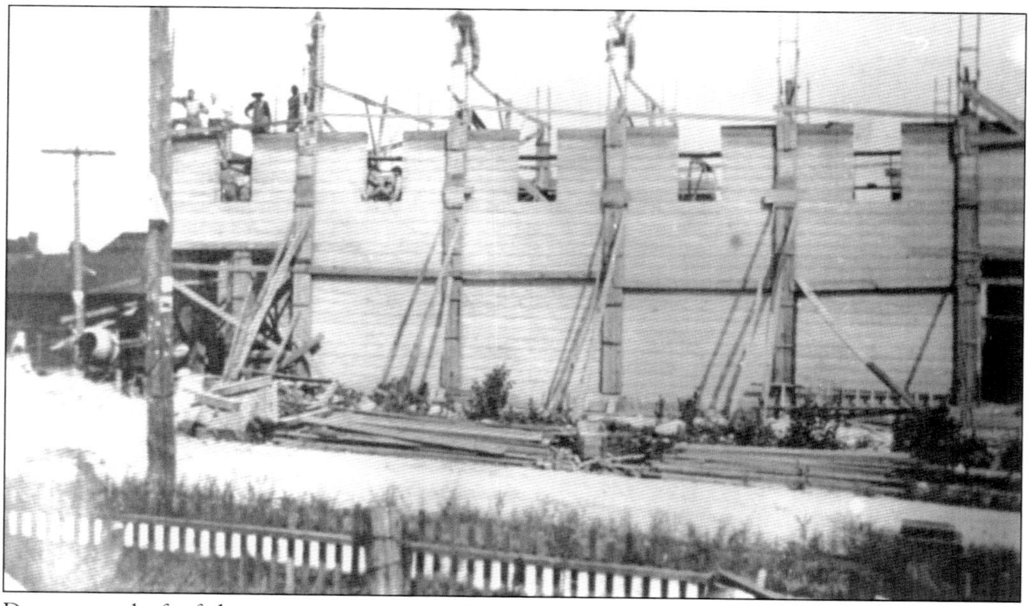

Due to crude firefighting equipment, wooden structures did not often survive a fire. Chase's answer to that problem was this two-story poured-concrete building, one of only a few constructed in Michigan. Built for the Odd Fellows and Rebekah lodge it was later used as a post office, general store, and community hall for basketball games and square dances. This 1914 photograph shows men hauling concrete to the second floor. (Courtesy of Tennis Trucks.)

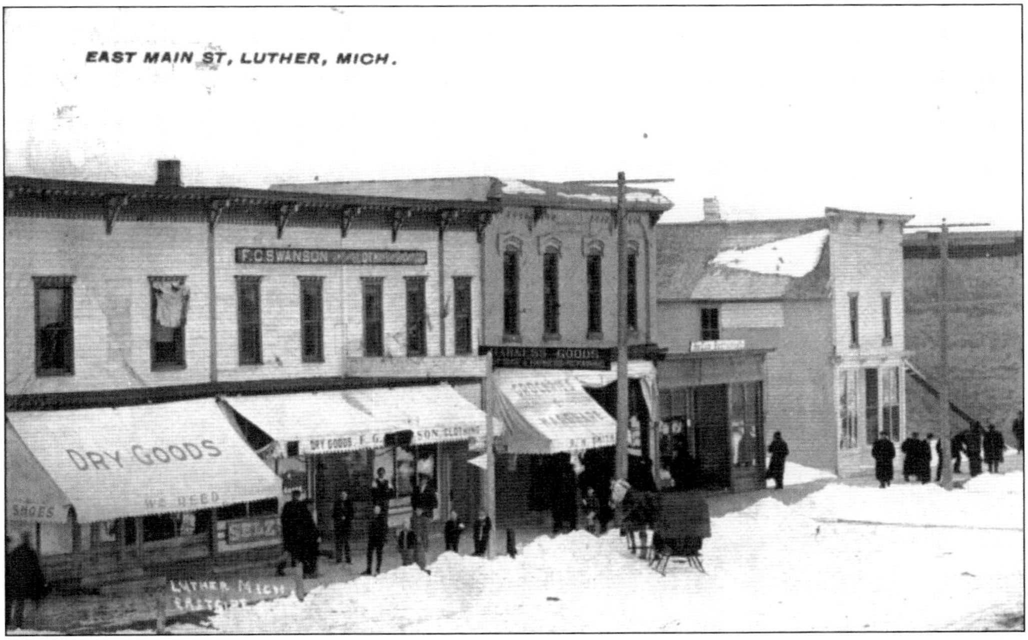

While Baldwin and Chase fought for the county seat, the village of Luther, in northern Lake County, became a roaring lumber town. Named for William Luther, the town had a variety of shops on East Main Street for its customers to buy their wares. In 1885, Luther had four saloons, several hotels, a newspaper, three doctors, an opera house, and four churches. (Courtesy of the Lake County Historical Society.)

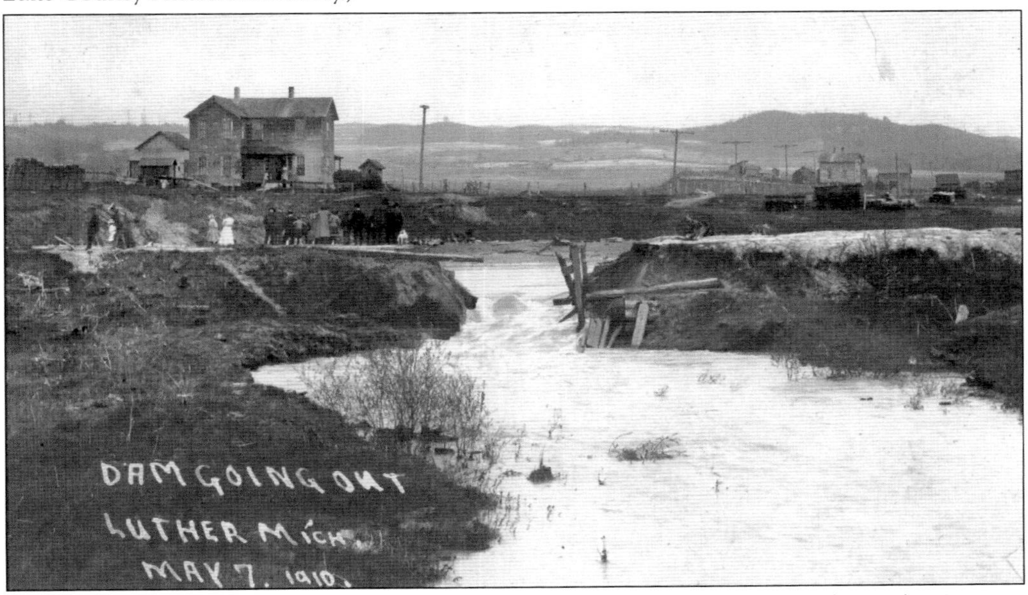

In 1881, the Wilson, Luther and Wilson Lumber Company built a mill beside the Little Manistee River south of Luther. A dam was constructed to furnish power and the millpond became a place to fish and relax. On May 7, 1910, the earthen dam broke as captured in this photograph by Allan Clark. The Vincent House, a boardinghouse for lumberjacks and businessmen, housed Clark's photography shop. (Photograph by Allan Clark, courtesy of Jerry Poprawski.)

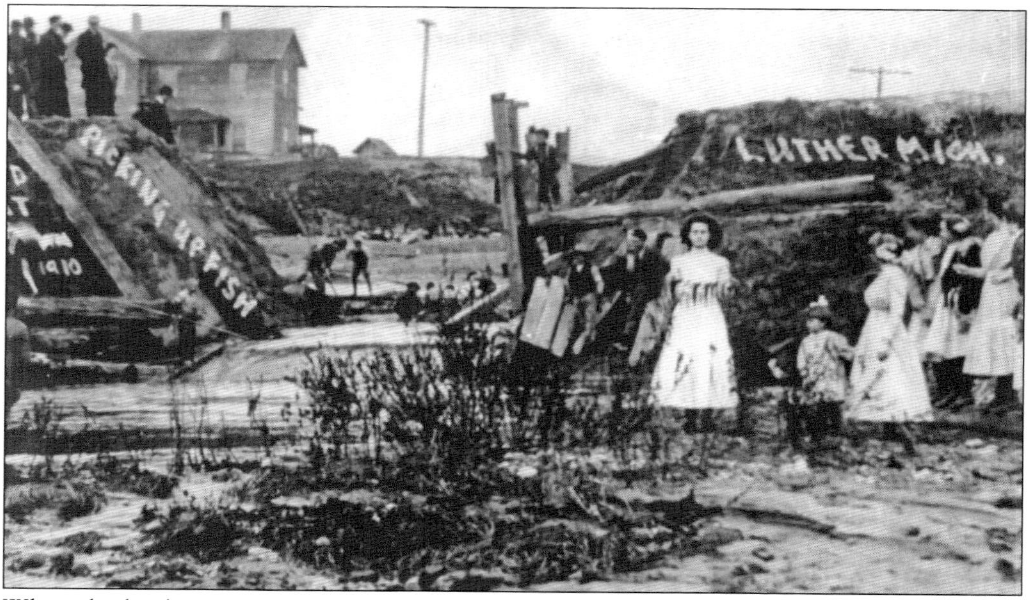

When the lumber company's dam broke, many of the 1,000 Luther residents came to harvest trout and other fish floundering on the sand. The dam was rebuilt and remains today as a reminder of earlier times. A three-story gristmill was also on the pond and in 1913, with the addition of a generator, produced electricity for the town. (Photograph by Allan Clark, courtesy Terri Jamison.)

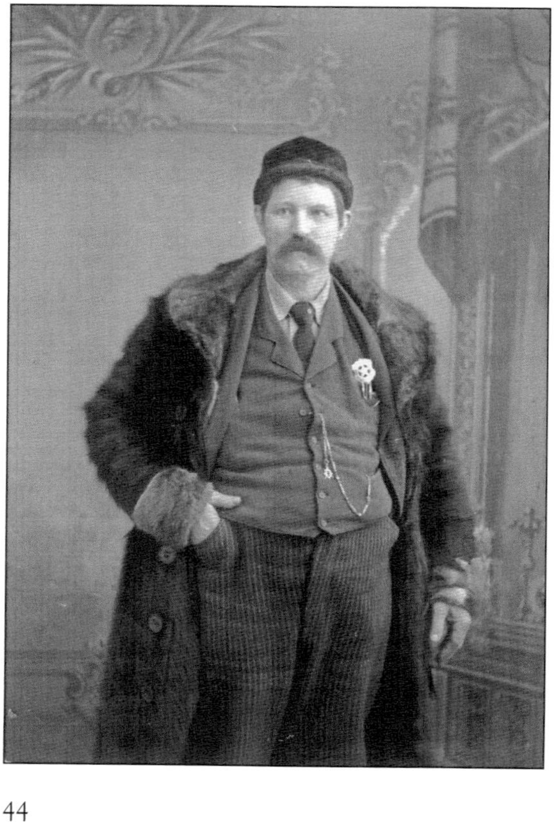

David Colton, in his bearskin coat, was the Lake County sheriff in 1898. A man reported to Colton that he had found his brother dead in an icehouse sawdust pile. But local resident George Bradford recognized the socks on the corpse and identified him as another man recently buried. Hal Cutler, prosecutor, charged the man reporting the crime with grave robbing. It had been the robber's intention to collect on an insurance policy. (Courtesy of the Lake County Historical Society.)

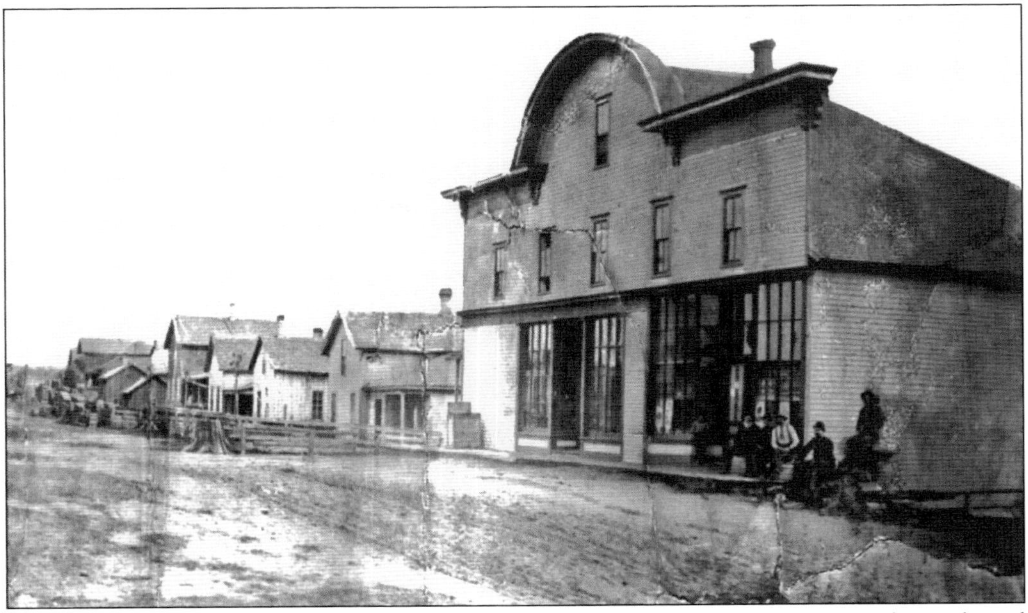

Founded in 1885 as a lumbering settlement on the Manistee branch of the Grand Rapids and Indiana Railroad in Pinora Township, Deer Lake grew to a town of 300 people. The general store, in the forefront, was owned by Osterhout, Fox and Company. This isolated settlement boasted a blacksmith shop, shingle factory, meat market, shoe shop, and roller rink. (Courtesy of the Lake County Historical Society.)

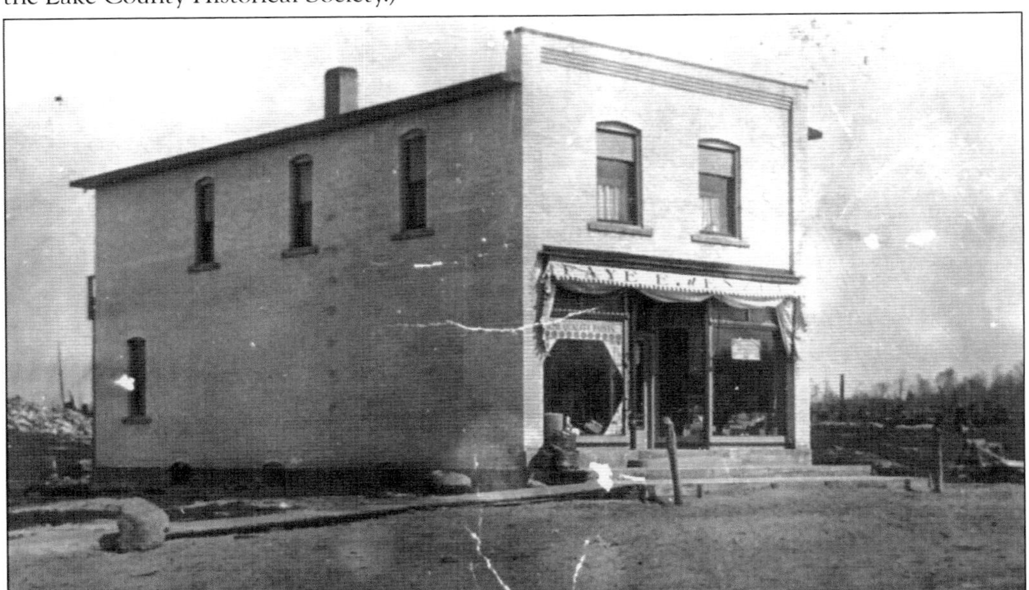

German immigrants William Greenwald, Matt Troge, and Albert Buss began farming in Lake County in the 1890s. In 1900, the Michigan East and West Railroad cut through their land and thus the town of Edgetts was established. The Faye Wenzel building was the railroad station, as well as a mercantile and post office. Two potato warehouses and a pickle station were also in town. (Courtesy of Tennis Trucks.)

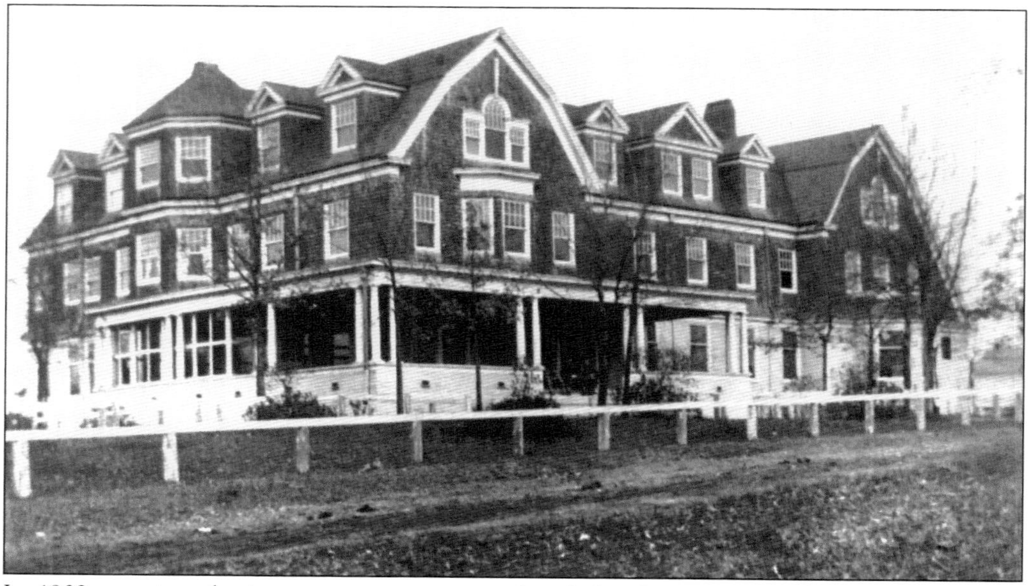

In 1902, a unique business venture was started in Lake County. Howard Parsons, a Detroit investor, founded the Great Northern Portland Cement Company south of Baldwin. Unlike lumber settlements, Marlborough (Marlboro) would have a strong cultural base influenced by Fredric Farnsworth, a Detroit banker and lover of the arts. Andrew Bradford helped supervised the construction of the majestic Marlborough Inn shown here. (Courtesy of the Lake County Historical Society.)

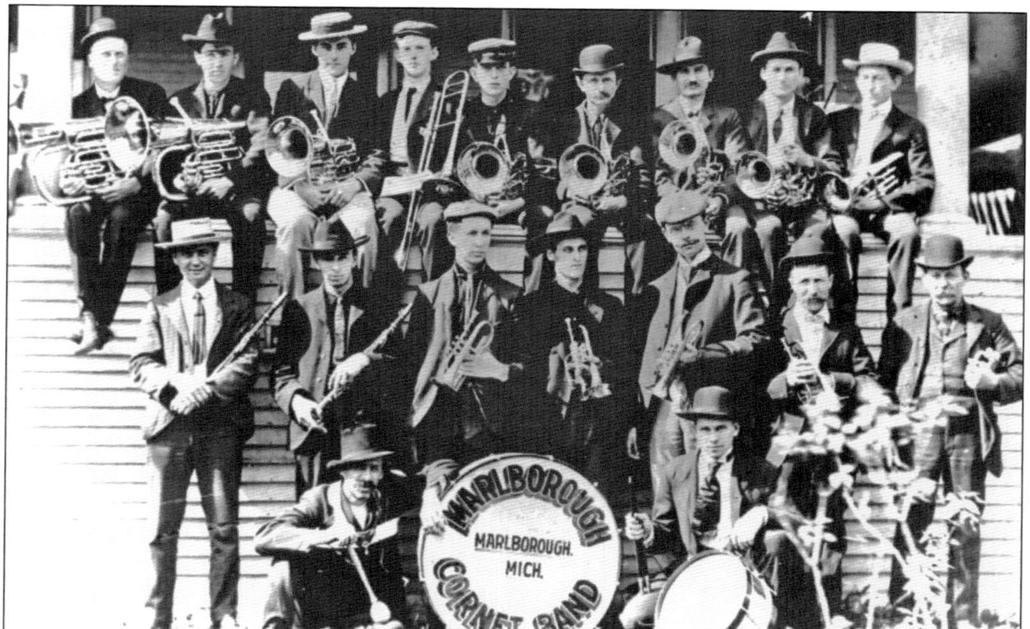

Towns such as Marlborough would often form a local band. The opera house provided a venue for the Marlborough Cornet Band to entertain local residents. Baldwin, Chase, and Luther also had bands that provided musical entertainment and a bit of culture to the community. (Courtesy of the Lake County Historical Society.)

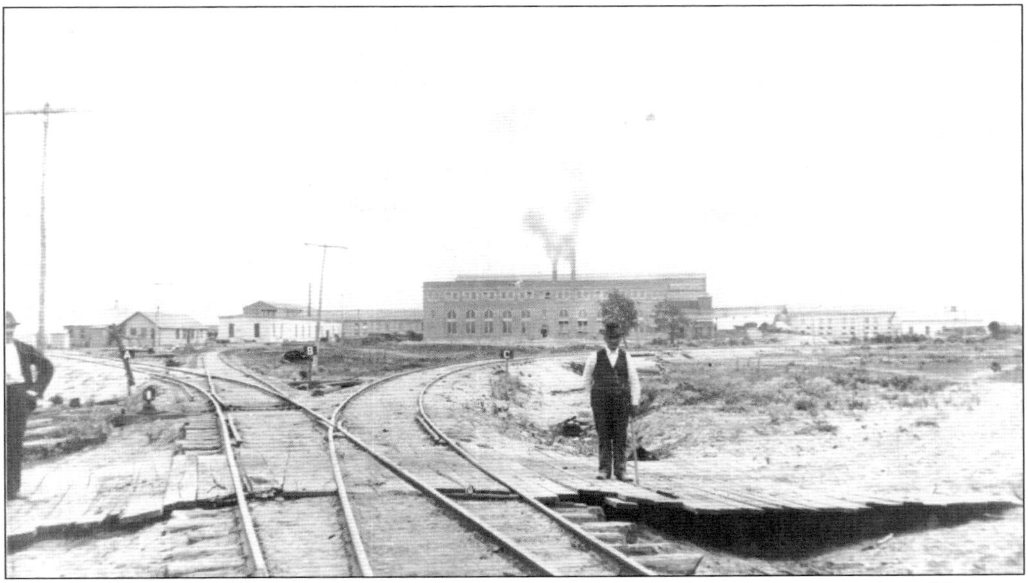

Capital stock of $5,000 created an industry employing 200 workers. Immigrants from Hungary came to the Northern Portland Cement Company to make 15¢ an hour. The company owned 8,000 acres of land, which was the home of the world's largest cement plant at that time. The railroad shipped the finished product from the Marlborough plant, seen in the distance. (Courtesy of the Lake County Historical Society.)

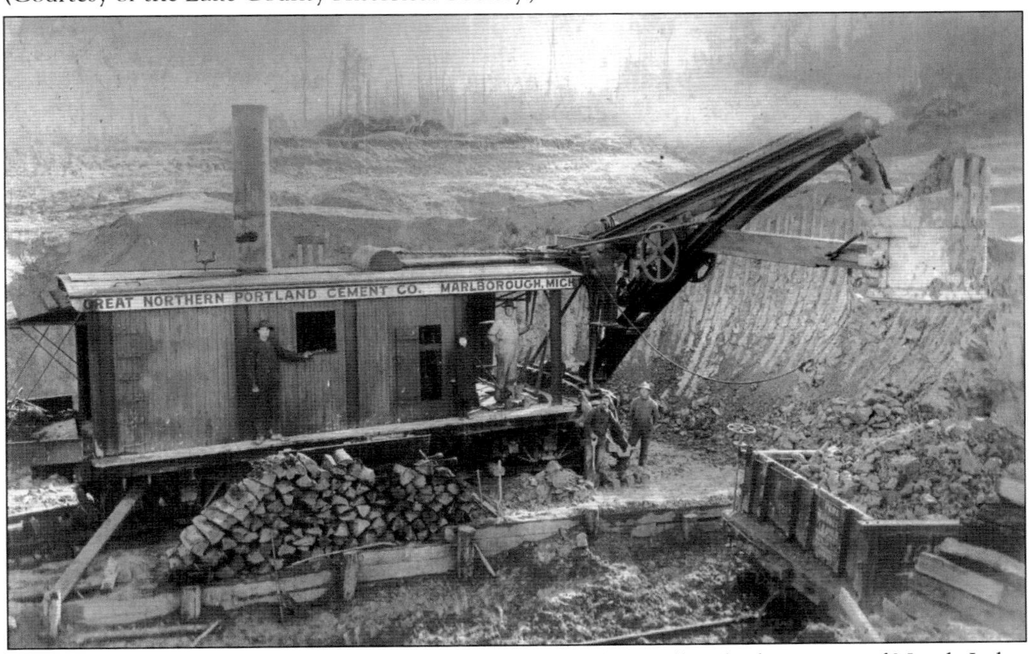

Marl, a component of cement, was dug by steam shovel as well as by barge out of North Lake. "Vast quantities of marl should last many years" was the claim of owners of the Great Northern Portland Cement Company. But a depletion of marl, as well as new ways of making cement, spelled doom for this industry and town in 1908, only six years from its inception. (Courtesy of the Lake County Historical Society.)

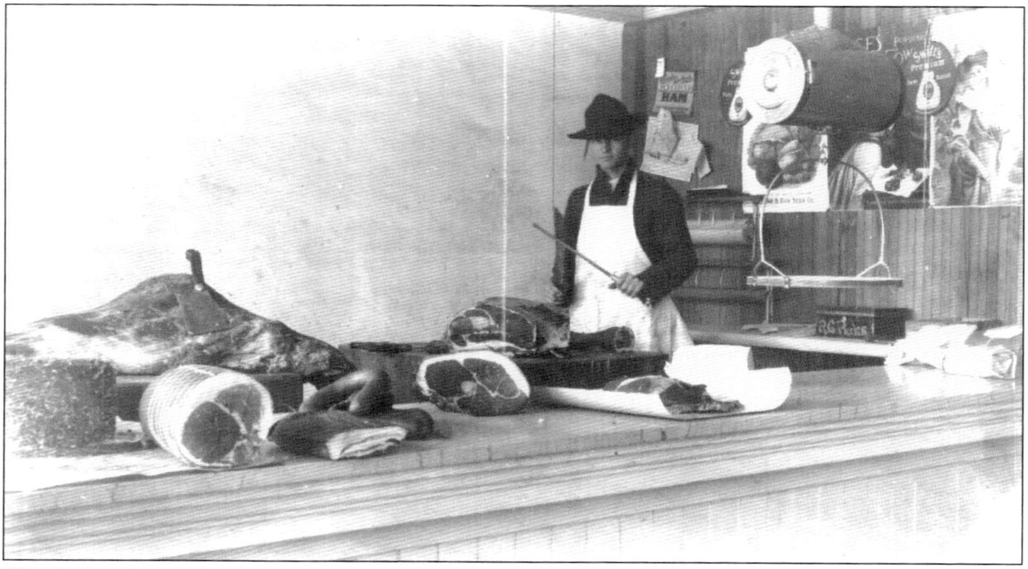

While the Great Northern Cement Company was still in business, Marlborough was a wealthy town with streetlights and stately homes. Numerous businesses served the residents including the butcher shop located in the mercantile building. The opera house, on the second floor, provided cultural entertainment. When the cement plant closed, Marlborough became a ghost town. (Courtesy of the Lake County Historical Society.)

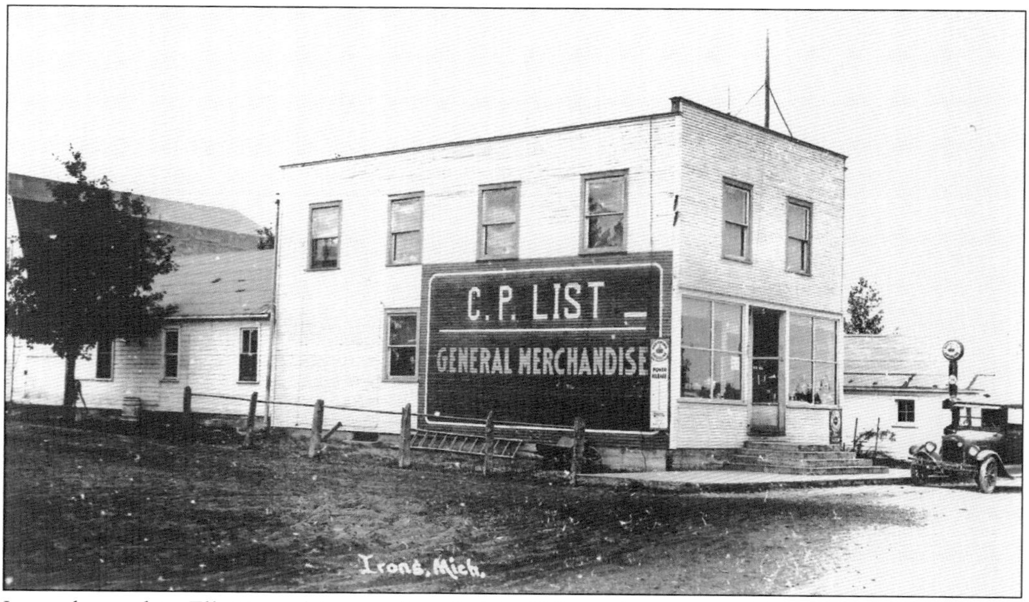

Irons, located in Elk Township, was founded in 1909 and was named for Wilford McIrons, an immigrant from Ireland. The family shortened the name to Irons, as was common for some families to do when coming to America. The C. P. List Store catered to immigrants from Europe who homesteaded in the area. The driver of the 1920s Model T has just filled his tank with Red Crown gasoline. (Courtesy of Jerry Poprawski.)

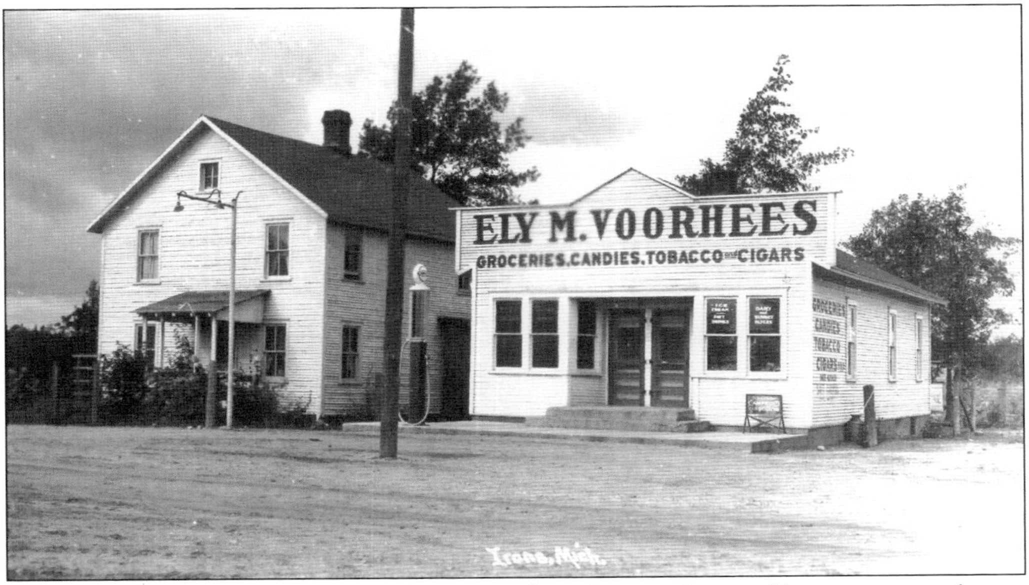

As was typical of small towns, the Ely M. Voorhees Store in Irons sold newspapers, tobacco, ice cream, and gasoline, as well as serving as the post office. It was conveniently located next to the tracks for the Chicago and Western Railroad, which later was purchased by the Pere Marquette Railroad. As many as four trains stopped in town daily in the 1940s. (Courtesy of Jerry Poprawski.)

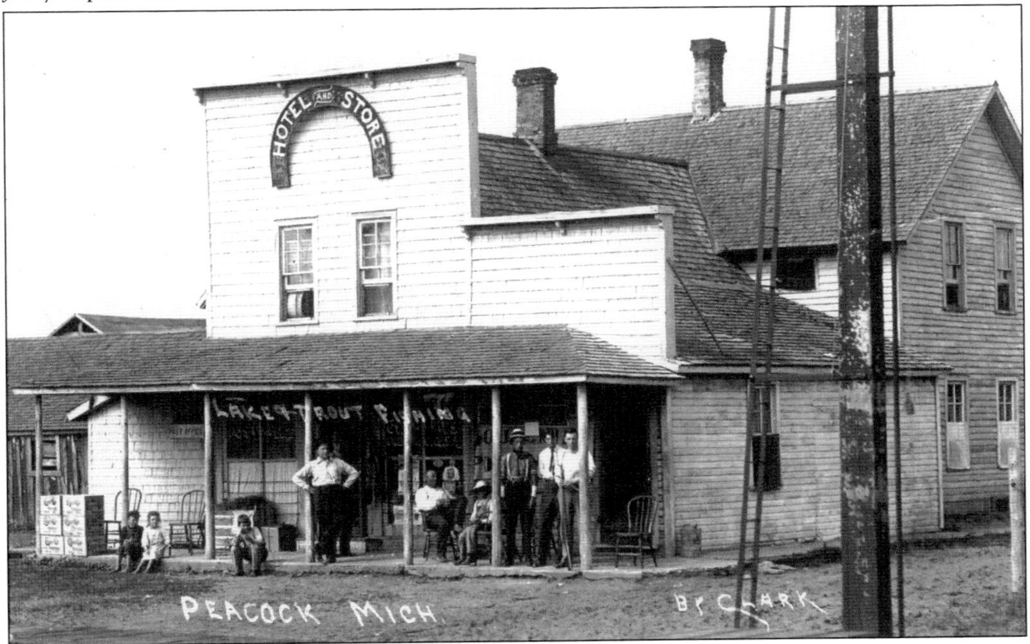

Another town on the railway line from Grand Rapids to Petoskey was Peacock. Settlers from many backgrounds, including African Americans, made their home here. The town was settled in 1897 and was named for its first postmaster, David Peacock. The post office was in the Hotel DeGale, which was operated by Joe Gale and his family. (Photograph by Allan Clark, courtesy of Jerry Poprawski.)

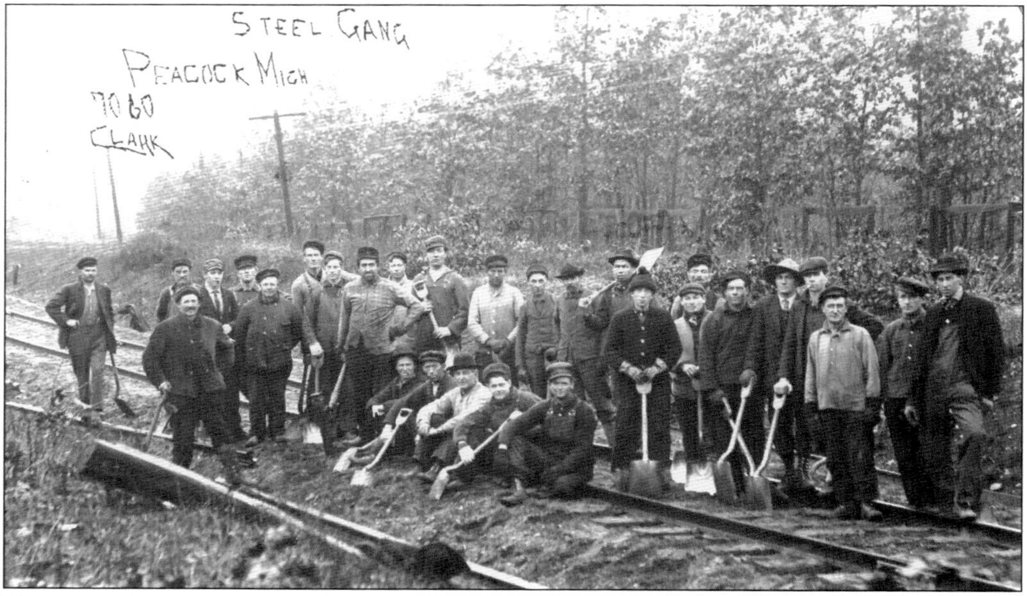

The town of Peacock provided room and board for many railroad workers. The steel gang, which laid the rails, employed Native Americans from two Chippewa families as well as European immigrants. The crews worked long hours for little pay. The three men on the right are probably supervisors. (Photograph by Allan Clark, courtesy of Jerry Poprawski.)

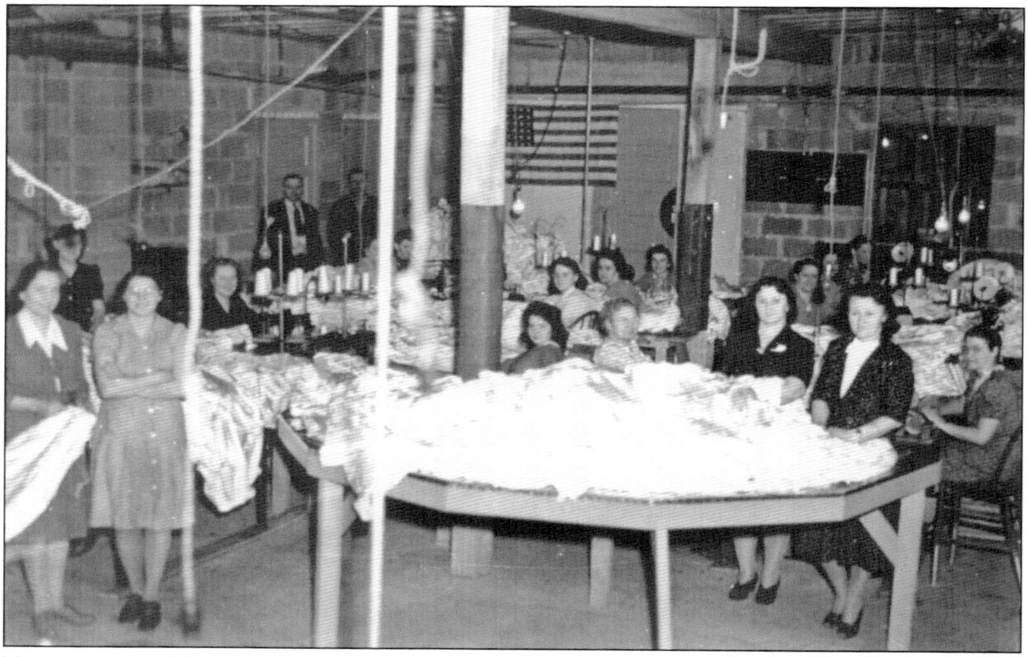

Nirvana, a Buddhist term for "highest heaven," was settled in 1874 and was supported by 12 sawmills. By the 1900s, all had disappeared except for a couple of stores. In the 1940s this town was reborn as women interested in assisting with the World War II effort started the Nirvana Parachute factory in the basement of an old candy factory. Local women sewed silk parachutes for the troops overseas. (Courtesy of the Lake County Historical Society.)

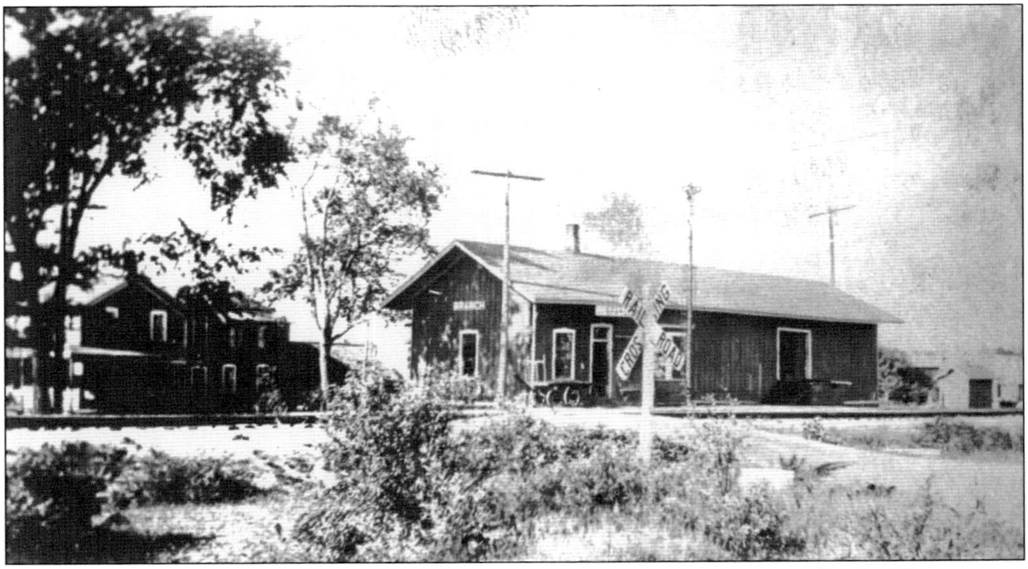

Branch was settled in 1873 by Benjamin Barnett who served as a sergeant for the Union army in the 20th Regiment, Company C, New York Calvary. Branch straddles the Lake and Mason county line. The 14-bedroom Barnett Hotel is seen behind the depot. The depot was originally west of this site, but, due to an uphill grade, the railroad moved it one mile east to a location called 12 Mile Place. (Courtesy of Paul Bigford.)

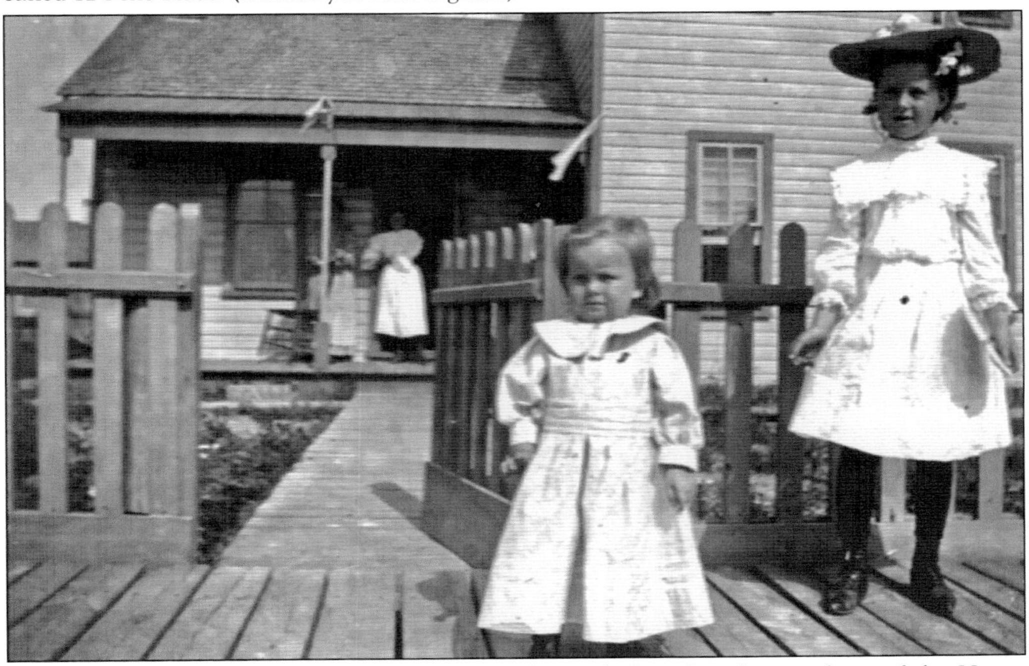

Baldwin town life in the 1890s called for ones finest clothes. Standing in front of the Henry Rudd residence are two young children. The youngster on the left is Clifton Rudd, son of a local saloon owner, seen with Hazel Weaver Wilkinson, daughter of a local store owner. It was not unusual for young lads to wear clothing resembling that of girls. (Courtesy of the Lake County Historical Society.)

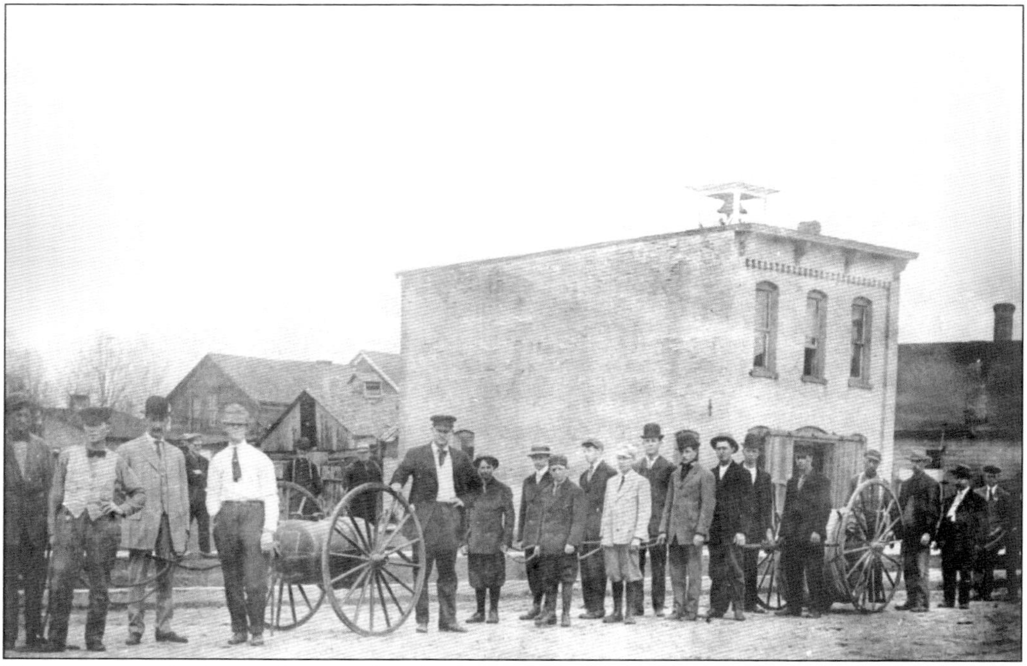

Many towns relied on volunteer fire departments. In this photograph, from the 1890s, local Baldwin men and boys are standing ready to pull the water wagon and hose cart. In the background is the town hall, which was converted to the fire hall by adding a wide door in the front wall and bell tower on the roof. (Courtesy of Tennis Trucks.)

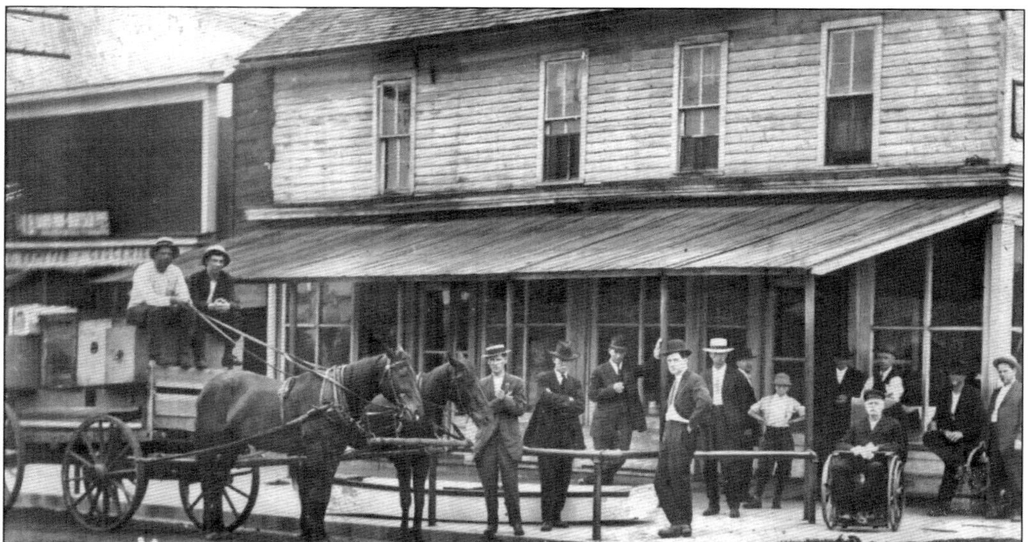

In the wheelchair is Robert Matthews, owner of Matthews Grocery and operator of an early tourist business. Lake County catered to groups coming north to fish. The Mahoning Camping Club members, who came by rail from Ohio to Baldwin in 1914 to camp on Matthew's property on Whalen Lake, have just loaded supplies for their two-month stay. (Photograph by Theodore Kestner, courtesy of the Lake County Historical Society.)

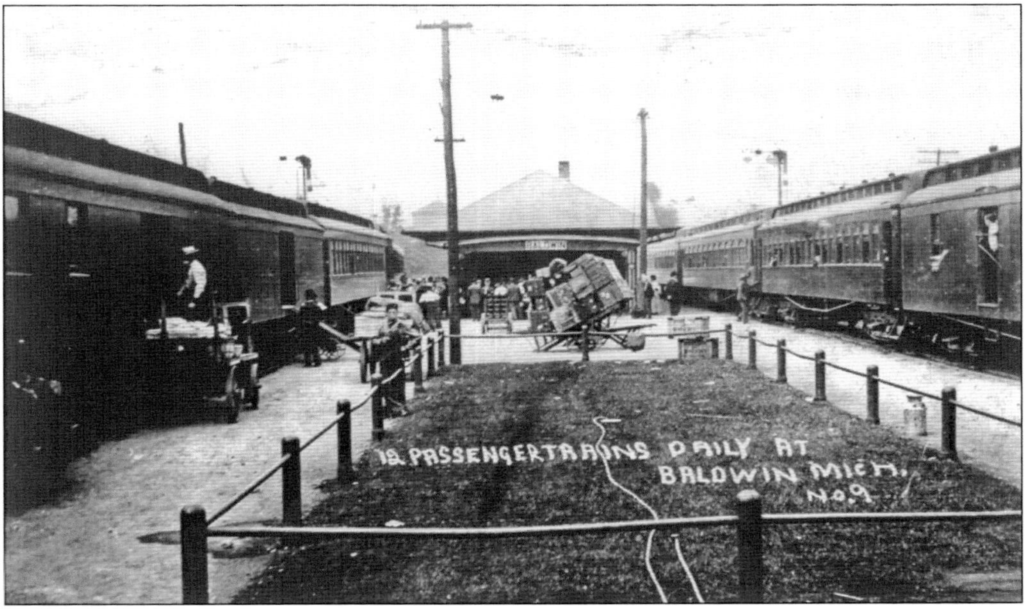

For Baldwin, the crossing of the Flint and Pere Marquette Railroad and the Chicago and West Michigan Railroad meant many jobs as well as a boom for tourism in town. In the early 1900s, as many as 12 passenger trains a day came through Baldwin, with most travelers riding the line from Grand Rapids to Petoskey. (Courtesy of the Lake County Historical Society.)

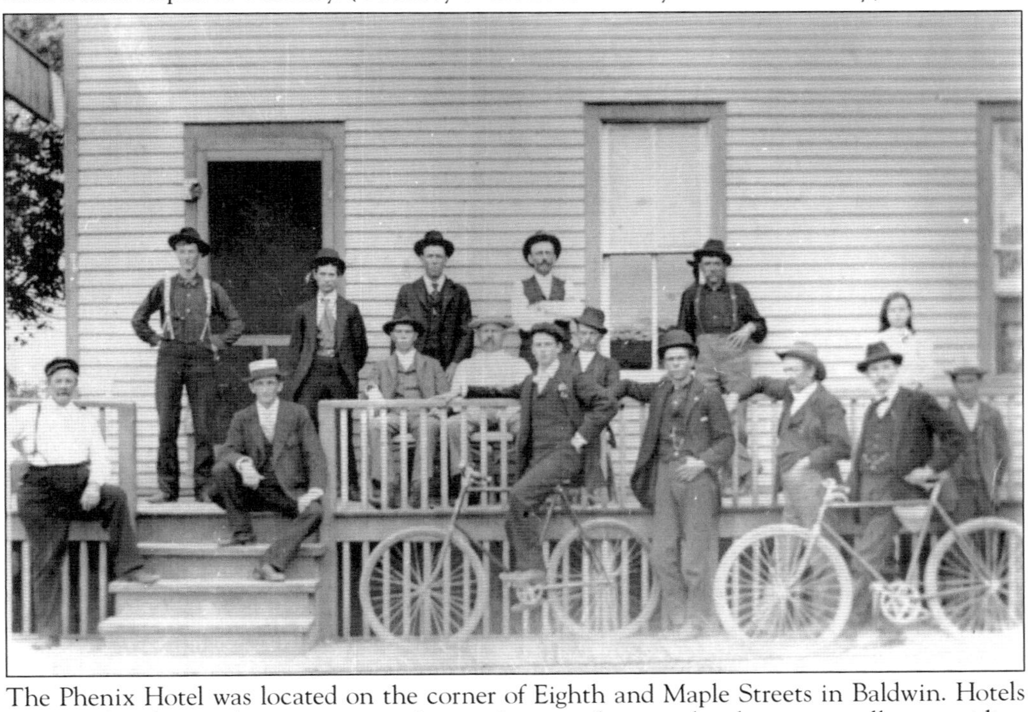

The Phenix Hotel was located on the corner of Eighth and Maple Streets in Baldwin. Hotels became the place to have a cigar on the porch or catch up on local news as well as providing overnight lodging. Standing with the bicycle on the right is Louis Caplan, who built the first store in Baldwin. (Courtesy of Tennis Trucks.)

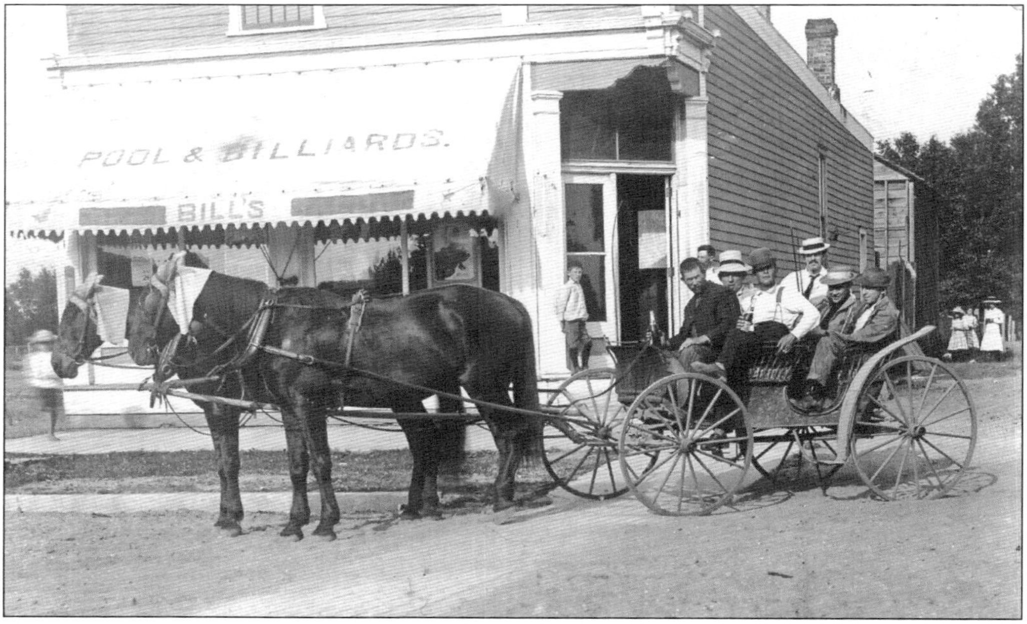

Another popular Baldwin place was the pool hall. The men in the wagon are enjoying a cold soda in front of Bill Wilkinson's Pool and Billiards and the boy in the doorway is Wilkinson's son. Near the back of the hall is the icehouse, filled with blocks of ice cut from local lakes in the winter—a necessity if one wanted cold drinks on a hot summer day. (Courtesy of Bruce Micinski.)

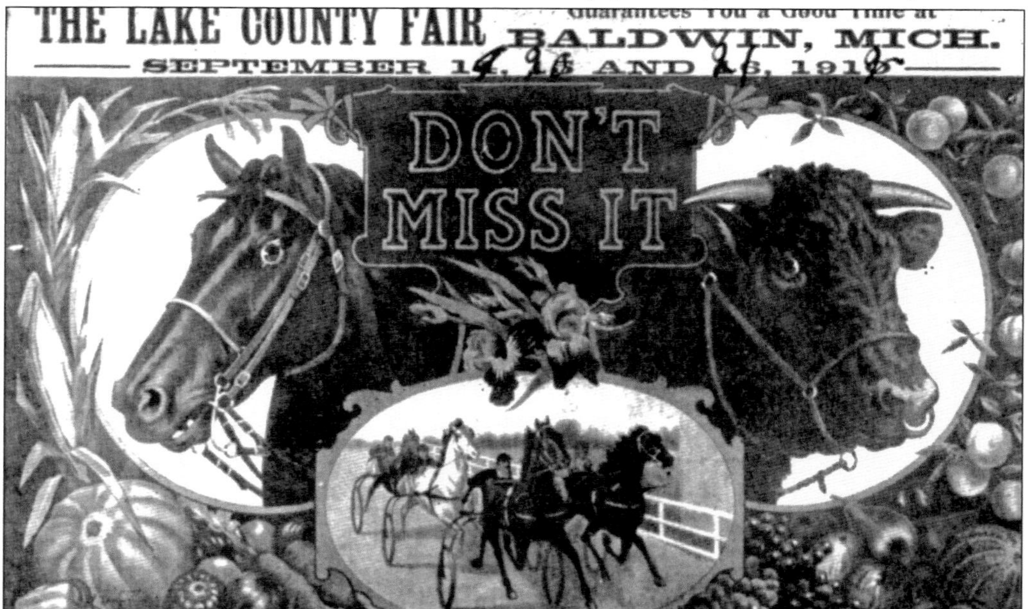

The county's early immigrants celebrated their harvest at the Lake County Fair in Baldwin. This postcard advertisement promotes horse racing at the fairgrounds east of town. The fair was started in 1905 and included vaudeville acts, baseball games, and a steam-powered merry-go-round. Local store owner Louis Caplan promised a suit of clothes to the farmer bringing the largest family to the 1912 fair. (Courtesy of Bruce Micinski.)

The key to economic growth is a bank. The Lake County Bank was founded in 1908 by Curtis W. MacPhail and Elias L. Cole. The original bank was located in the Messenger Building in central downtown Baldwin. Robert J. Smith became the first employee and took over as president following MicPhail's death. The bank provided the financial means for much of Baldwin's growth through the years. (Courtesy of Deborah Smith-Olson.)

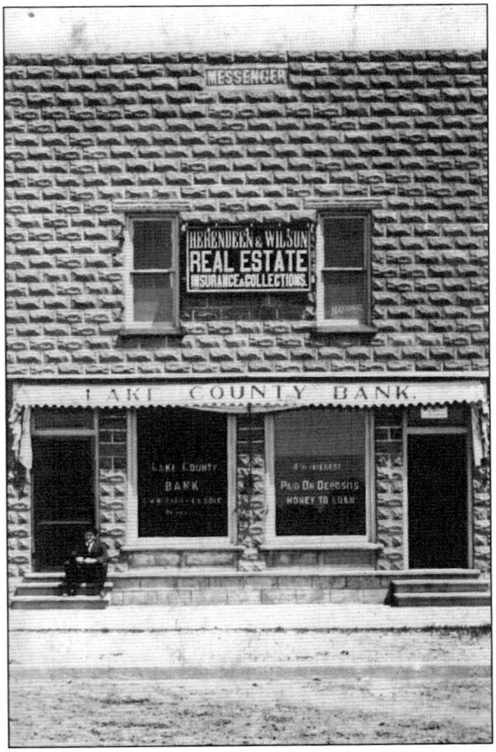

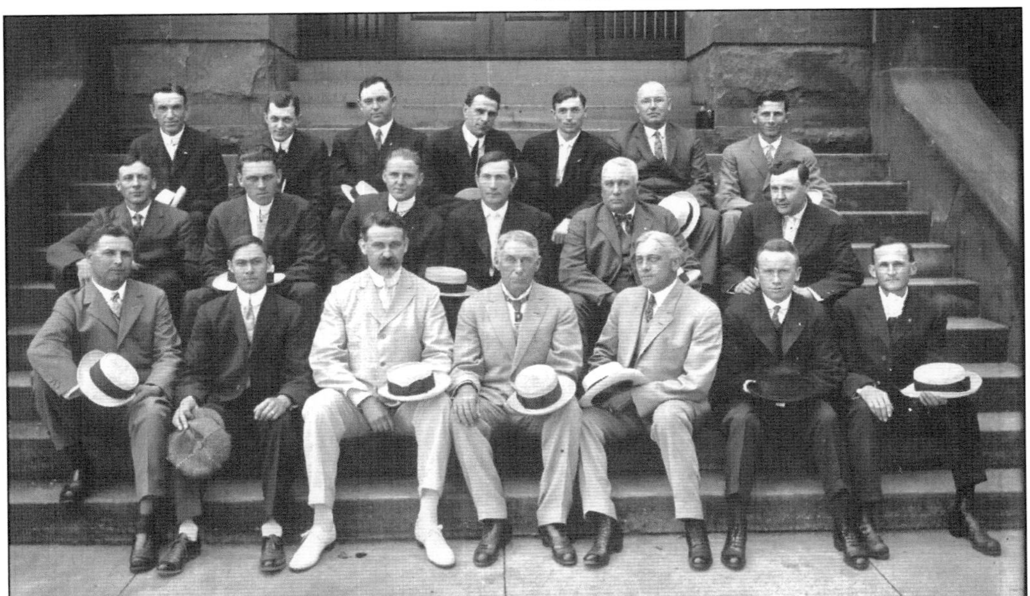

Looking quite distinguished and posing for this c. 1910 photograph on the steps of the Mason County Courthouse in Ludington is financier Curtis MacPhail, center, first row, with bankers who worked in his 13 banks. In the second row, fifth from the left, is Elias Cole who partnered with MacPhail in the Lake County Bank. Fourth from left, second row, is Robert J. Smith, their first employee. (Courtesy of Deborah Smith-Olson.)

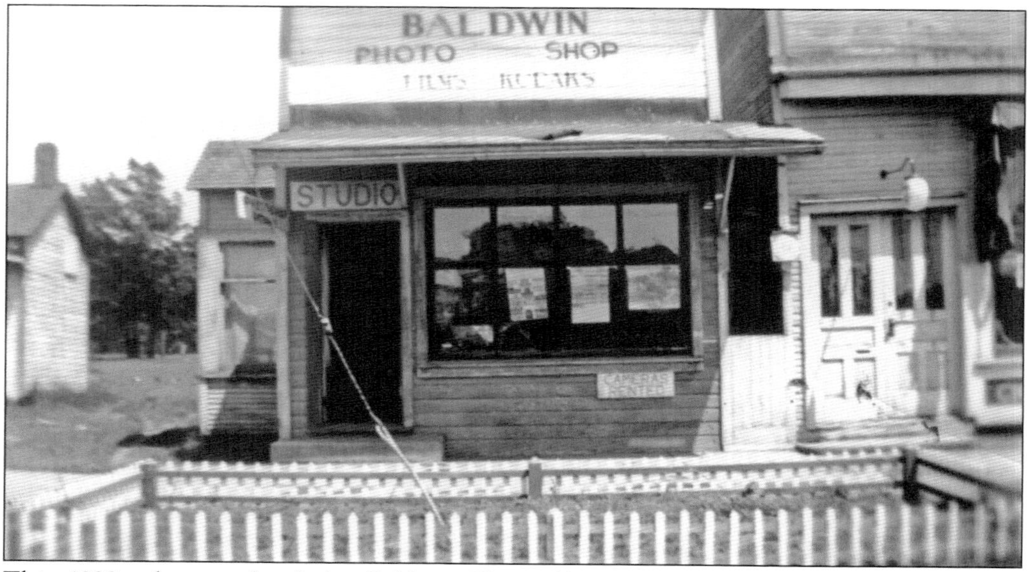

This 1920s photograph of the Baldwin Photo Shop was taken by owner Kurt J. Kahl. Kurt P. Kahl followed in his father's footsteps. Their photographs froze time by capturing not only subjects of commissioned photographs but everyday life situations as well. Group photographs of organizations and sports teams were mixed with documentaries of personal life—a summer celebration, a fishing expedition, and more. (Courtesy of Tennis Trucks.)

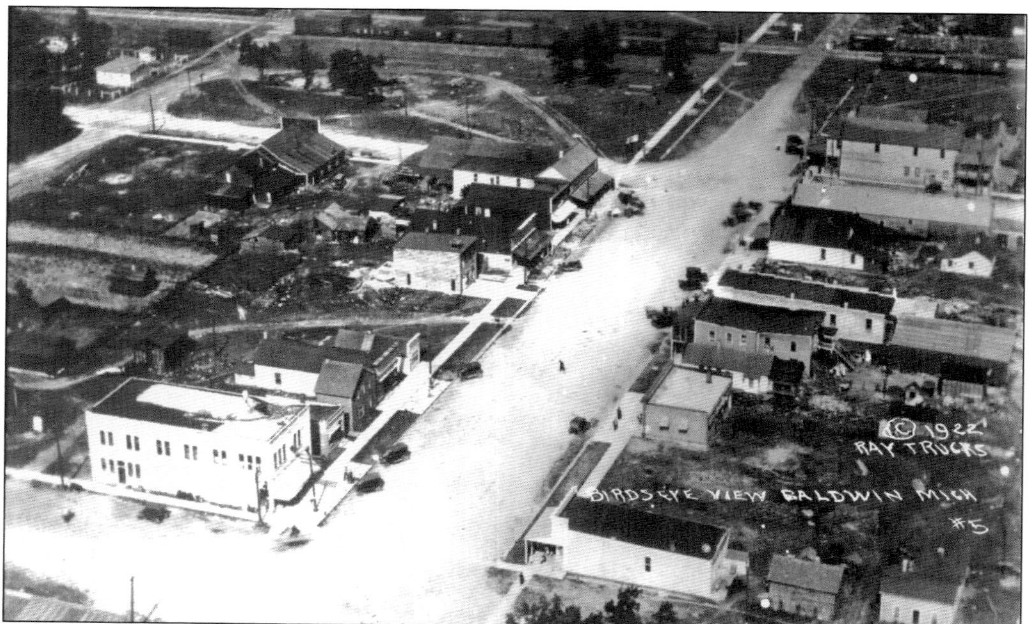

This aerial view of Baldwin looking north shows Michigan Avenue at the intersection of Eighth Street (at the top of the photograph). The first building on the west side is the Odd Fellows building and Duffing's Hardware. Baldwin Lumber Company is on Eighth Street in the middle of the block, west of Bradford's Market on the northwest corner of the intersection. The opera house is on the northeast corner. (Photograph by Ray Trucks, courtesy of Gordon Allison.)

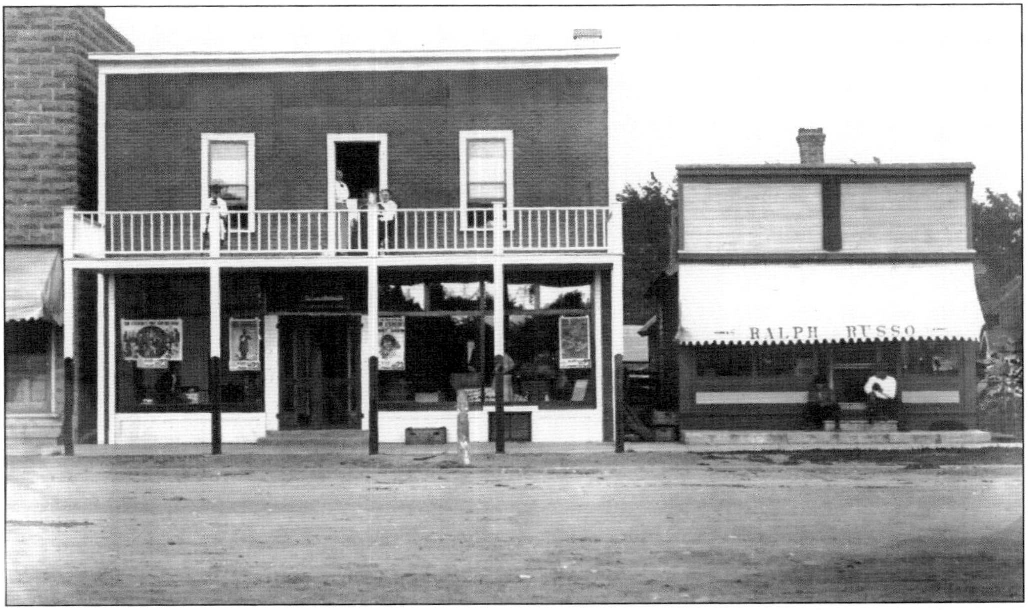

The posters in the front windows of the Fenner Hotel in Baldwin announce that Tom Atkinson's Pony and Dog Show, as well as his Dixie Minstrels Show, would be coming to town. In the 1920s, many small circus groups would come to entertain residents from Baldwin and the surrounding area. To the right of the hotel is Ralph Russo's Shoe Repair Shop. (Courtesy of the Lake County Historical Society.)

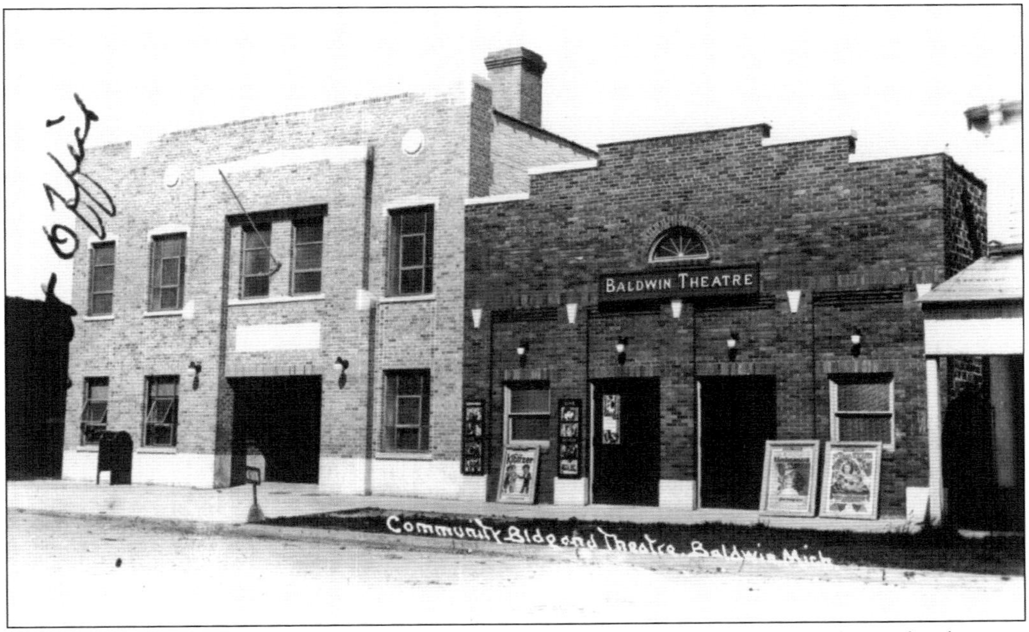

The advertising poster on the left announces that *The Kibitzer*, a 1929 film, will soon be showing at the Baldwin Theater. The community building next door, with a raised stage, hosted not only plays, vaudeville acts, and musical entertainment but also served as the court for the Baldwin High School basketball games. (Courtesy of Gordon Allison.)

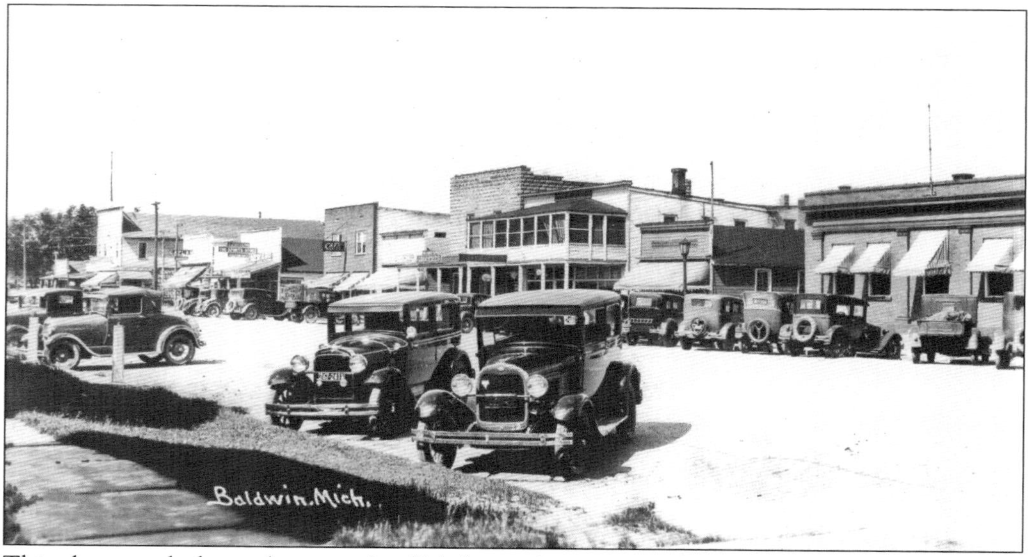

This photograph shows the east side of Michigan Avenue in Baldwin. On the far left is Caplan's Drygoods, in the center with its second-floor enclosed porch is the Fenner Hotel, and on the far right in its new building location is the Lake County Bank. Although most of the automobiles in town are 1928–1930 Model As, one can see the hitching posts that remain for the occasional horse-drawn wagon or carriage. (Courtesy of Gordon Allison.)

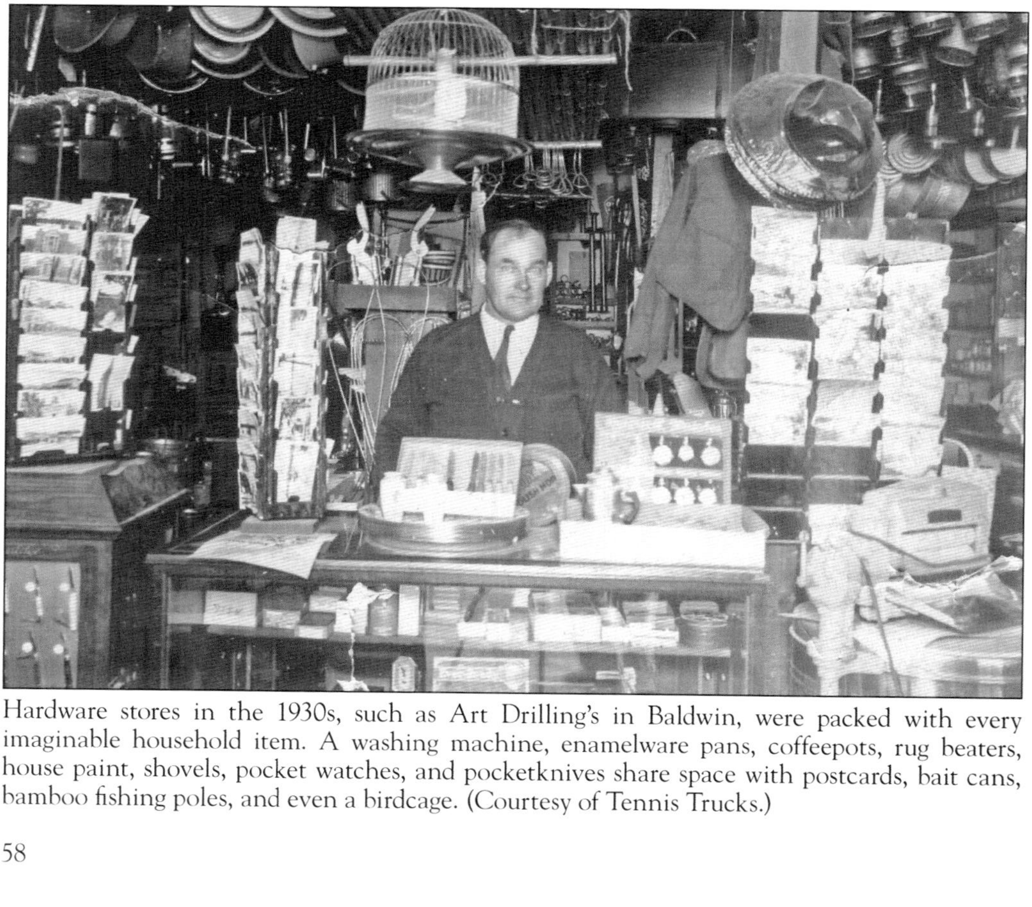

Hardware stores in the 1930s, such as Art Drilling's in Baldwin, were packed with every imaginable household item. A washing machine, enamelware pans, coffeepots, rug beaters, house paint, shovels, pocket watches, and pocketknives share space with postcards, bait cans, bamboo fishing poles, and even a birdcage. (Courtesy of Tennis Trucks.)

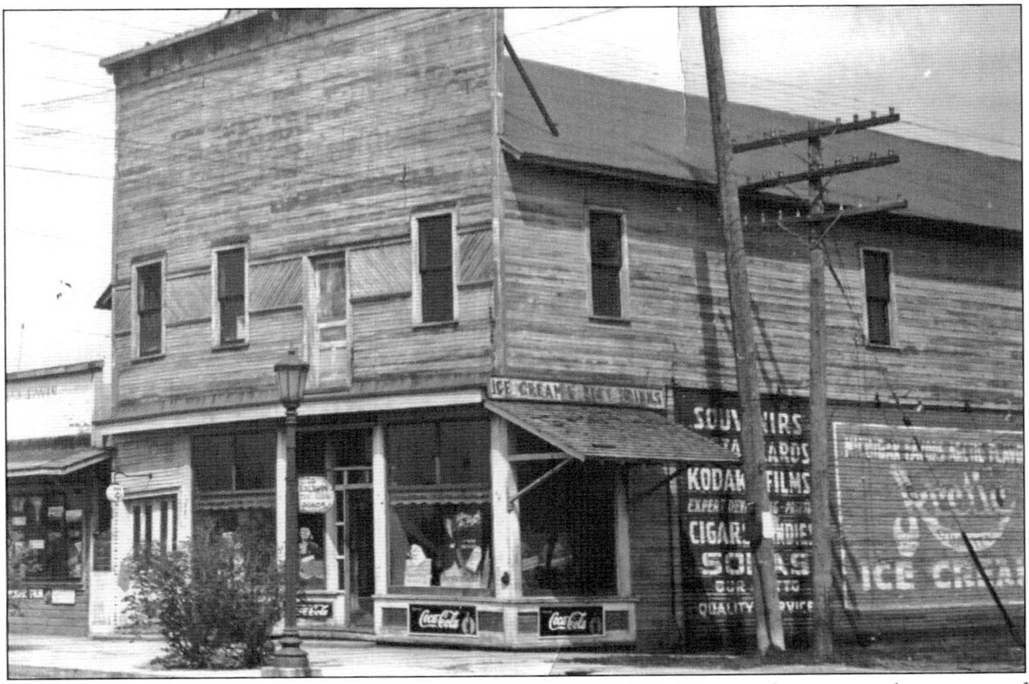

D. D. Pattie opened his drugstore in Baldwin in 1932 in the old opera house, on the corner of Eighth and Michigan Streets. Four years later, he moved southward down the street. Mary Pattie, in 1936, was one of the first females to graduate from Ferris Institute with a bachelor's degree in pharmacy. She took over operation of the pharmacy upon her father's death in 1940. (Courtesy of Tennis Trucks.)

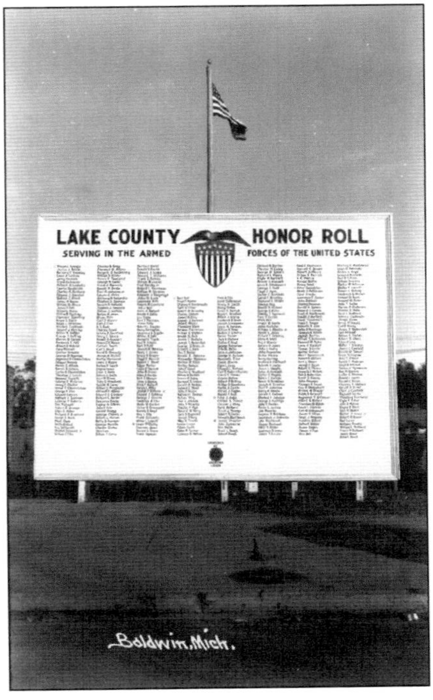

The impact of World War II was seen on the Lake County honor roll billboard in Baldwin, sponsored by the American Legion. Nearly 400 names were listed, which is noteworthy for a county this size. Fortunately only six were identified as killed. Many immigrants showed strong loyalty by serving this country in times of war. The billboard was removed when the vacant lot was needed for a building project. (Courtesy of Gordon Allison.)

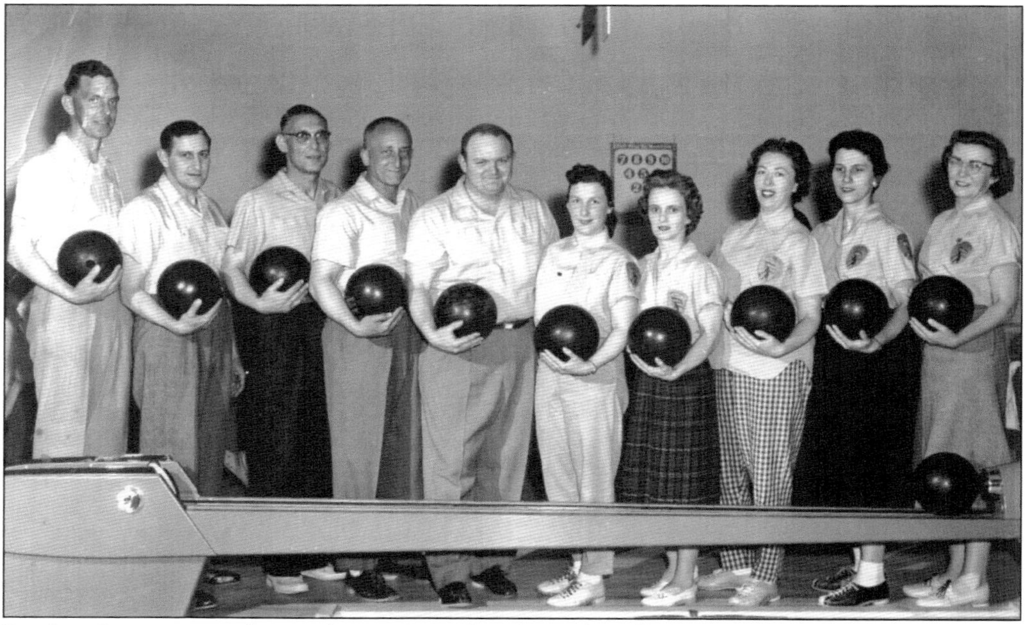

Bowling became popular in the 1940s and 1950s. Ed Sedlecky and Zimmie Nolph operated the Baldwin Bowling Alley. This 1958 photograph shows local bowlers, from left to right, Ray Meinke, Fritz Mistelli, Rollo Branch, Ed Kreidler, Don MacDougall, Denise MacDougall, Ruth Bradford, Mary Burns Gibson, Elva Heyd, and Dorothy Trucks posing with their bowling balls. (Courtesy of Diana Hipshier.)

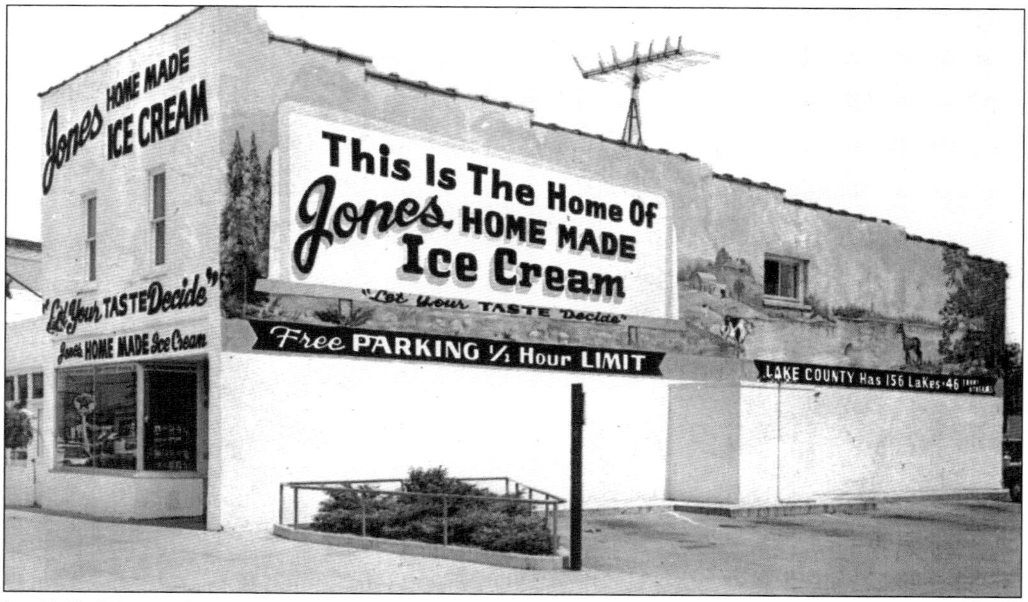

In 1942, Marcus Jones started Jones Ice Cream Store in Baldwin. He purchased the Messenger Building, which had been the original home of the Lake County State Bank, and outfitted it with the latest soda-fountain equipment. This c. 1960 postcard shows the hand-painted sign advertising Lake County's 156 lakes and 46 trout streams. Jones is a favorite stop for locals and tourists alike. (Courtesy of Jill Engelman.)

Five

A Community Affair

For many years and generations, the people of Lake County have enjoyed and revered their community affairs and activities. Whether they are organizations, churches, schools, or family activities, these are the places that foster camaraderie and support.

Music traditions have been, and always will be, a part of Lake County. The role of music was to be entertaining, comforting, and inspirational. During times of war, music played an important role in keeping the spirits up of soldiers and the folks at home. Bands marched in parades, put on concerts to entertain the community, and supplied background music for numerous parties and picnics. The towns and villages of Baldwin, Luther, Chase, and Marlborough all had their own bands and ensembles. Churches in Lake County had their own inspirational choruses. Jazz, rhythm and blues, and gospel music are part of Idlewild's rich tradition. Lake County also had talent shows and dances, with much of the music provided by Leonard Keller and James Brown.

Towns and settlements in Lake County also enjoyed special events in the form of homecomings, picnics, and socials. The Baldwin homecoming is one example where old friends and relatives would journey for miles to Hollister Park to enjoy each other's company and good food. The heyday of the Baldwin homecoming was during the 1920s and 1930s, when approximately 200–300 people would attend this affair.

Many organizations have contributed to the social and supportive network of Lake County. These have included the Masons and Eastern Star, the Odd Fellows and Rebekah lodge, the Boy Scouts, the Girl Scouts, and the Rotary Club. Lake County businesses and local governments have also played an integral role in providing events, activities, and community support.

There is a great legacy of family values and memories, found in occasions of frivolous fun as well as those of solemn duty. This essence is captured in the photographs of the life of Lake County. Cultural diversity has been supported and celebrated. Individuals who have lived in the area for a time and have moved away or those who have established families have all left their imprint on the history of Lake County.

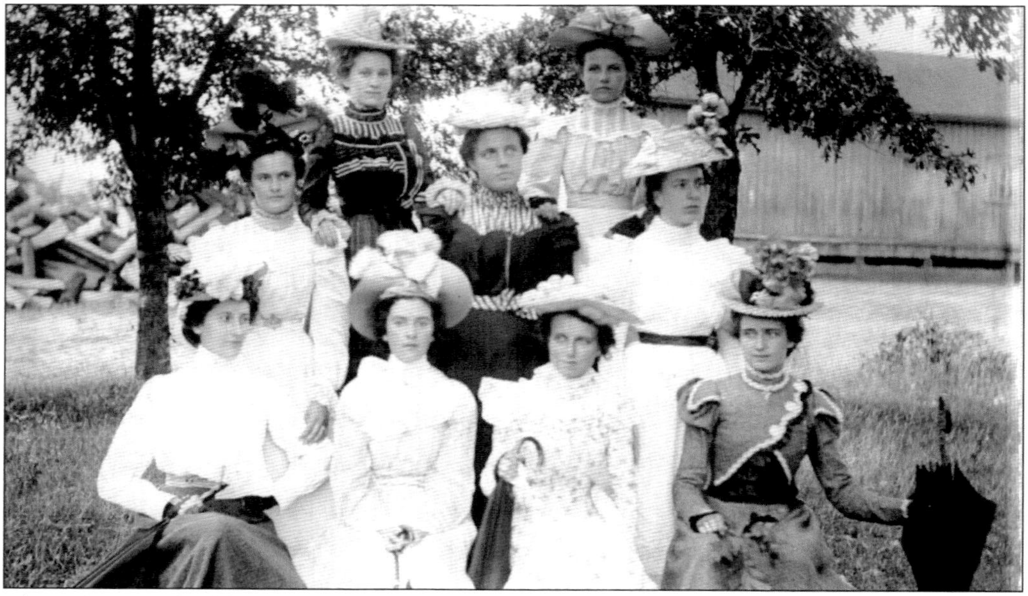

These women of Baldwin had gathered for a social occasion in the late 1890s. Were the umbrellas sun protection, or was a shower possible? How about those hats! The socialites are, from left to right, (first row) Lilly Fray, Edith (Matthews) Moore, Millie (Weavers) Baker, and Jennie (Bradford) Cashion; (second row) Nellie Mathews, Ethel (Bradford) Potter, and Fanny Waterman; (third row) Florence Carpenter and Mable (Drilling) Trick. (Courtesy of Jane Miller.)

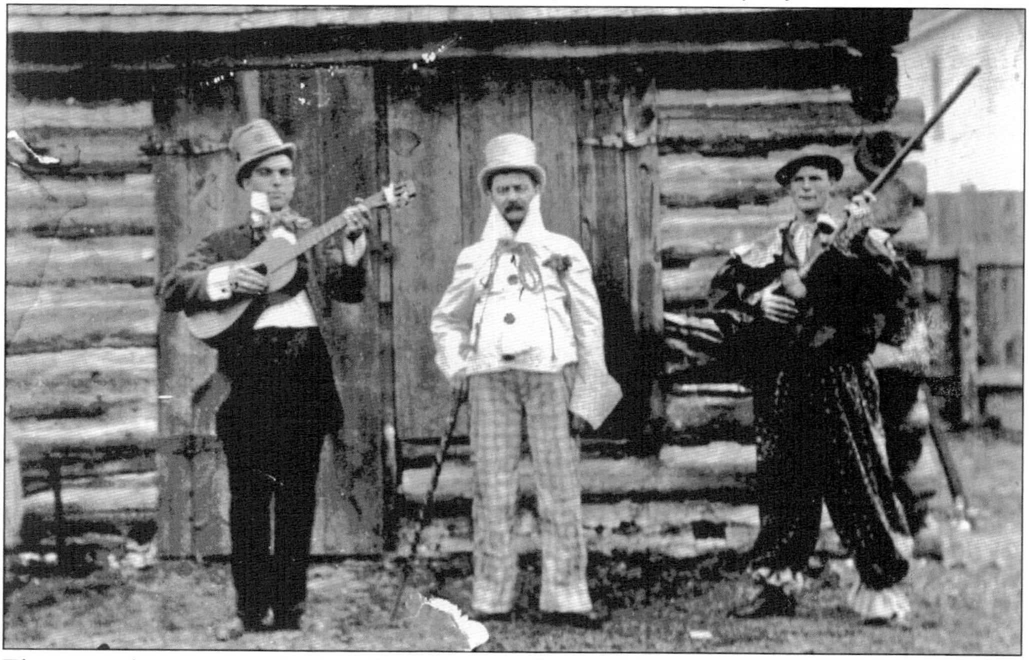

Three gentlemen are enjoying themselves, and providing entertainment to passersby, in Baldwin. In 1904, there were many early log structures on the main street like the one shown. The gentlemen getting ready for a town celebration or possibly a parade are, from left to right, George Stoors, William Rudd, and John Updegraff. (Courtesy of Jane Miller.)

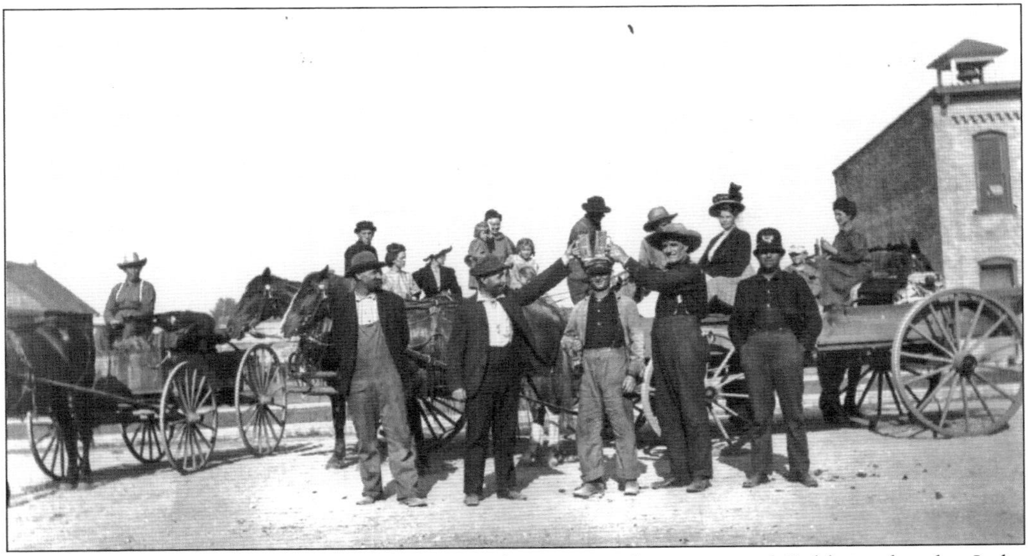

In 1908, men, women, and children are gathering on the streets of Baldwin for the Lake County Fair. Some of the men seem to already be celebrating the occasion. The tall building in the background is the town hall and fire hall. Town meetings were held upstairs and the fire equipment was housed on the ground floor. On the roof the fire bell can be seen. (Courtesy of Tennis Trucks.)

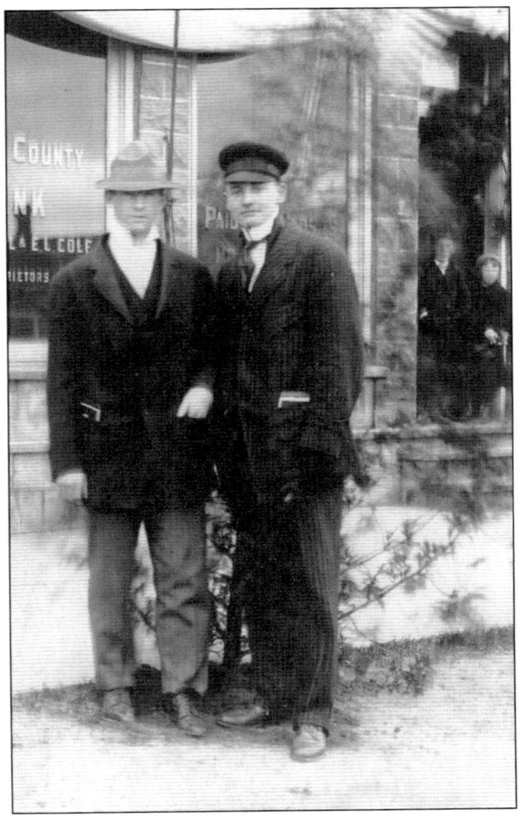

The Lake County Bank, known today as Lake-Osceola State Bank, has always been a vital part of the area. Since the bank's inception in 1908, it has supported individuals and organizations alike in their community activities. Customers Elgar Bradford, left, and Ely Campbell are seen standing in front of the windows with their bank books in their pockets. (Courtesy of Susan Bradford Tripp.)

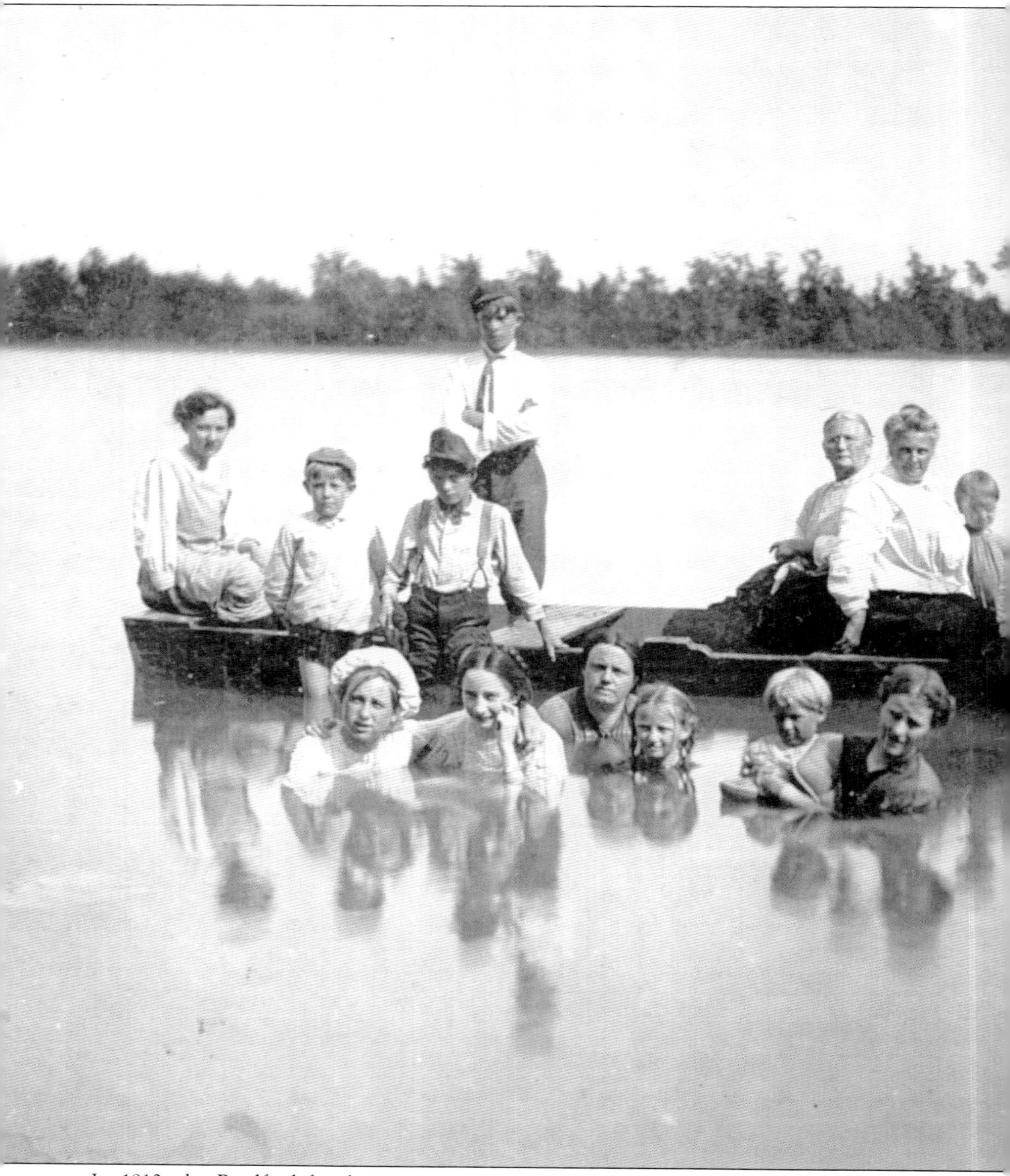

In 1910, the Bradford family camping gang has taken to the water at Little Star Lake just outside Baldwin. From left to right are (in front of the boat) Rhea (Shane) Heselscwerdt, Hazel (Wilkinson) Updegraff, Ethel (Bradford) Potter, Agnes (Bradford) Gibson, John Bradford, Agnes (Updegraff) Bradford, Clarence Baker, Maria (Bradford) Weavers, Louise (Trick) Bradford, Mabel (Drilling) Trick, Alice (Updegraff) Wilder, Ila (Updegraff) Gibson, Sarah (Updegraff)

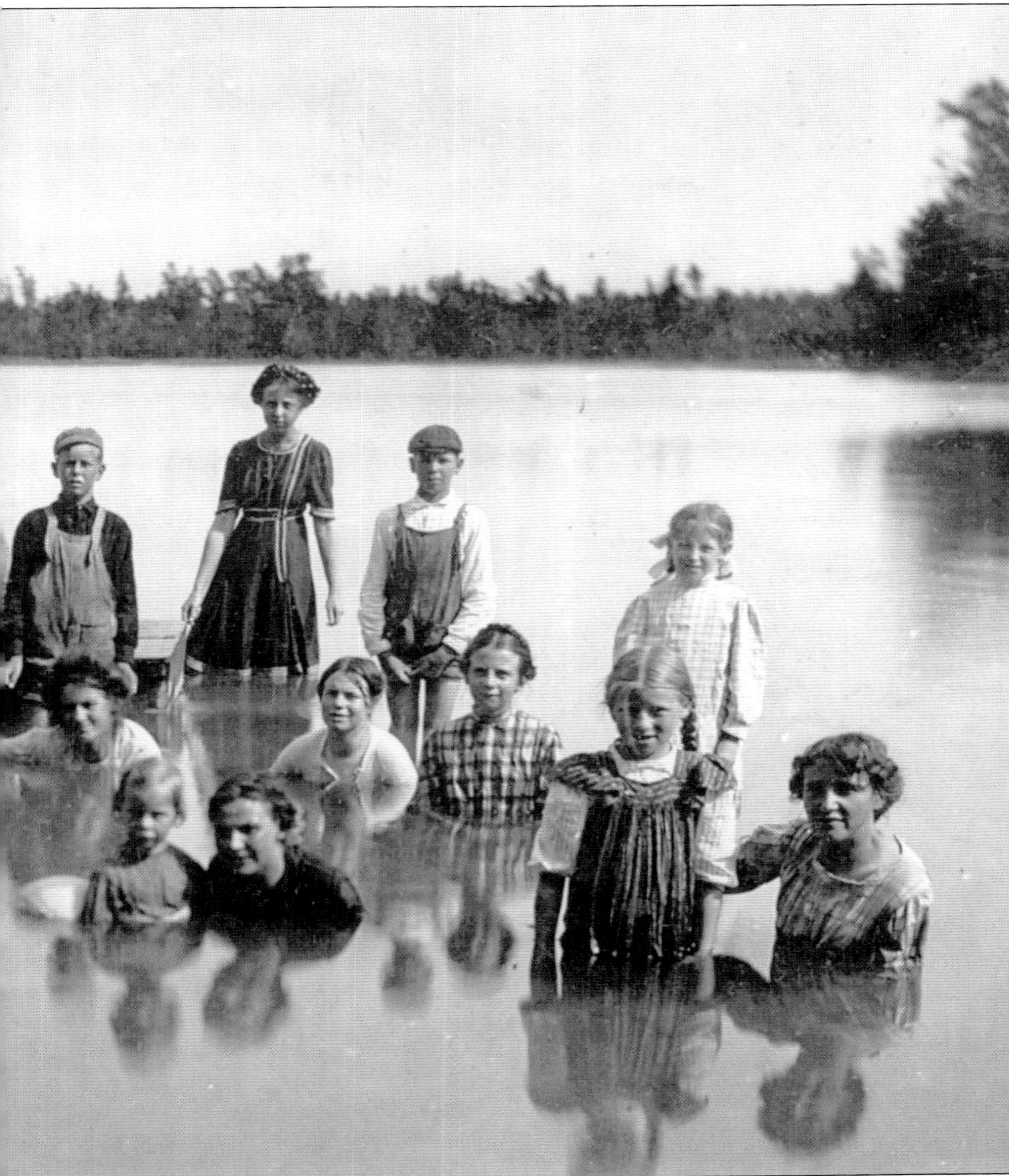

Thomas, and Jennie (Bradford) Cashion; (standing by the boat) Bill Wilkinson Jr., Tim Drilling, Wayne Esterling, Clifton Rudd, Mildred (Shane) Allen, Ping Wilder, and Anstice (Bradford) MacLeod; (in the boat) Myrtle Rudd, unidentified, Jane Updegraff, Sarah (Bradford) Drilling, and Kenneth Baker. (Courtesy of Jane Miller.)

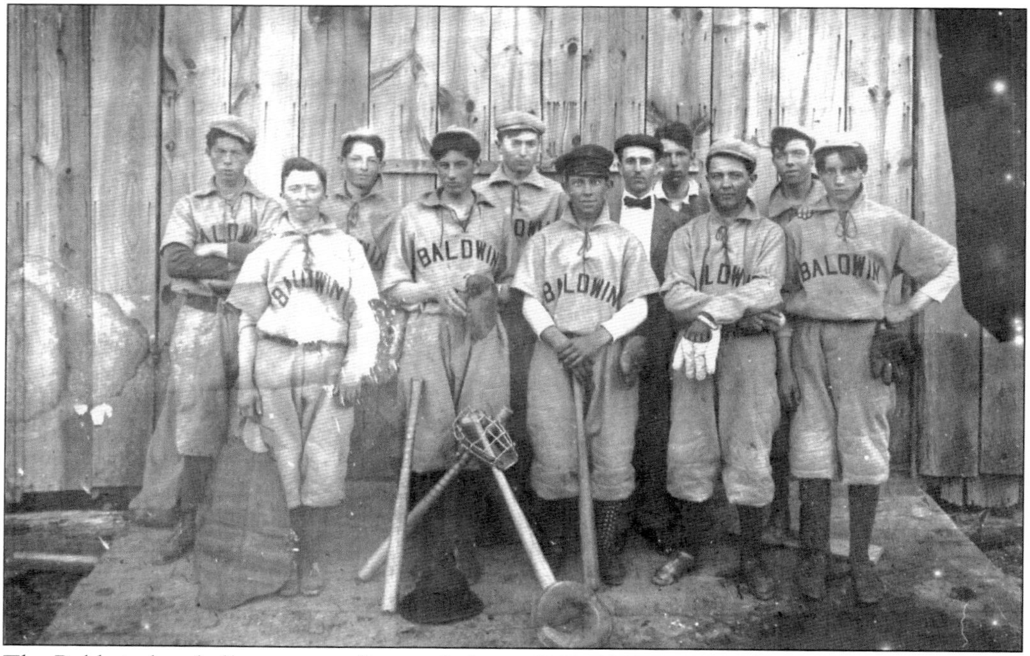

The Baldwin baseball team proudly stands for its 1909–1910 season's photograph. The members from left to right are (first row) Max Moore, Clyde Wilkinson, Alfred Beatty, Albert Beatty, and Glen Wilkinson; (second row) Martin Duffing, Harry Bradford, Howard Hollister, team manager Herb Davis, unidentified, and Art Wallace. (Courtesy of Noel Duffing.)

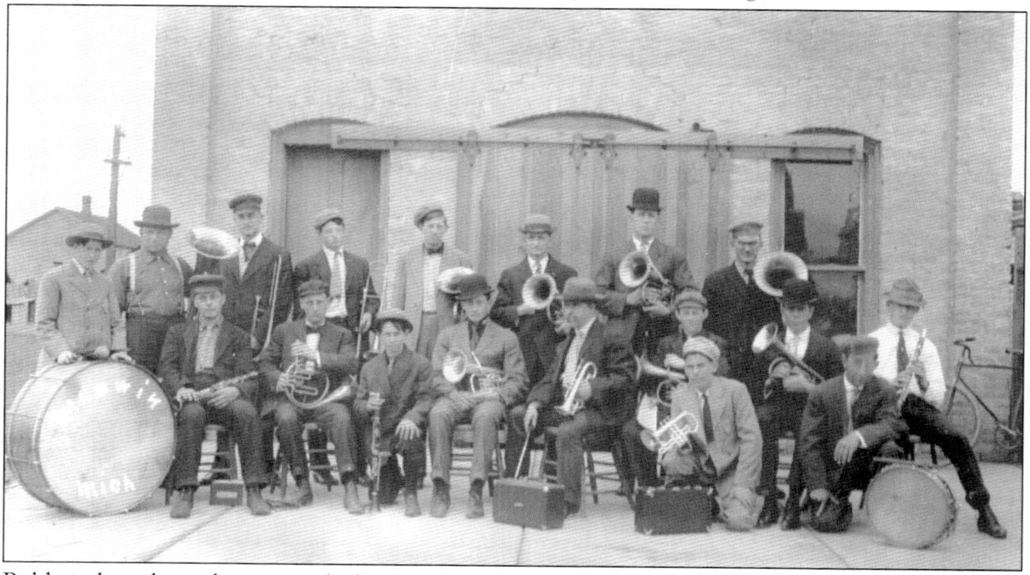

Baldwin has always been proud of its bands and musical traditions. This group was photographed in front of the fire hall in 1910. Band members from left to right are (first row) two unidentified members; (second row) three unidentified members, Glen Wilkinson, director Clifford Branch, Fred Bradford, Lewis Duffing, and Elgar Bradford; (third row) Harold Fisher, Jack Bradford, unidentified, Andy Bradford, unidentified, William Potter, and two unidentified members. (Courtesy of Chris Bunch.)

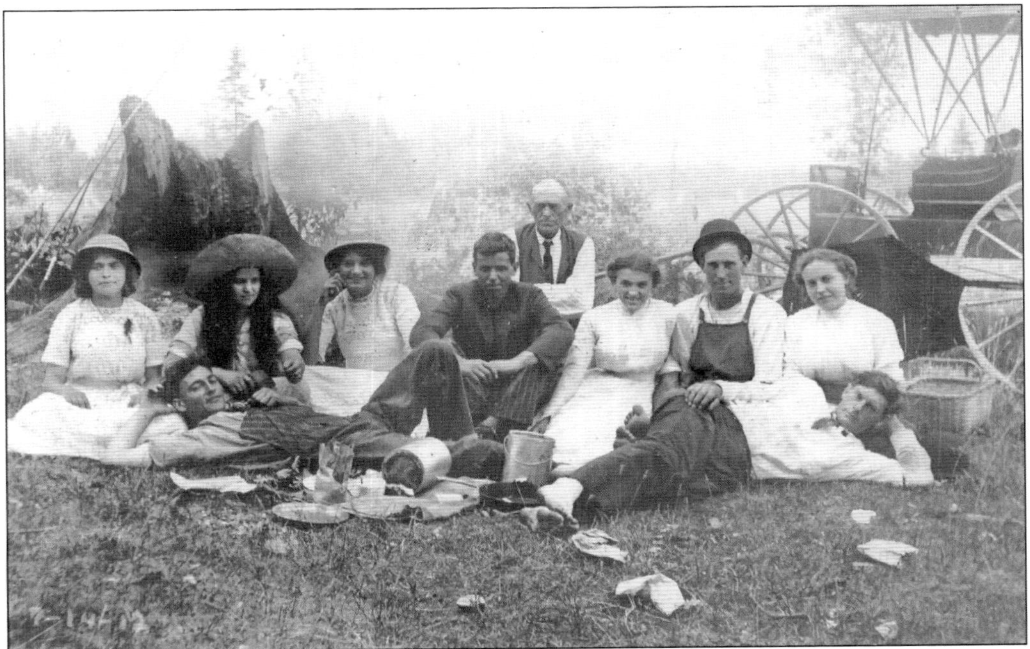

A "poverty social" was held on church grounds in Nirvana on September 14, 1912. The ladies brought box lunches filled with homemade delicacies to be auctioned to the highest bidder. There was a 5¢ fine for wearing good clothes. It appears that everyone present is having a great time, and that some followed the suggested attire for the day. (Courtesy of the James Woods family.)

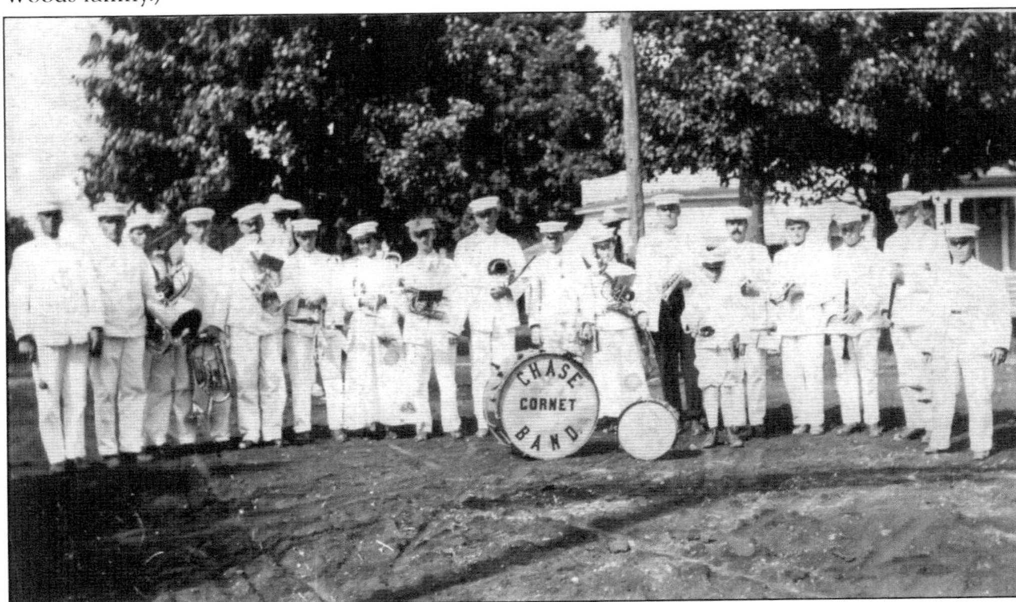

This photograph, dated September 5, 1913, is of 20 men, women, and children of the Chase Cornet Band. Dressed in their crisp, white uniforms and hats, this band marched in parades for national holidays and put on concerts to entertain the community. A brass trumpet and small drum from the band have been archived at the Chase Library. (Courtesy of Dennis Ellison.)

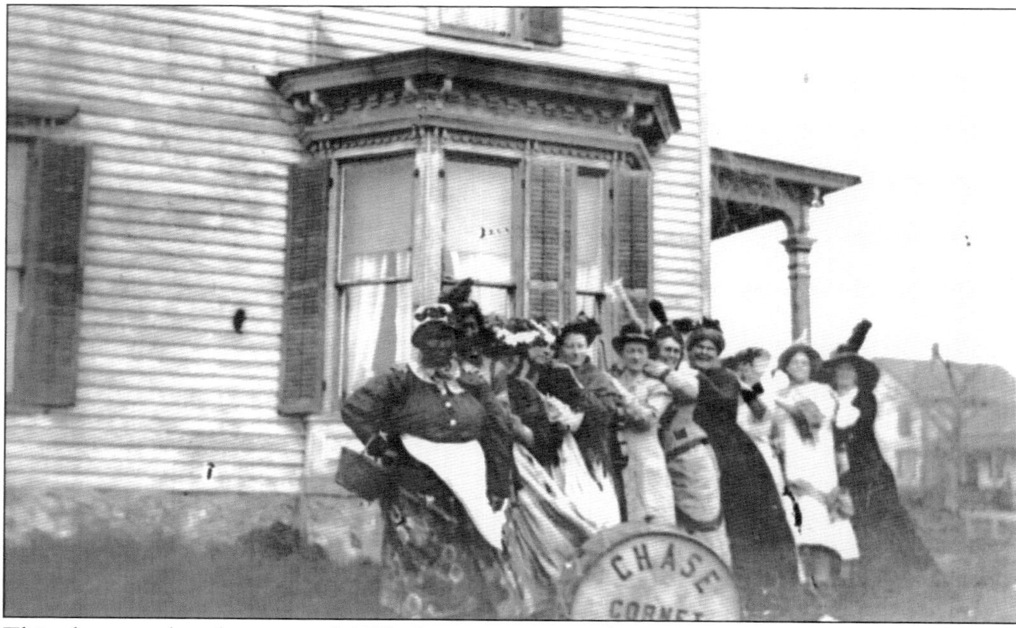

This photograph, taken around 1918, showcases 11 members of the Chase Cornet Band. These ladies were dressed in costume and preformed with other band members. Early bands consisted almost entirely of men, but during World War I, with so many of them serving their country, the women stepped in so the music would continue. (Courtesy of Dennis Ellison.)

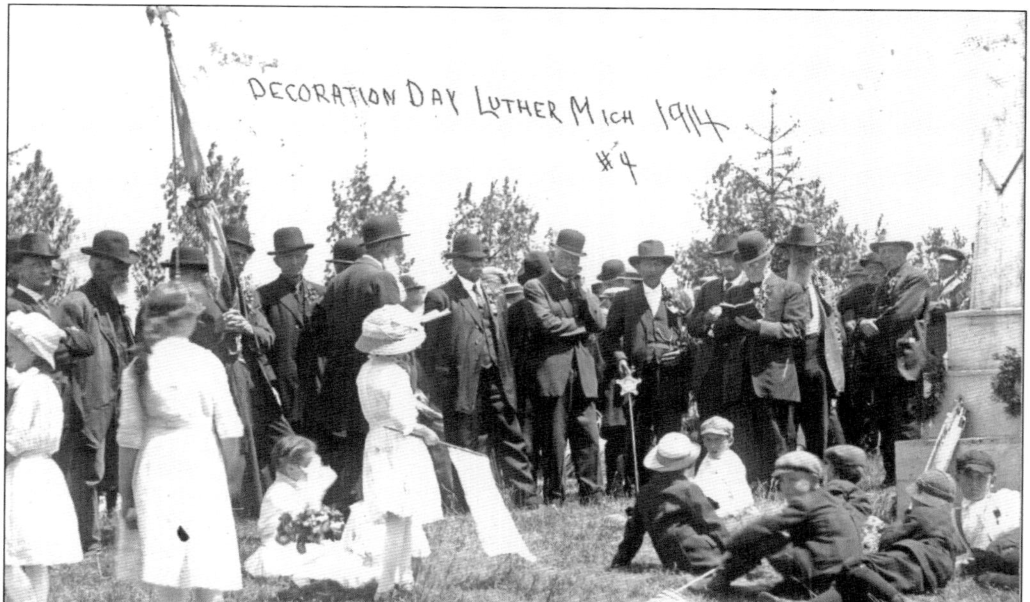

Decoration Day, now known as Memorial Day, was celebrated in a grand but solemn manner to remember those who had died for the country. Well-dressed veterans attended the observance in the cemetery next to a possible Civil War marker. The gentleman in the center is holding a Grand Army of the Republic five-pointed star, which most likely will be placed at a gravesite. (Courtesy of Jerry Poprawski.)

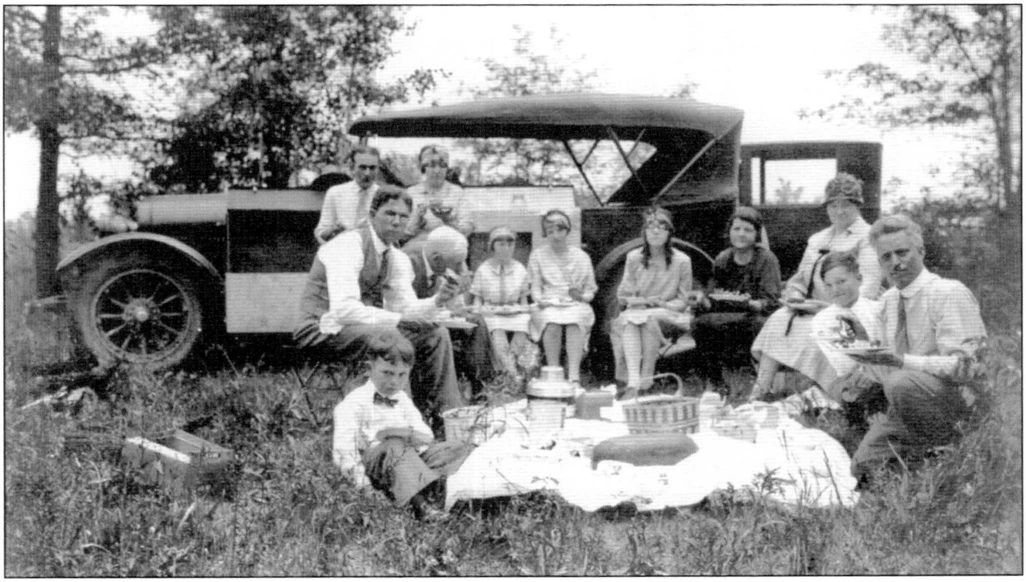

In this 1925 photograph, the George and Irene Duffing family is enjoying a picnic carefully laid out on a cloth on the ground next to its touring car. Everyone appears well dressed for this outdoor outing, and the picnic feast looks like it will conclude with the carving of a watermelon. Family time is the hallmark of the day. (Courtesy of Chris Bunch.)

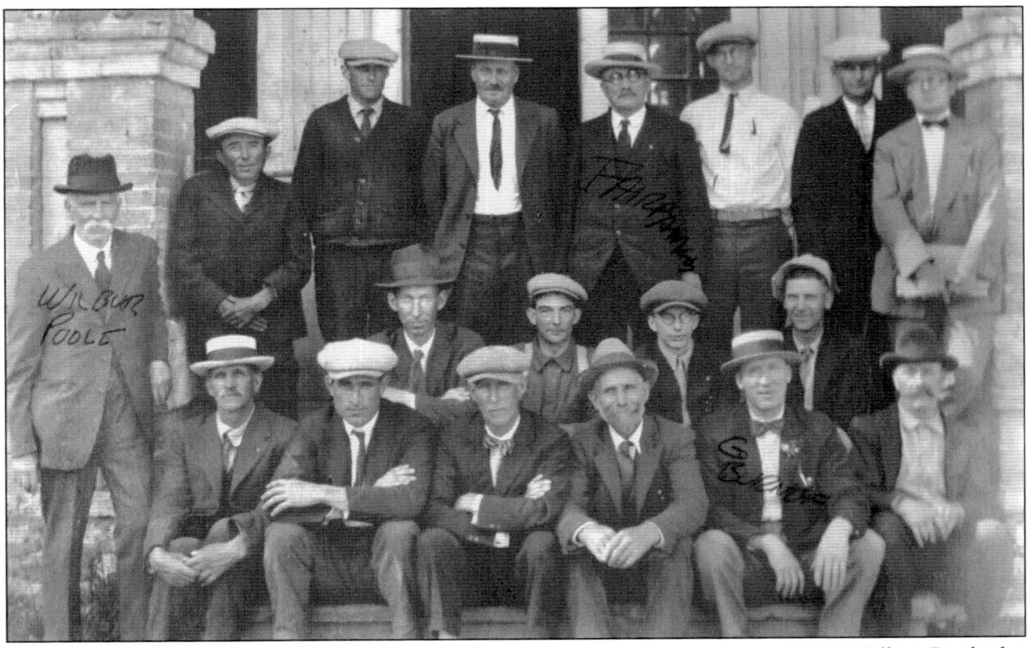

This photograph of the Lake County commissioners was taken prior to 1927. Wilbur Pool, the prosecuting attorney, is standing on the left. From left to right are (first row) commissioners James Evans, Jack Woolsey, Andres Loree, unidentified, Gary Burnett, and John Avery; (second row) G. Robertson, Harry Bartlett, John Weck, and Oscor Matson; (third row) unidentified, Henry Miller, Mat Stevensen, Dr. Fairbanks, Jesse Bradford, Alex Sauntman, and county clerk Emil Johnson. (Courtesy of Jane Miller.)

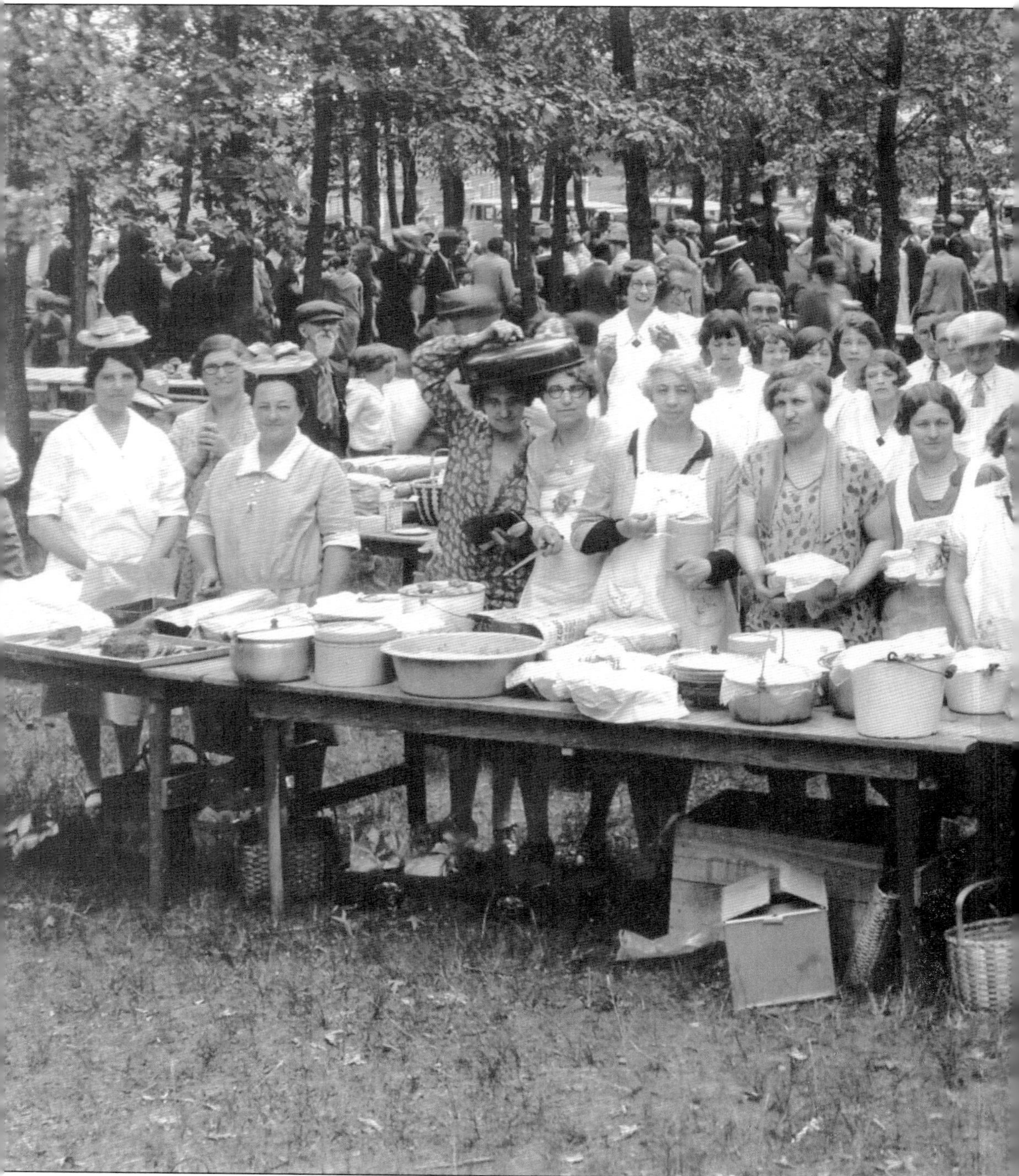

The annual Baldwin homecoming picnic in 1920 was held at Hollister Park. People journeyed for miles to enjoy a Sunday afternoon with friends and relatives. The food table was surely the center of attention. The ladies completing the final preparations seem to prefer clowning around to having their picture taken. Those at the table, from left to right, are Hazel Foster, Lerene Trucks, Pearl Thompson, Jen Cashion and Maria Weavers with the roaster pan lid on their

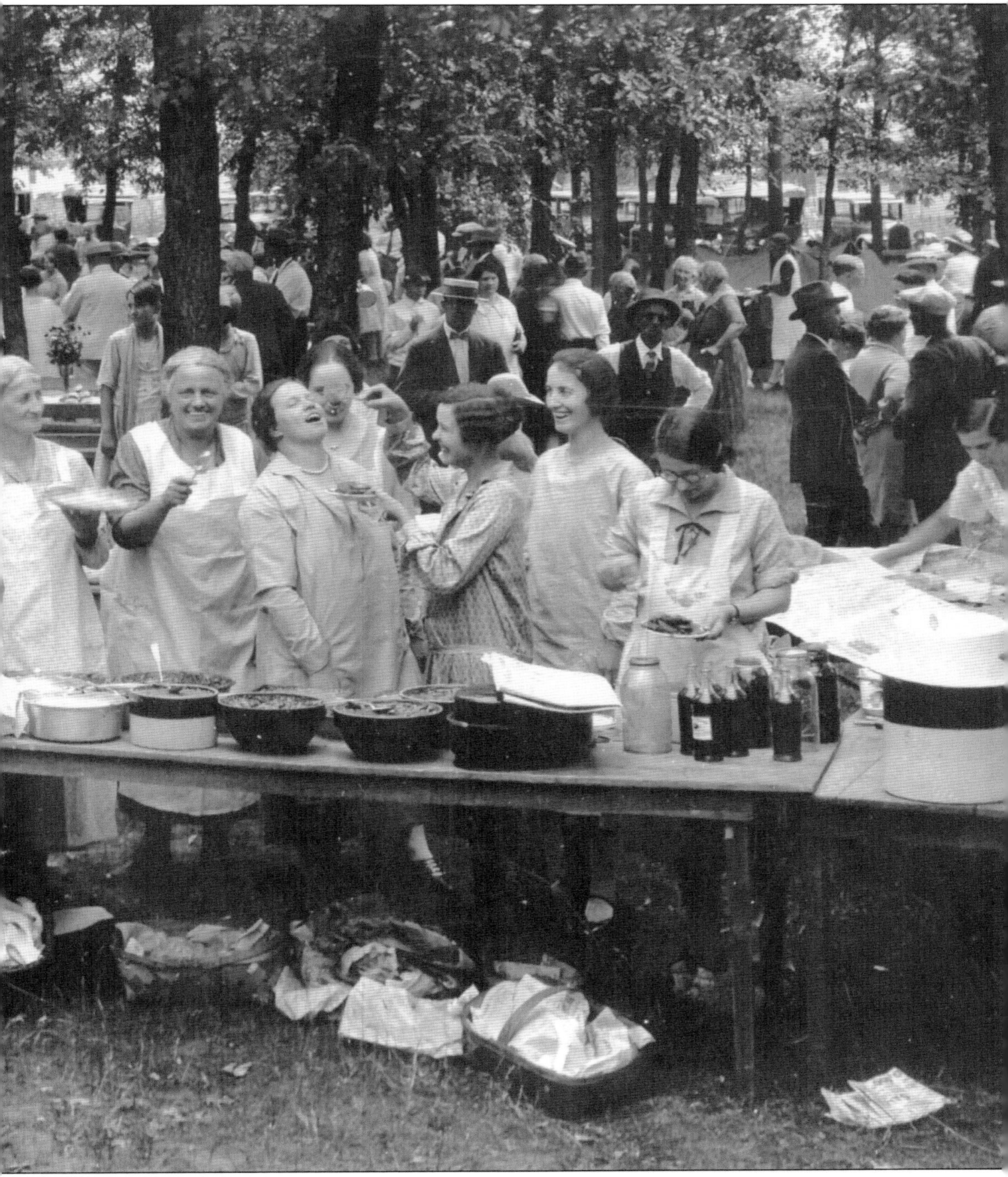

heads, unidentified, Mrs. Brott, Agnes Bradford, Blanche Fisher, Clara "Cad Brad" Bradford, Ethel Potter, Alice Wilder being fed pie by Bessie Merrill, Mrs. West, Betty Hollister, and Annie Duffing at the far right around the corner. Others in the background include, generally from left to right, Edna Bradford, Julia Fields, Emily Wilkinson, Glen Drown, Lenore Gleason, Francis Strayer, and Howard and Marie Updegraff. (Courtesy of Jane Miller.)

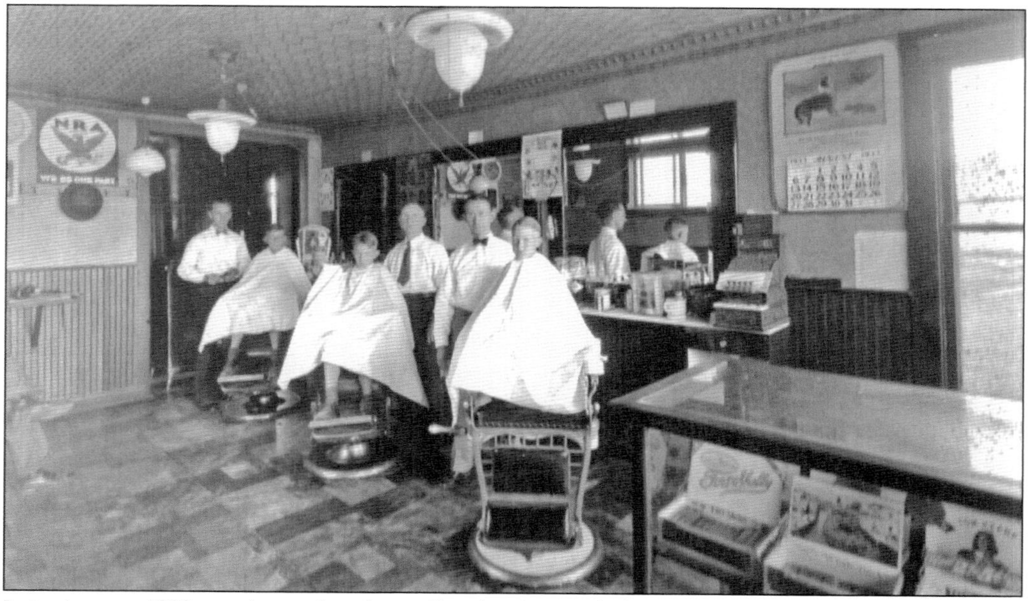

It is August 1933, as shown by the wall calendar, and three young men are seated for their haircuts in Duffing's Barbershop in downtown Baldwin. This three-generation barbershop has never moved from its original location and continues to be a source of social activity, informed conversation, and a good haircut. The barbers from left to right are Farl Duffing, Norm Crysler, and Farl's father, Harry Duffing. (Courtesy of Noel Duffing.)

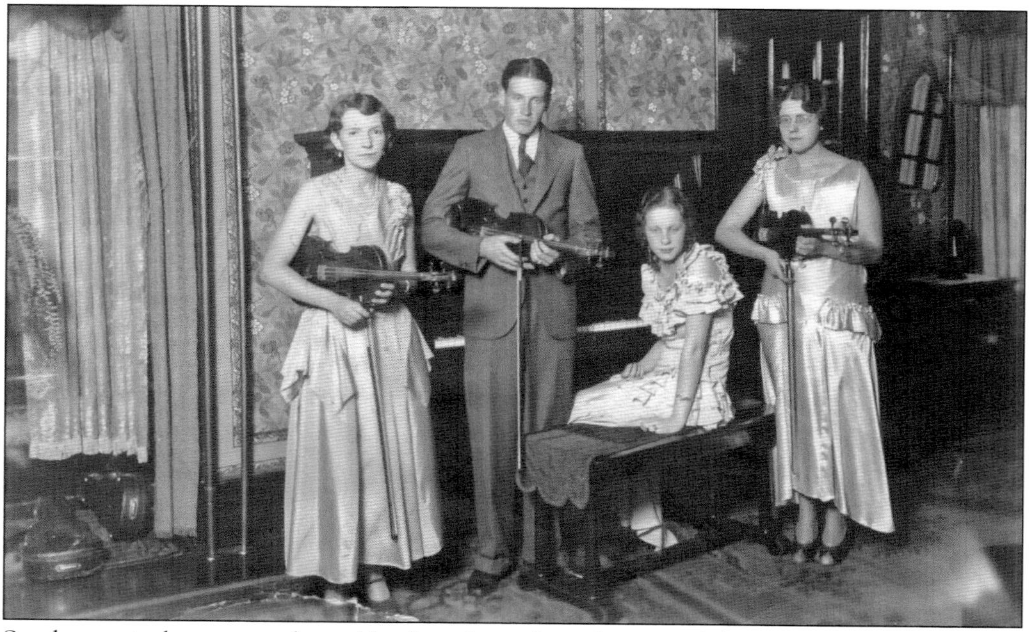

Sunday musicales were performed by these four talented young adults in 1934. This photograph was taken in the George Duffing home in the village of Baldwin, on the corner of Seventh and Maple Streets. Appearing from left to right are Gladys (Duffing) Bradford (violin), Varl Wilkinson (violin), Ruth (Wilkinson) Leeson (piano), and Georgene (Duffing) Anderson (violin). (Courtesy of Chris Bunch.)

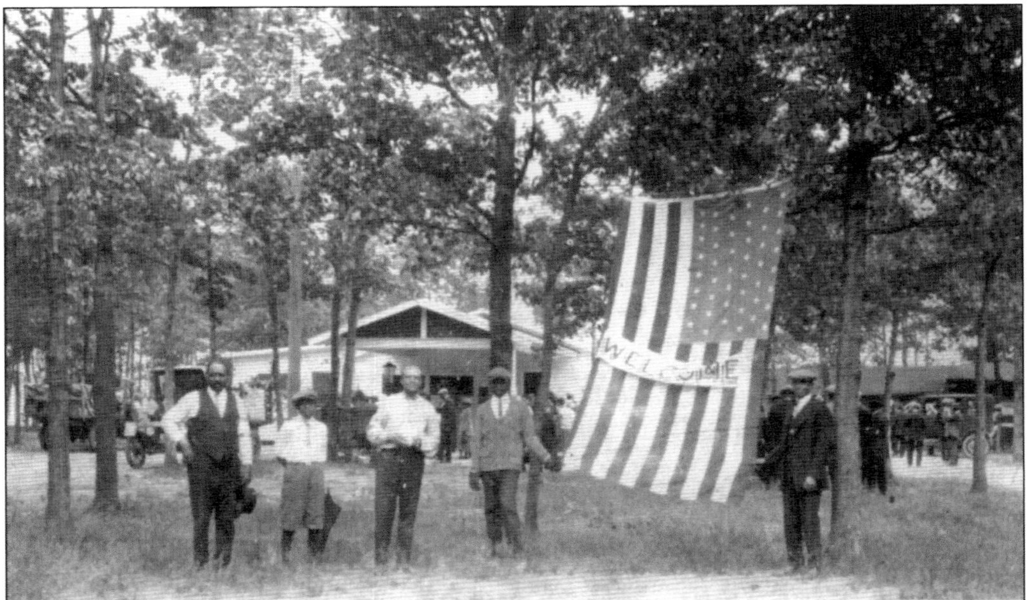

Scenes In Paradise Park, Baldwin, Mich.

Community gatherings with opportunities to join in the fun, celebrate, and share common sentiments are evident in both of these images from two different areas of Lake County. The photograph for the pictorial postcard above, titled "Scenes in Paradise Park, Baldwin, Mich.," was actually taken in Idlewild in the late 1920s. This historic African American resort includes both Paradise and Idlewild Lakes. The large American flag, with its 48 stars, suggests a patriotic celebration is in the offering. The pictorial postcard below was taken in the Irons area at Lake Nataka, also known as Big Bass Lake. The *c.* 1925 gathering includes men, women, and children enjoying a beautiful summer day. (Above, courtesy of Gordon Allison; below, photograph by Allan Clark, courtesy of Tennis Trucks.)

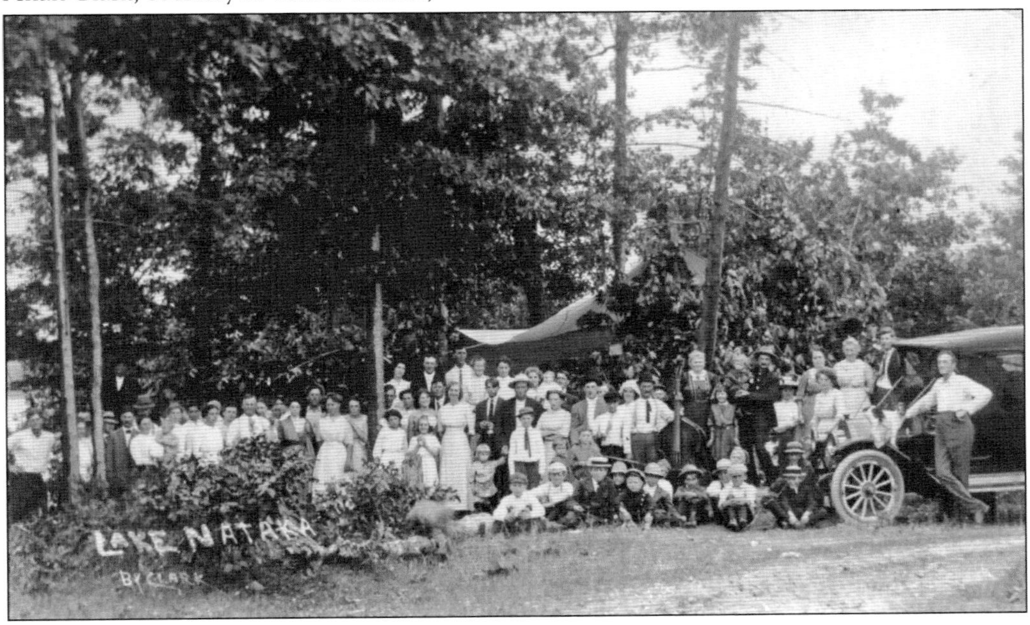

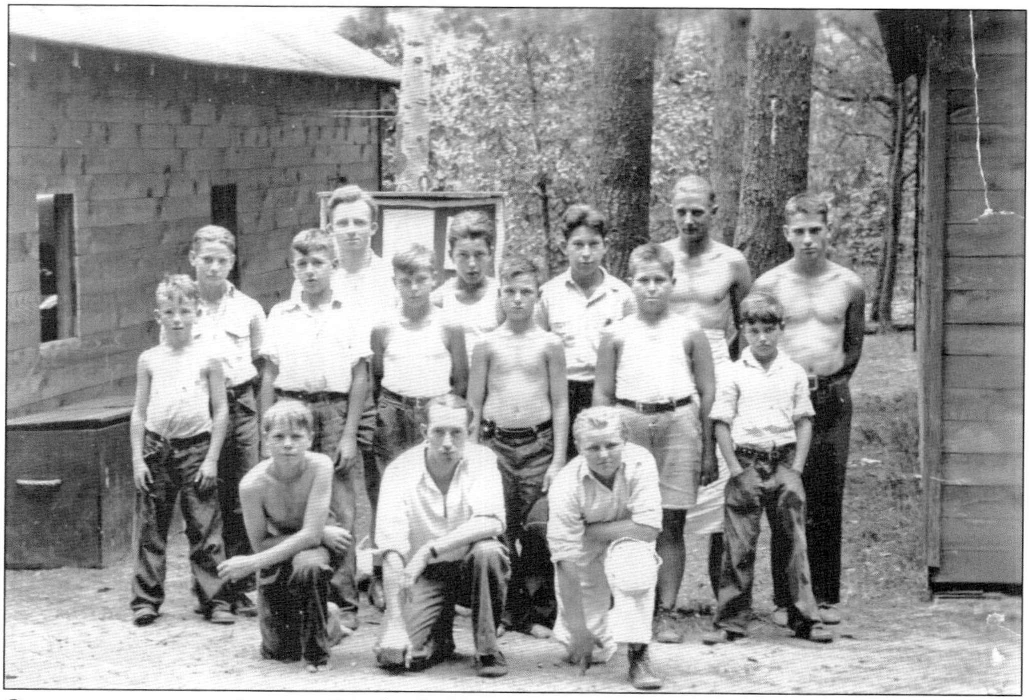

On a warm summer day in 1934, the Baldwin Boy Scout Troop, on a camping trip, poses for a group photograph. They are, from left to right, (first row) Bucky Wallace, Scoutmaster Fred Bradford, and Paul Gibson; (second row) Charles Bradford, Fred Felt, Bud Castle, Donald Johnson, Dormand Fenner, ? Cameron, and Junior Ebmeyer; (third row) Robert S. Smith, Warren Smith, Kurt P. Kahl, Russell Burkett, and Jim Felt. (Courtesy of Jane Miller.)

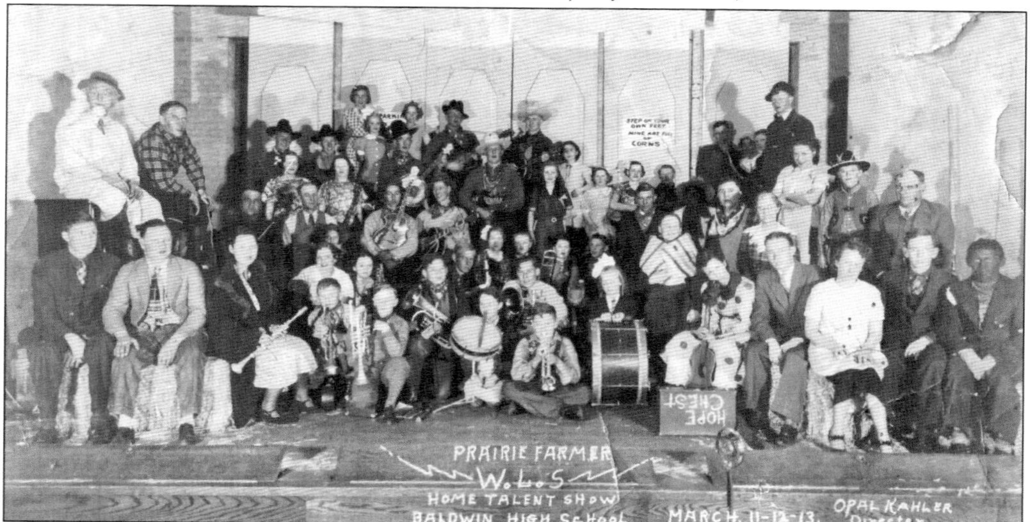

Chicago's WLS radio ran a talent contest where winners were to travel to Chicago for a radio broadcast. Glenn and Martin "Bud" Dietel with the black Stetson hats (left side) and Alberta and Kathleen Shoemaker (standing directly in front of them) took second and first place, respectively. Depression finances kept them from traveling to Chicago. Leonard Keller, in the plaid shirt, is sitting on the piano. (Courtesy of Phyllis Dietel.)

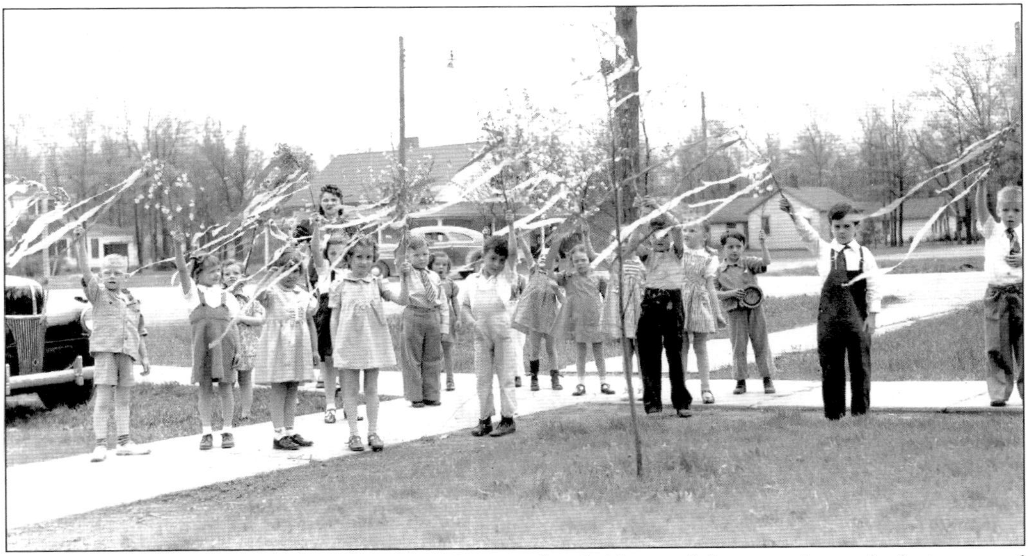

May Day celebrations were a festive rite of spring for children celebrating the end of winter and the beginning of a new season's growth. The students of Baldwin School, located at the corner of Oak and Seventh Streets in the village, appear to be eagerly participating in the joyful activities. The photograph above was taken at a May Day celebration, around 1945, where Baldwin school children are happily waving the traditional ribbons. The photograph below, around 1950, shows the results of the schools' election of the king and queen of the May. The queen, seated on the right side of the stage, was Judy Drilling. (Courtesy of Kris Trucks.)

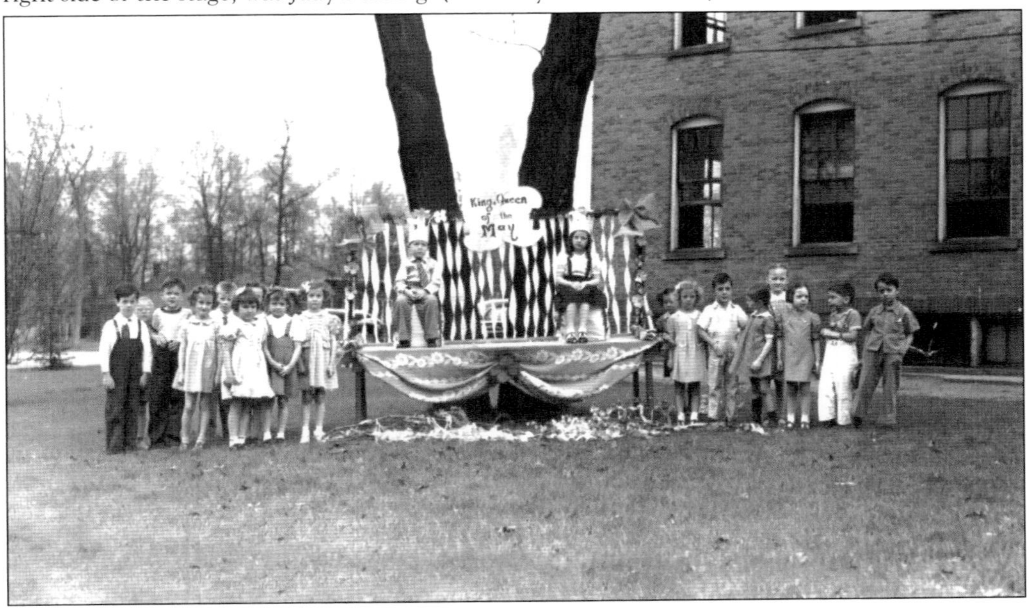

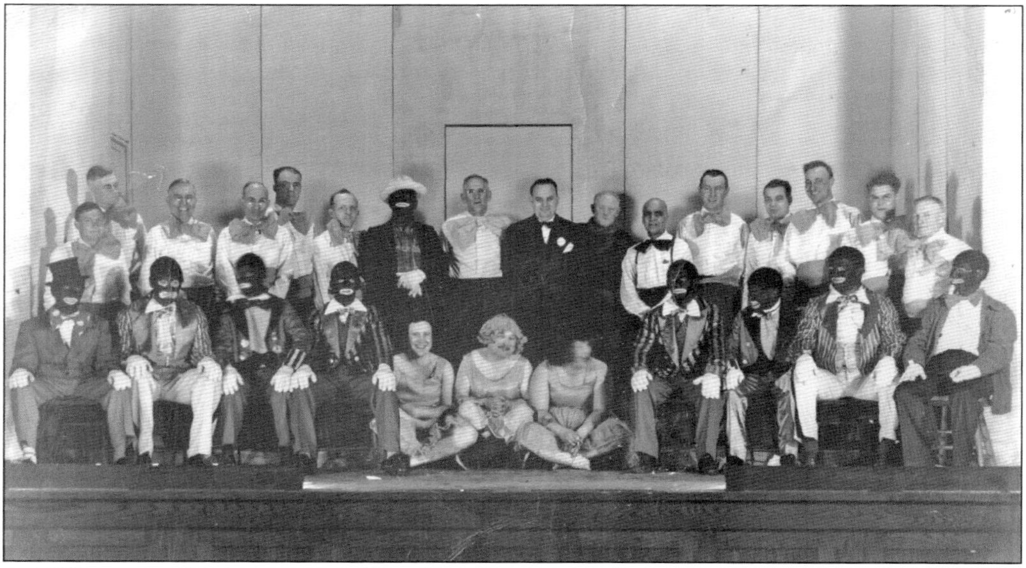

A 1950s vaudeville show was performed at the community center. The "women" in the center, from left to right, are Howard Russell, Darcy Weaver, and Max Oswald. The seated men in blackface are not identified. Standing from left to right are Robert Leeson, Jesse Bradford, Max Brail, Lowell Thomas, unidentified, Robert S. Smith, unidentified, Leonard Keller, unidentified, Fred Fairburn, James Brown, Lou Williams, David Snyder, Ernie Loucks, Joel Bartlett, and Earl Gibson. (Courtesy of Deborah Smith-Olson.)

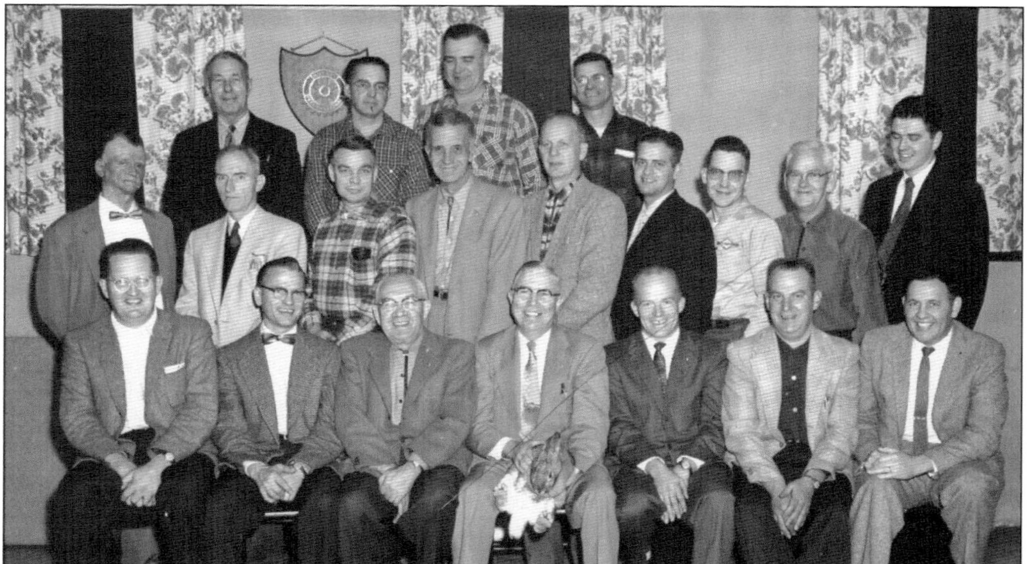

The Baldwin Rotary Club's member who missed the last meeting had to care for the rabbit. Seated from left to right are 1960s members (first row) Vernon Moordyk, Emil Wenger, Dinty Moore, Max Brail (with rabbit), Curtis Smith, Edward Timm, and Charles Wickens; (second row) Dic Cooper, Dwight Jackson, David Snyder, Tom Carnahan, Taft Utter, Guy Hunt, Millard Johnson, Wallace McGarr, and Fred Lawless; (third row) Harry Murphy, Al Patterson, Robert Brophil, and Don Young. (Courtesy of Deborah Smith-Olson.)

Six

TEACHING THE CHILDREN

Traveling down long, dusty roads in Lake County today one will often still find one-room schoolhouses. For many settlements, one of the first items of business was to build a school, usually housing kindergarten through eighth grades in one room. There was one teacher for all those grades and sometimes the teacher was younger than the oldest student. Some, like Ellen Stevensen of Branch, taught for 45 years and dedicated their whole lives to the communities. For a small salary, a teacher had enormous duties. In addition to teaching, the schoolmarm was the janitor and also had to report to the school board on the conditions and needs of the building. Early schools had no indoor plumbing. Water was pumped from the outdoor well and put in a wash basin or fountain at the entryway. All drank from one dipper. The schoolhouses were often heated by a large round parlor stove, stoked in the morning by the schoolmistress. On bitter cold days, students would leave their coats on and study by the woodstove. In 1911, Lake County boasted 48 schools with 1,237 students attending.

Schools also often served as neighborhood centers. Church and Sunday school were sometimes held in schools such as Marlborough (Marlboro) and Cherry Valley. Dorothy Johnson Hibberd of Marlborough traveled from school to school teaching Bible studies, something unheard of today. Marie Moore of Big Bass Lake School had a Christmas program that took months to prepare, complete with hand-sewn costumes. Box socials were a way to raise money for special class projects.

Churches have deep roots in Lake County. Jane Gibson Miller attends Baldwin Congregational Church and recently told churchgoers that seven generations of her family have attended the church. Idlewild, the African American resort community, remains a stronghold of black Baptist churches. Even the roads there instill a message with names like Hope and Charity. The Methodist Church of Luther celebrates 135 years of existence, while St. Ann's Catholic Church in Baldwin is a full-time parish that had its start as an early mission.

As time has passed, the old country schools have evolved into more up-to-date buildings with modern technology giving students the best opportunity possible. Church congregations have grown, necessitating newer and larger structures.

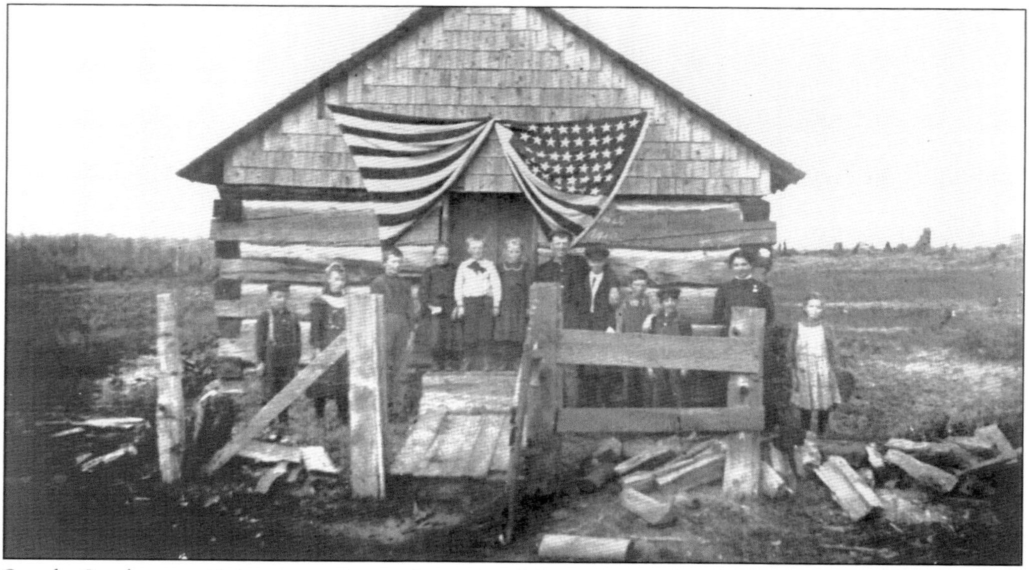

Swede Settlement School was located north of Branch, on the flatlands east of Ward Hills. Families coming from Norway and Sweden to farm and run small sawmills sent their children to this 1900s log schoolhouse. Ten students, from left to right, Fred Zwiegle, Amelia Zwiegle, Ed Olson, Alice Olson, Seymour Thorsen, Ellen Stevensen, John Thorsen, Ben Anderson, Bert Olson, and William Zwiegle, are standing with their teacher, Ida Olson. Mabel Clemenshaw is seen standing at the right. (Courtesy of Paul Bigford.)

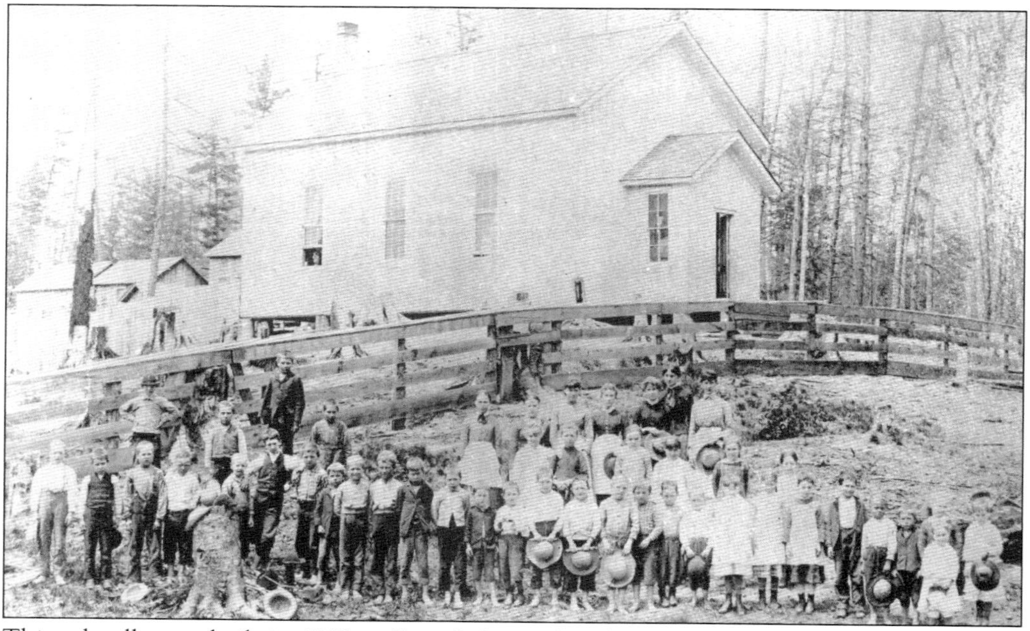

This schoolhouse, built in 1885 at Deer Lake, replaced the first structure, which burned. In 1900, Deer Lake became a ghost town and the school was moved east to Deer Lake Road. Some families stayed in the area to farm. George Bates, a log scaler, bought 735 acres in Deer Lake for $7 an acre. George had nine sons who all attended Deer Lake School. (Courtesy of the Lake County Historical Society.)

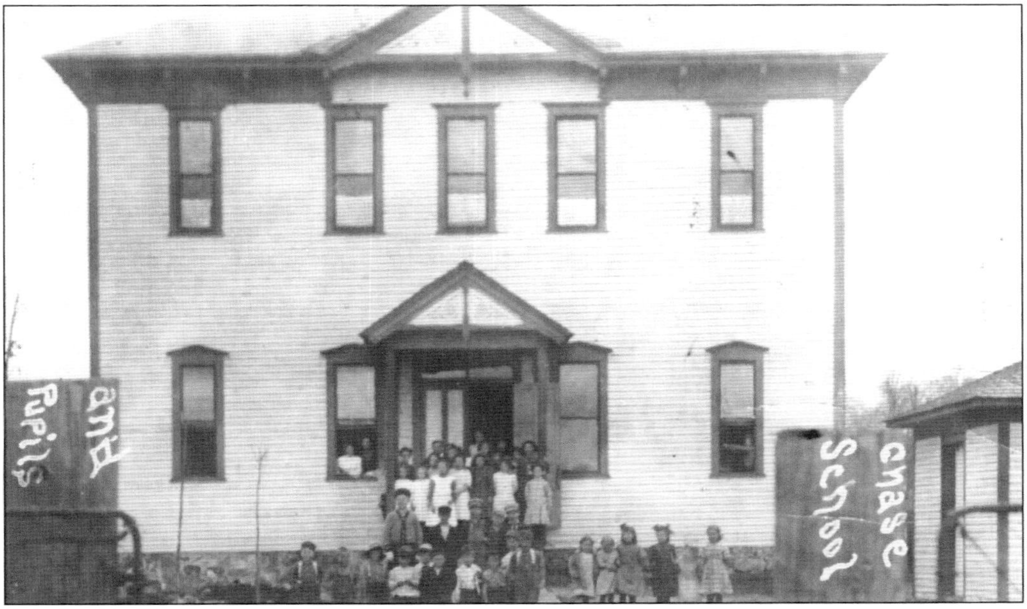

This postcard of the Chase School and its pupils is dated July 16, 1913. The two-story wood frame structure was built in 1882 and was in use until 1935, when it was demolished. A new brick building replaced the outdated schoolhouse. The school closed in 1969, and the building now houses the Chase Township Library and Chase historical archives. (Courtesy of Dennis Ellison.)

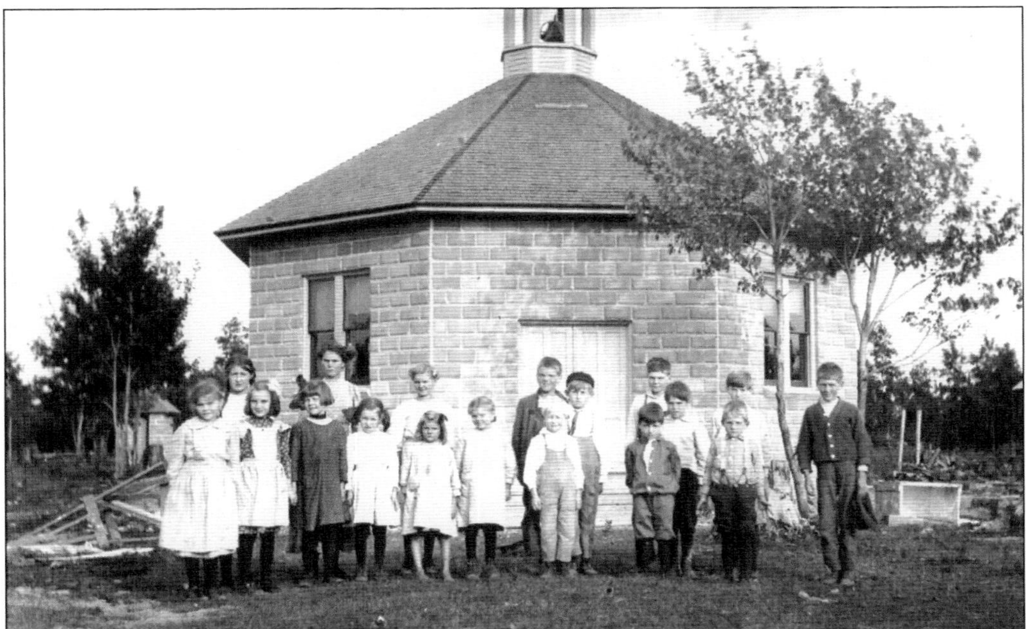

In 1918, the population of Sauble was 40. The rather unique octagon Sauble School was built just south of Sauble Station, a railroad stop on the Manistee and Grand Rapids Railroad north of Branch, and served the town and the surrounding area. This tiny hamlet was first called Goodrich, then Sheepdale, and finally Sauble. (Courtesy of Albert George.)

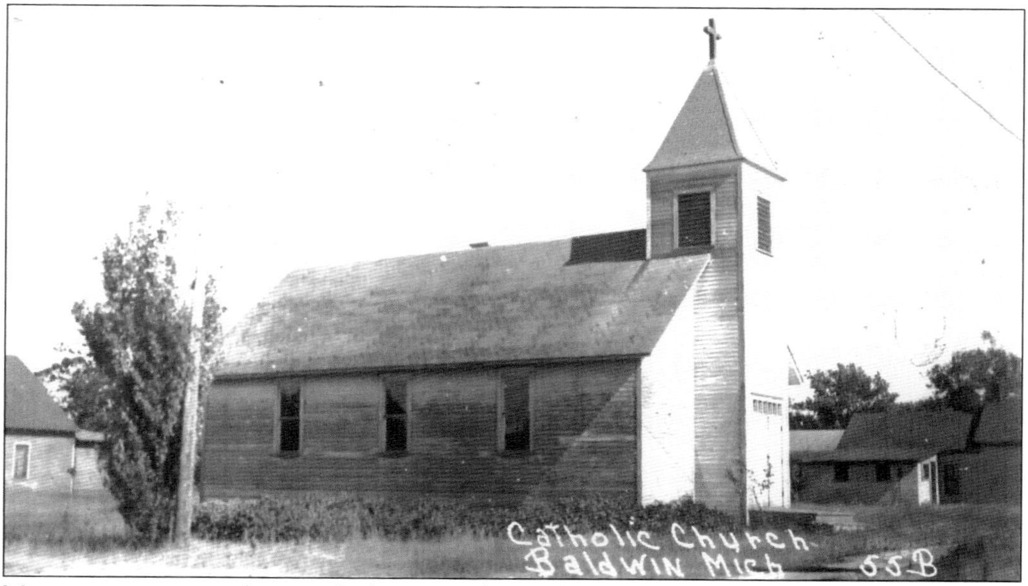

Many immigrants to this area had strong religious beliefs, which resulted in mission churches being started. St. Ann's Catholic Church in Baldwin, seen here in the 1930s, was visited twice a month by a mission priest from Grand Rapids. Most of the early priests were of Polish descent. St. Ann's still stands today. (Courtesy of Bruce Micinski.)

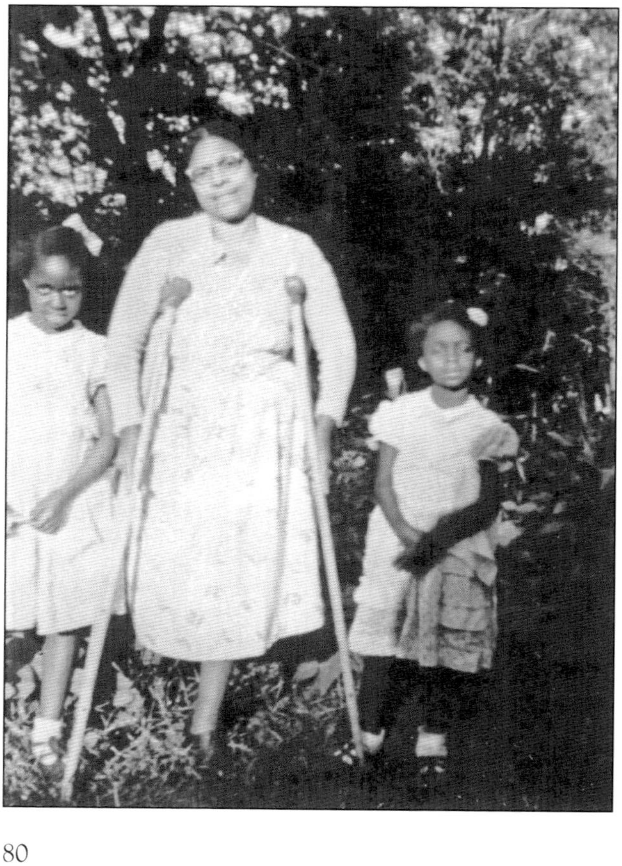

Standing with her grandchildren, Arizona (left) and Georgia, Willie Mae Hunter, who had a leg amputated, ran an advertisement in a Grand Rapids newspaper in 1954 pleading for a garden tractor. Jane Roodvoet, a member of the Netherlands Reformed Church of Grand Rapids, came to Baldwin and gave Hunter food and money. The Bethlehem Mission Church was started that day and has continued to help the less fortunate of Lake County. (Courtesy of Elder John Groenedijk.)

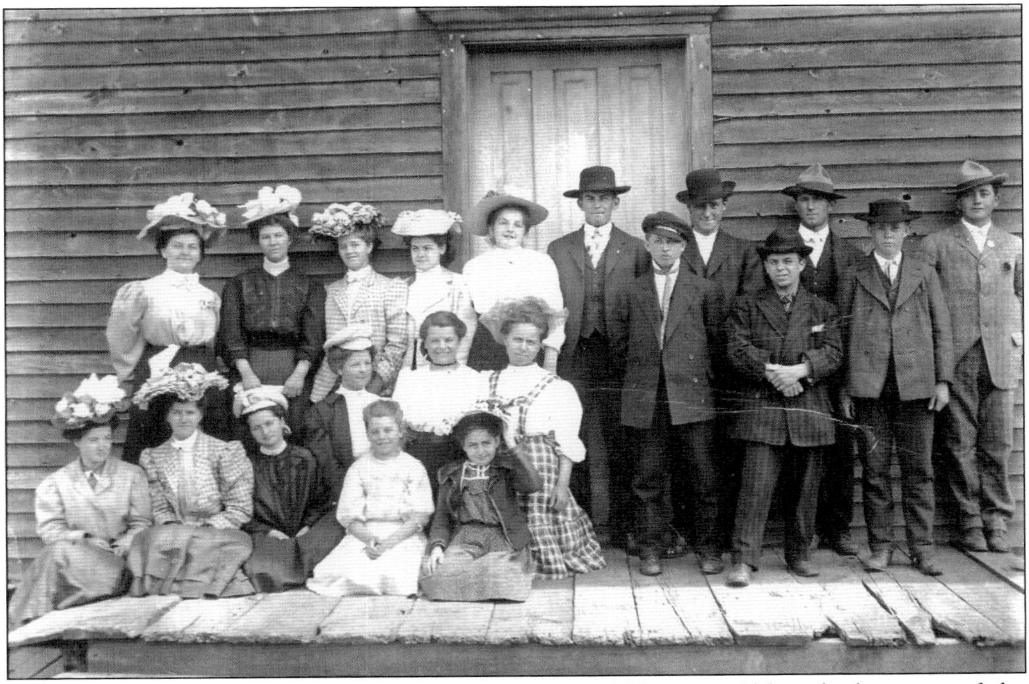

This photograph was taken in 1908 by Francis Lacy of Nirvana. Although the name of the church is not known, it is believed to be in the Nirvana area. Men and women dressed in their finest to attend services. (Photograph by Francis Lacy, courtesy of the James Woods family.)

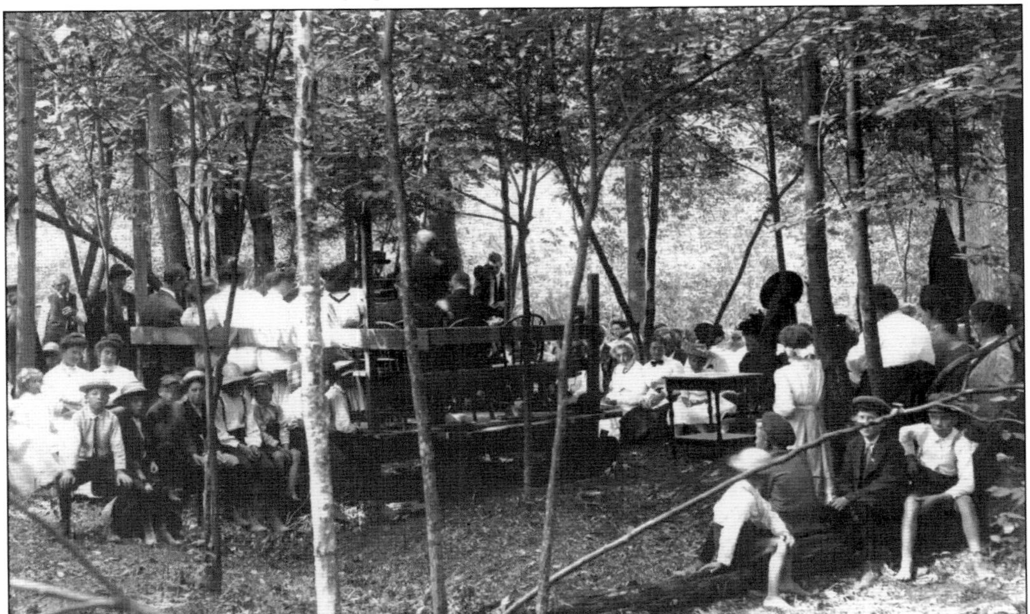

Church services in Luther were held in schools, halls, and vacant buildings. Circuit preachers would make the rounds to rural communities throughout the summer to preach the word of God. This photograph was possibly taken at Edgetts, near Luther, as they held church revivals there during the 1920s. (Courtesy of Jerry Poprawski.)

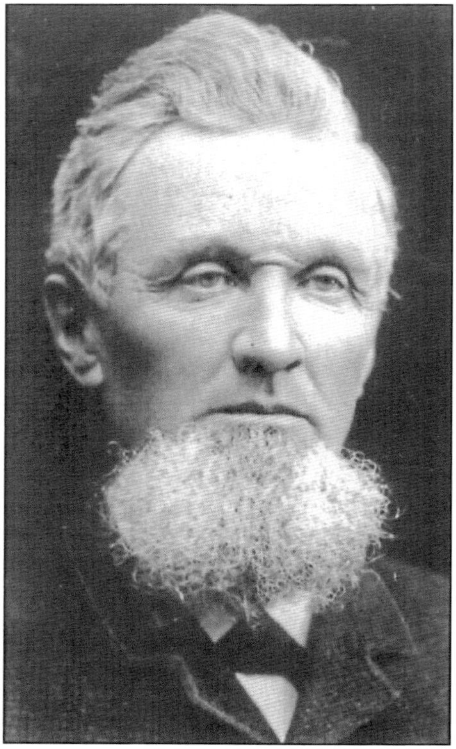

Before Lake County was organized, the settlement of Chase had several schools. In 1868, David Lathrop was the first teacher in the Oliver School District No. 1. This first school stood east of the village of Chase. In 1871, Lathrop was also the first county clerk and registrar. (Courtesy of the Lake County Star.)

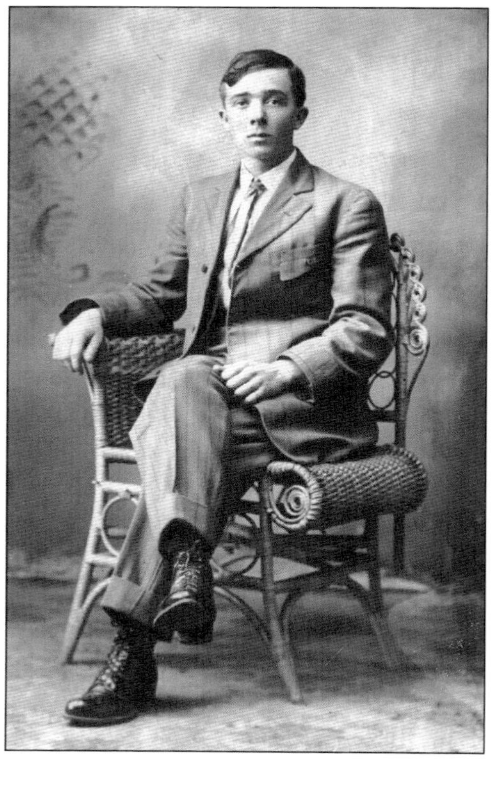

A surprise was the number of male school teachers in Lake County. Charles Eldred, born in 1891, was teaching at Spears Grove School in Pinora Township when he was 20. Eldred would be one of nine male teachers to preside at this one-room schoolhouse. The first teacher at this school was Julia Lathrop, wife of David Lathrop. (Courtesy of the James Woods family.)

The majority of school teachers, however, were young, single women, such as Ella F. Jennings. Female teachers in Michigan were not allowed to be married in the early 1900s. This student souvenir was presented by Jennings, teacher at the Lake Township School. Carr Settlement, which was founded by Union soldiers after the Civil War, was the location of the school. (Courtesy of the Lake County Historical Society.)

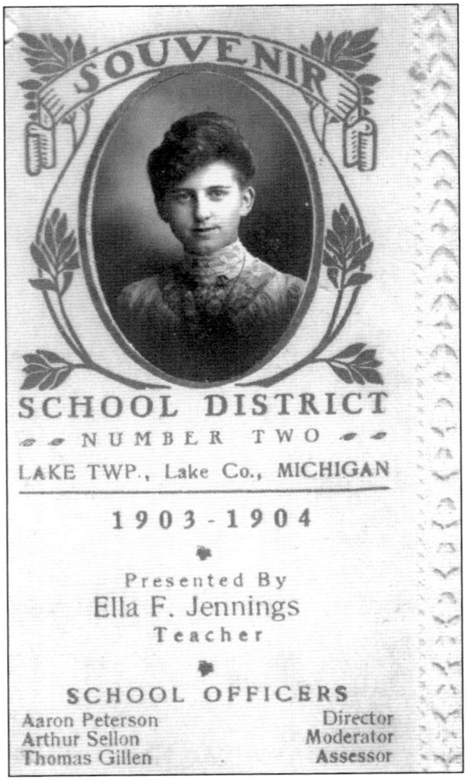

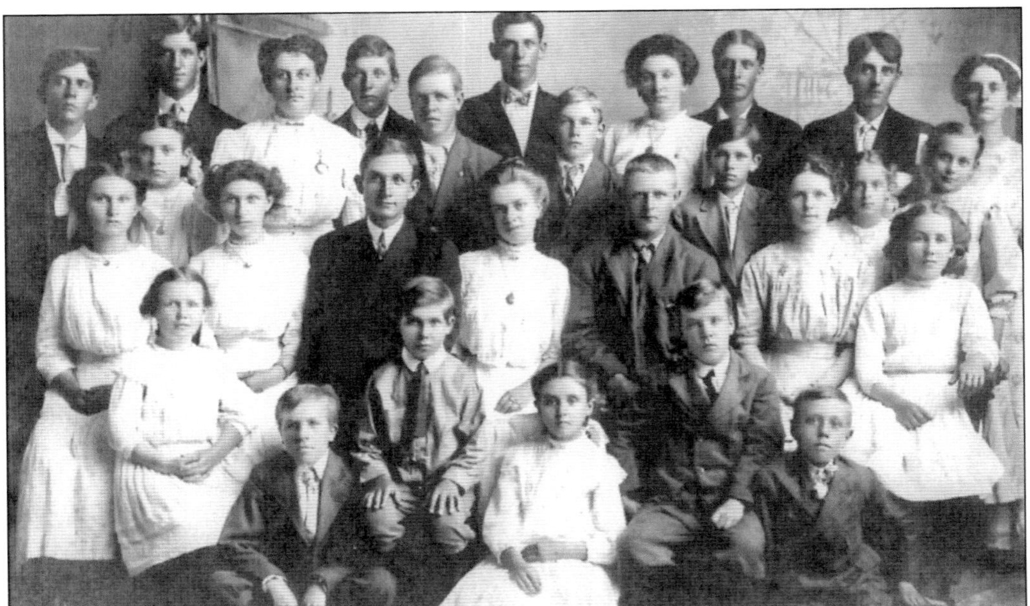

The Cornell School started in 1881 in Chase Township. Early school life included formal plays that cast all students. Pictured are cast members from a 1910 play. In the first row, center, is Magdalena Shoemaker; in the third row, second from left, is Chlorinda Lidquist; and in the fourth row, first on the left, is Velma Haree. (Courtesy of the Lake County Star.)

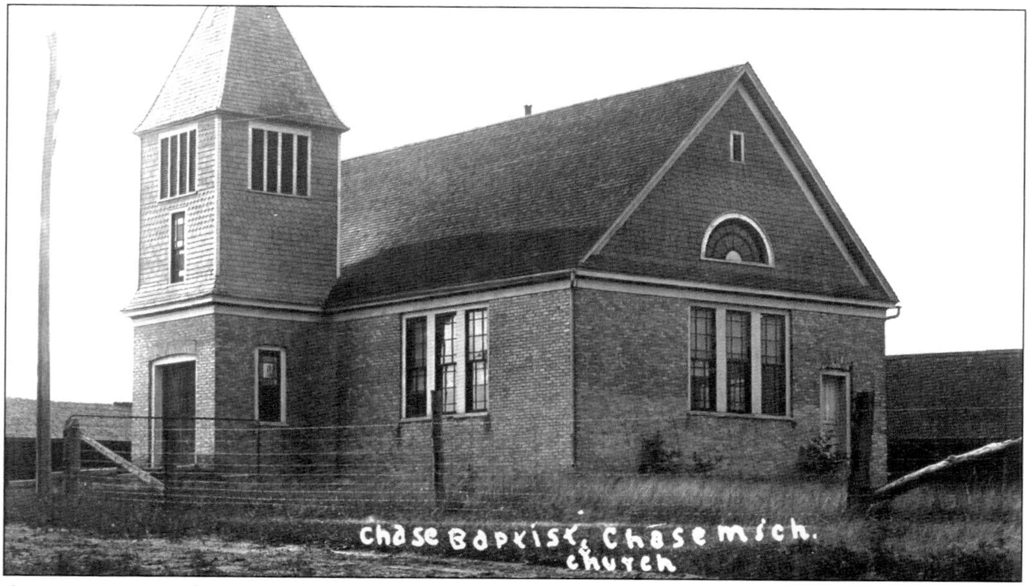

As congregations became established and membership grew, churches often built modern houses of worship to replace earlier ones. The Chase Baptist Church was located on North Street in town. The new church, photographed about 1910, was constructed of brick and included an enclosed entry hall and bell tower. (Courtesy of the James Woods family.)

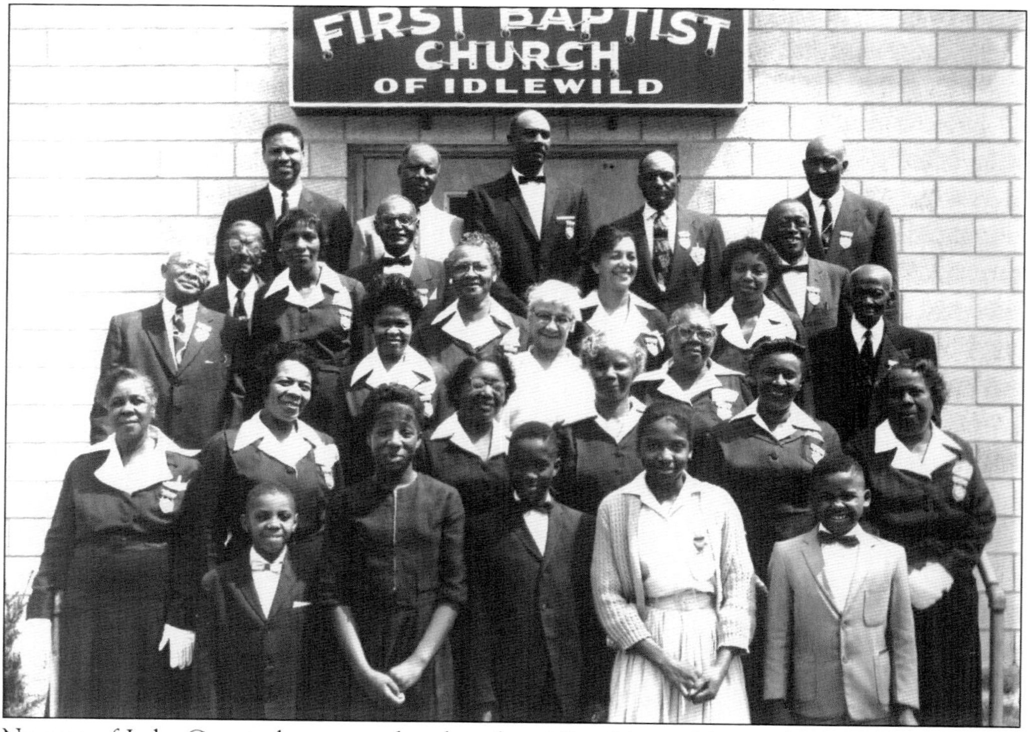

No area of Lake County has more churches than Idlewild, an African American community, founded in 1912. Sunday was a day of worship for young and old, as seen in the photograph of the First Baptist Church of Idlewild. (Courtesy of Tennis Trucks.)

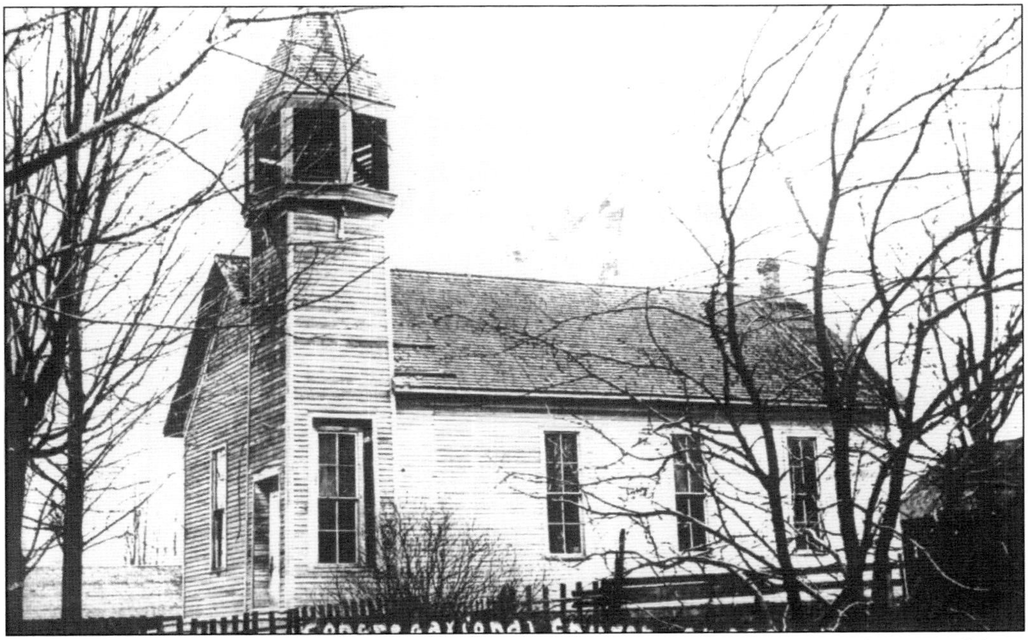

The reformation of the Church of England brought the Protestant movement to America. Many Congregational churches were formed in the late 1800s to early 1900s in Michigan. Photographed here is the Chase Congregational Church, around 1900, with its unusual octagon bell tower. (Courtesy of the James Woods family.)

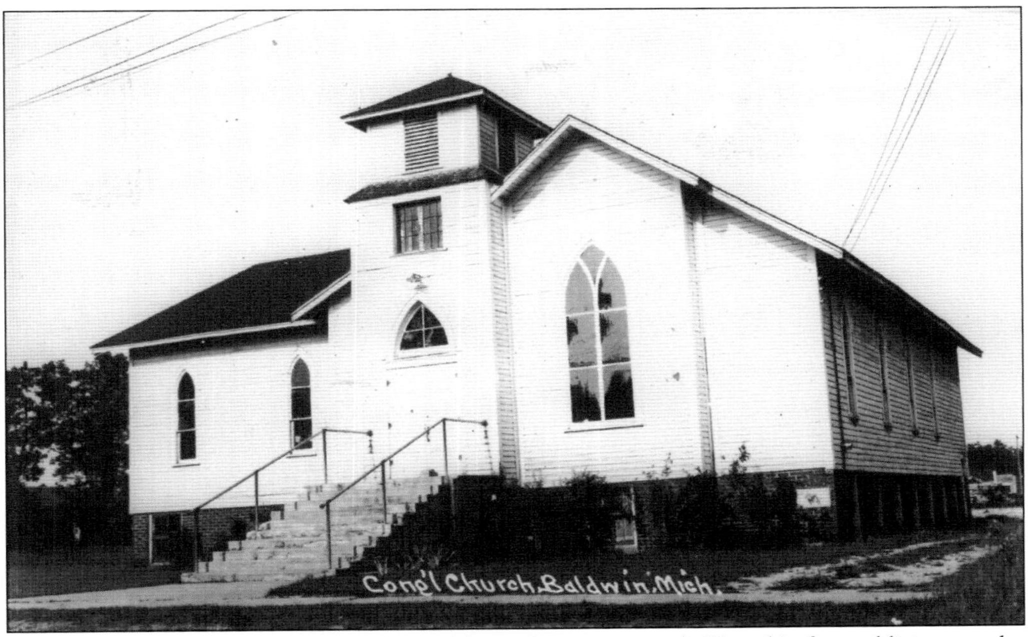

This undated photograph shows the Baldwin Congregational Church's first addition to the original church. The steeple was removed, as part of the renovation, which was common with churches during this time. This church remains active today and once again has a steeple. (Courtesy of Gordon Allison.)

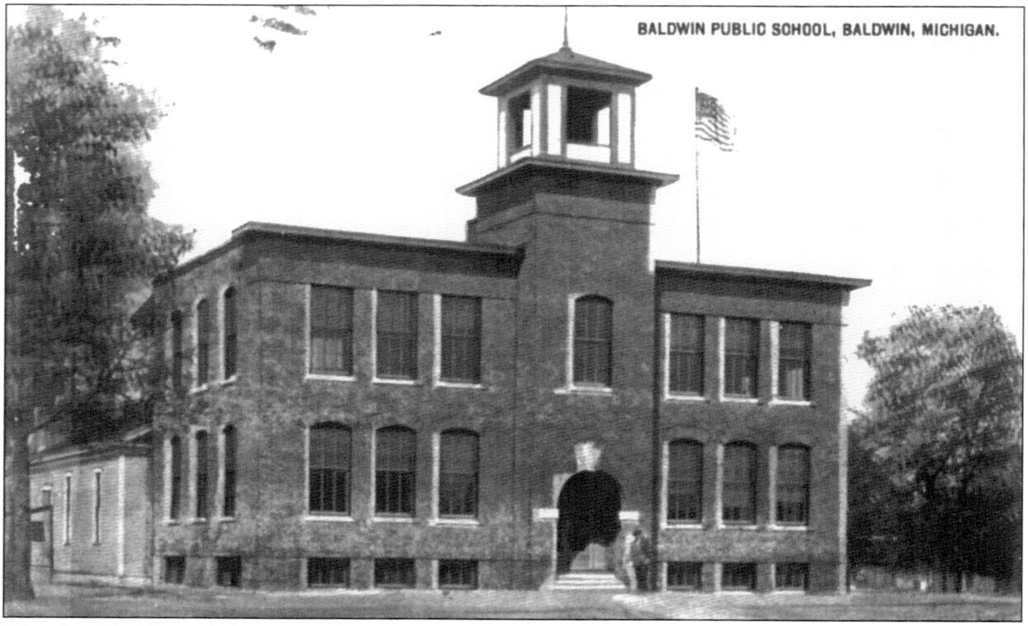

The first Baldwin School was built in 1875 of logs. When it burned in the late 1890s, it was replaced by a wooden frame structure that can be seen to the rear of the new brick school. Built around 1920, the new schoolhouse held grades 8 to 12. This building was closed in 1958 to move students into the current facility. (Courtesy of Paul Bigford.)

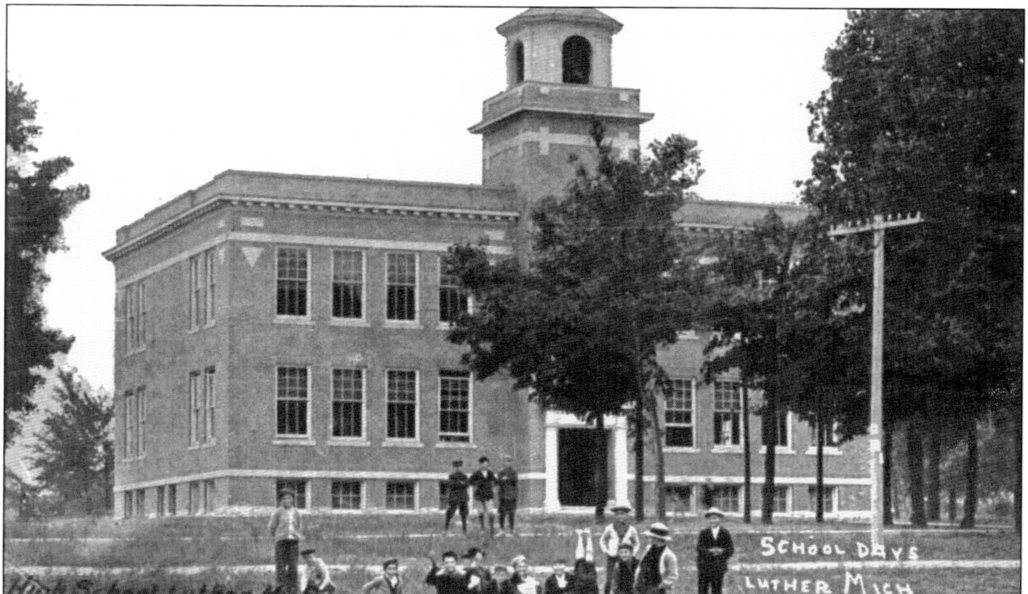

Appearing to be a twin of the Baldwin High School was the Luther Agricultural School. The Luther school was built in 1909 after the original wooden building was destroyed by fire. The school's name was chosen as it offered a fine farm program with Future Farmers of America. This photograph shows one boy standing on his head goofing off. (Photograph by Allan Clark, courtesy of Bruce Micinski.)

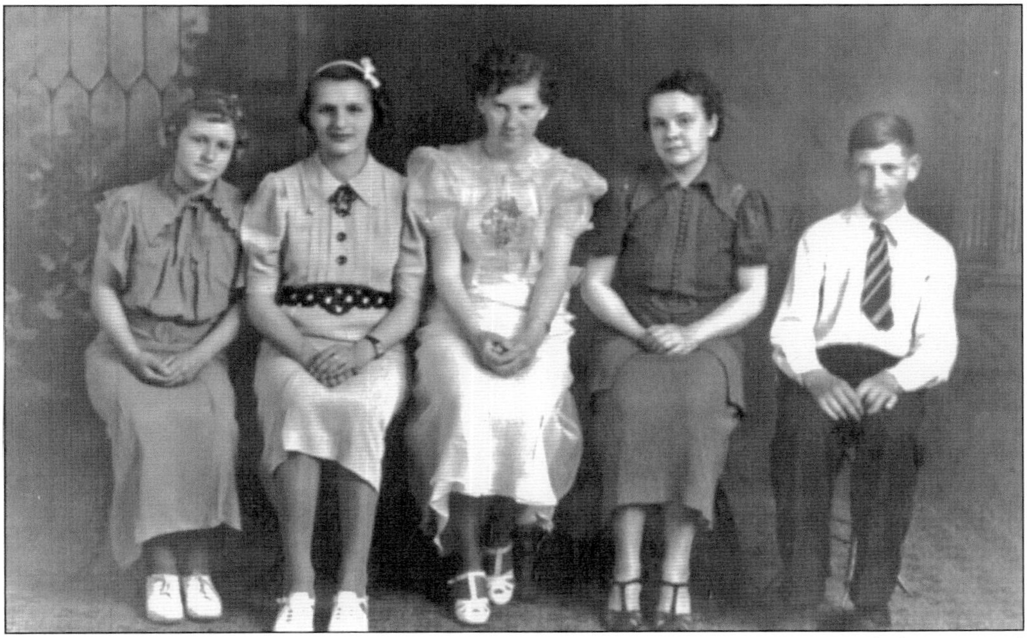

To complete eight years of schooling was a milestone in 1937. A copy of the original commencement address at the Spears School speaks to the proud parents of these four graduates. "We have battled fractions and fought our way through the Civil and Revolutionary Wars" states the unknown writer. From left to right are Lillian Spears, Evelyn Draminski, Lucille Fetzer, teacher Marjorie Sauntman, and Louis Morlock. (Courtesy of the James Woods family.)

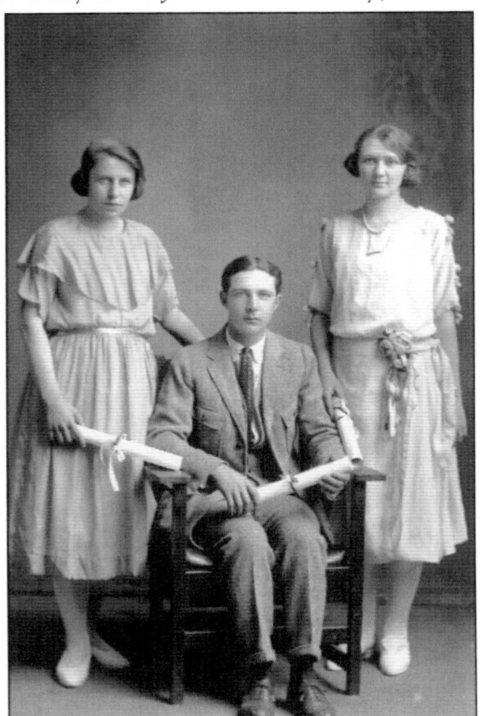

This photograph is believed to be of the first graduating class of the Baldwin High School. The 1923 graduates are, from left to right, Lottie Murlock, Lester Bradford, and Violet Chant. Graduating from high school was considered quite an achievement in 1923. (Courtesy of Jane Miller.)

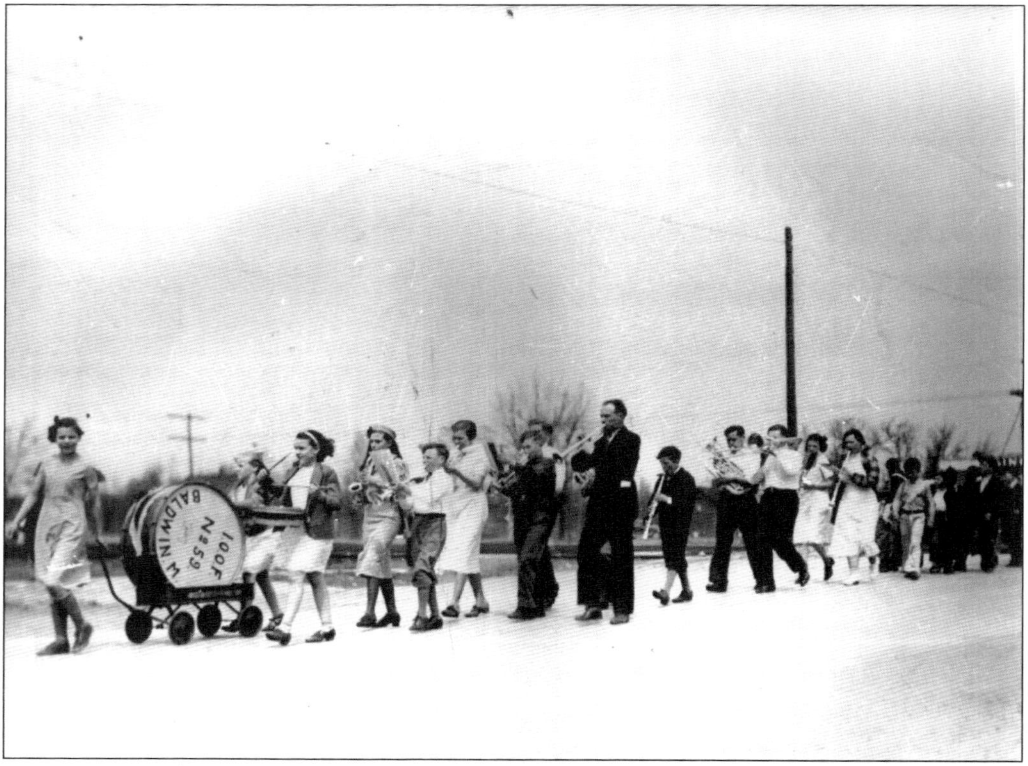

History was made in 1935 when Mr. Updegraff, a local music teacher playing the trumpet and walking mid-group, led a group of students down the main street in what would become Baldwin's first school band. The mothers of the children, with Updegraff's help, borrowed instruments to outfit the band, such as the drum from the Independent Order of Odd Fellows played by Jane (Gibson) Miller. (Courtesy of Tennis Trucks.)

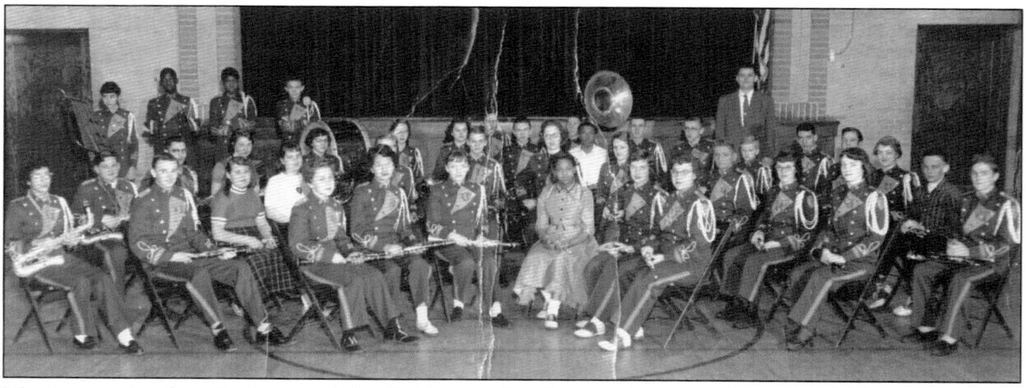

Music remained a vital part of the Baldwin school system's curriculum. Progress was certainly made since the first band was formed in 1935. A diversity of instruments, and formal band uniforms, can be seen in this 1950s photograph of the band at the Baldwin Community Center. (Courtesy of Tennis Trucks.)

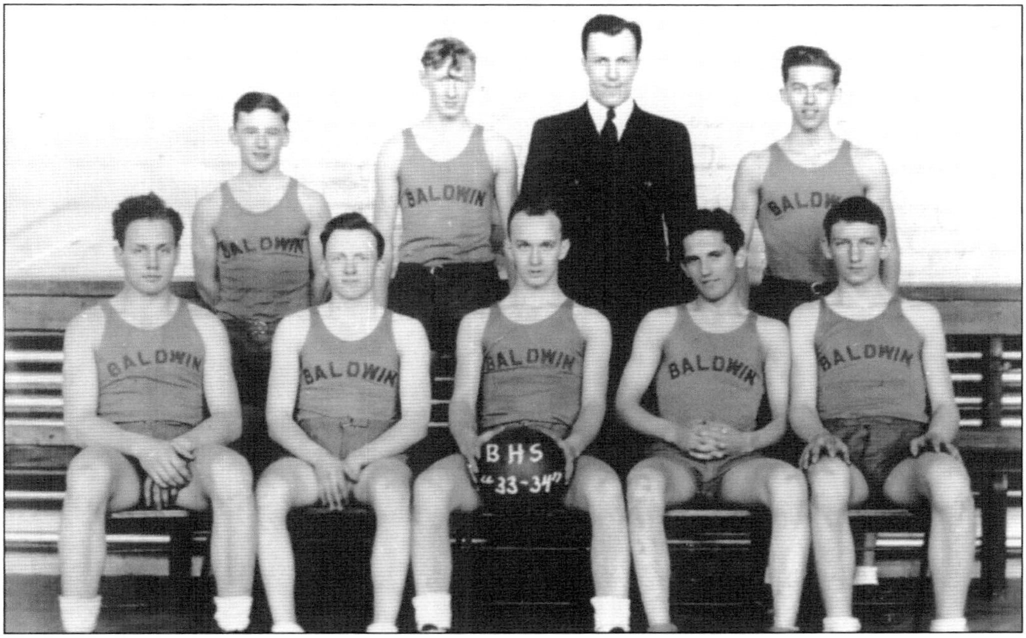

Sports were another way to enrich young people. This photograph shows the Baldwin Basketball team of 1933–1934. From left to right are (first row) Max Field, Robert Smith, Farl Duffing, Stan Bayak, and Don Hodgins; (second row) Jim Rouse, Bob DeLong, coach Dugald Munro, and Bruce Davis. Smith would later become president of the Lake-Osceola State Bank (formerly the Lake County Bank). (Courtesy of Deborah Smith-Olson.)

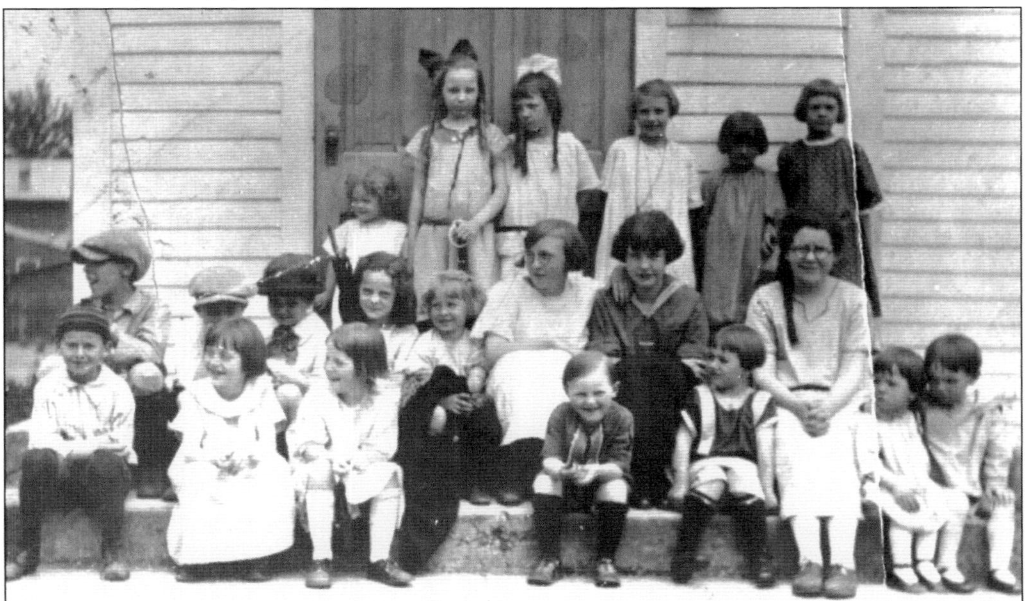

This group photograph is of the Baldwin Congregational Church Sunday school class in 1925–1926. The children learned about the Bible while sitting in pews in a portion of the sanctuary until the north addition to the church was built around 1930. Several years later, Sunday school was moved to a room on the lower level. (Courtesy of Tennis Trucks.)

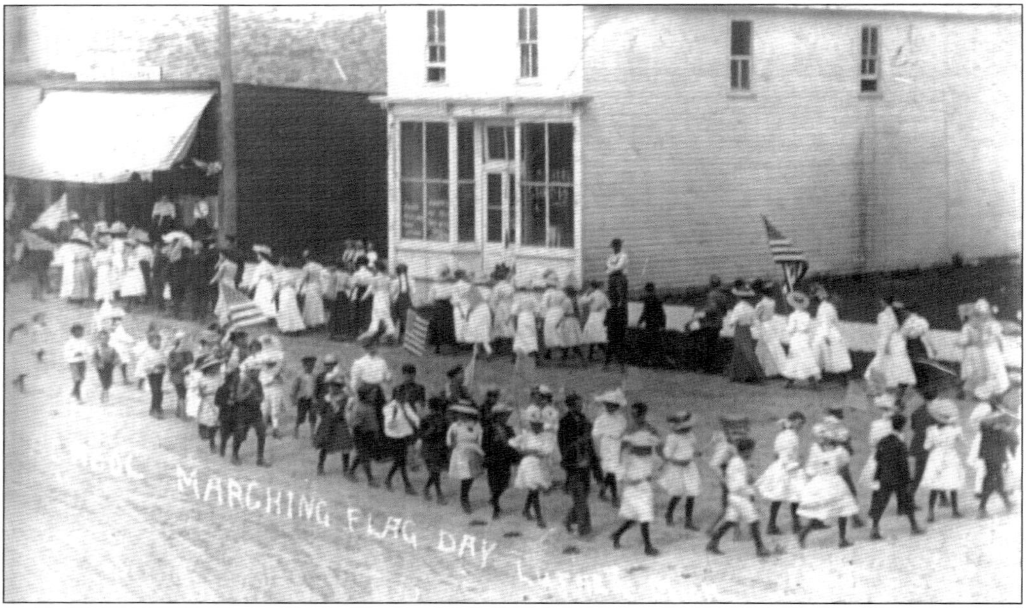

Luther school students celebrated Flag Day in 1911 by parading down the main street. Honoring the country was a vital part of education. Originating in 1885 with an elementary school teacher in Wisconsin, Flag Day was meant to be a day for children to honor the Stars and Stripes. As seen in the photograph, which was made into a postcard, students are proudly waving small American flags. (Courtesy of Jerry Poprawski.)

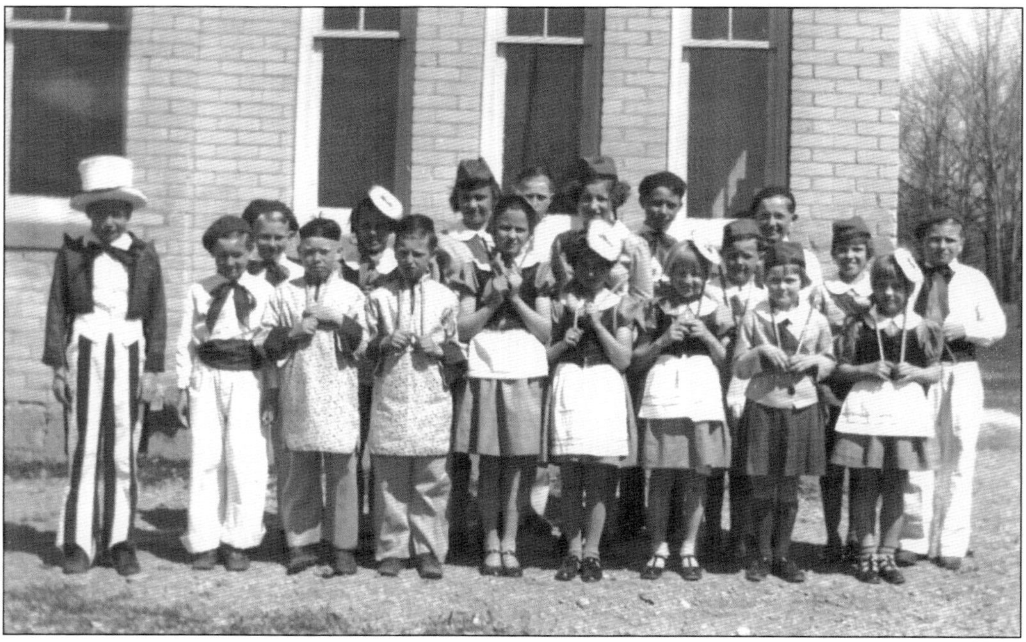

Marie Moore, the teacher at Big Bass Lake School, was creative in her lesson plans. Her students standing at the side of their schoolhouse appear to be wearing homemade costumes depicting various world countries. Young John Urban is dressed as Uncle Sam. (Courtesy of the Lake County Historical Society.)

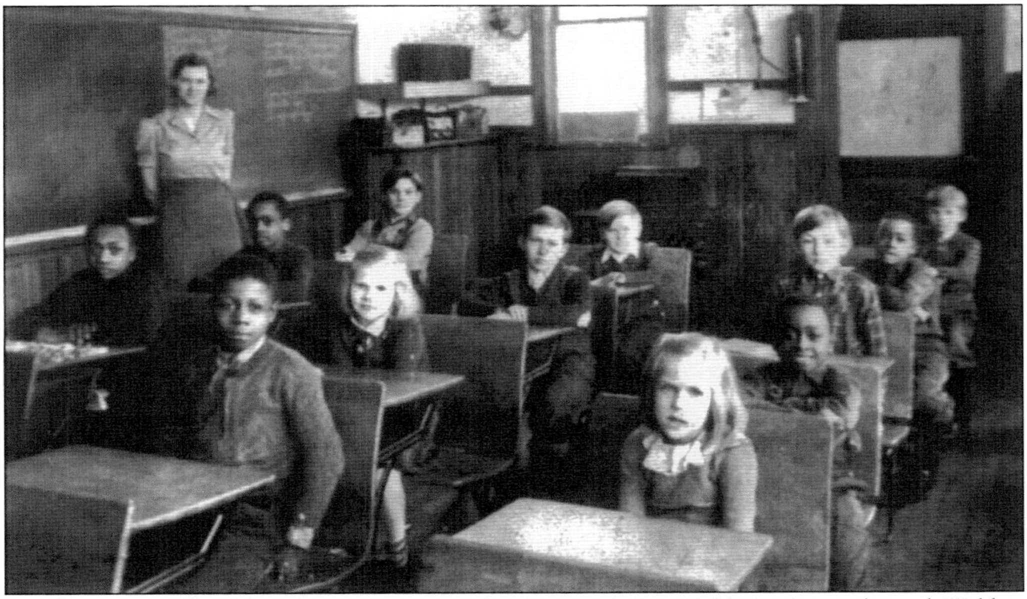

In addition to Idlewild, African American families settled in Baldwin, Peacock, and Webber Township. Hazel Bartlett, standing at the chalkboard, taught at the Eden Township School Unit 1 near Irons. From front to back are (left row) Hartwell Beane, Hiram Beane, and Leonard Maresch; (second row) Isaac Williams, Mary Jane Kabor, Frank Digovama, and Anton Zoubek; (right row) Lillian Kabor, Fred Beane, Joseph Kiannis, Herbert Beane, and David Kessel. (Courtesy of the Martin Johnson Heritage Museum.)

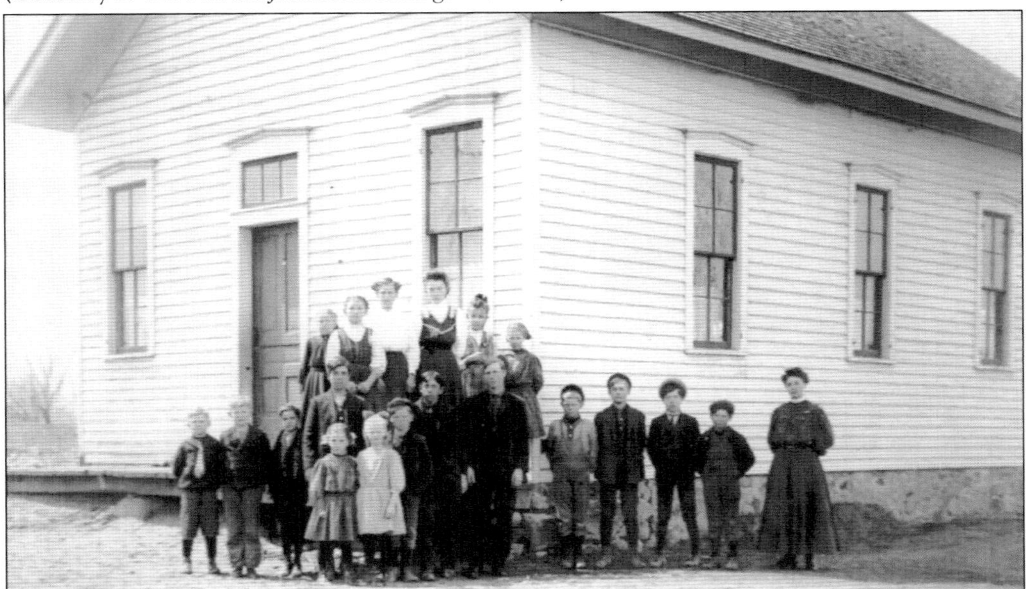

This photograph is of a class of students from the 1890s. When one-room schoolhouses were the norm, Samis School was one of six operating in Chase Township. Built in 1876, it was located on the southwest corner of Hawkins Road and Eightieth Street and served students from Barton Township in Newaygo County as well. The school closed its doors in 1960. (Courtesy of Betty Gawne.)

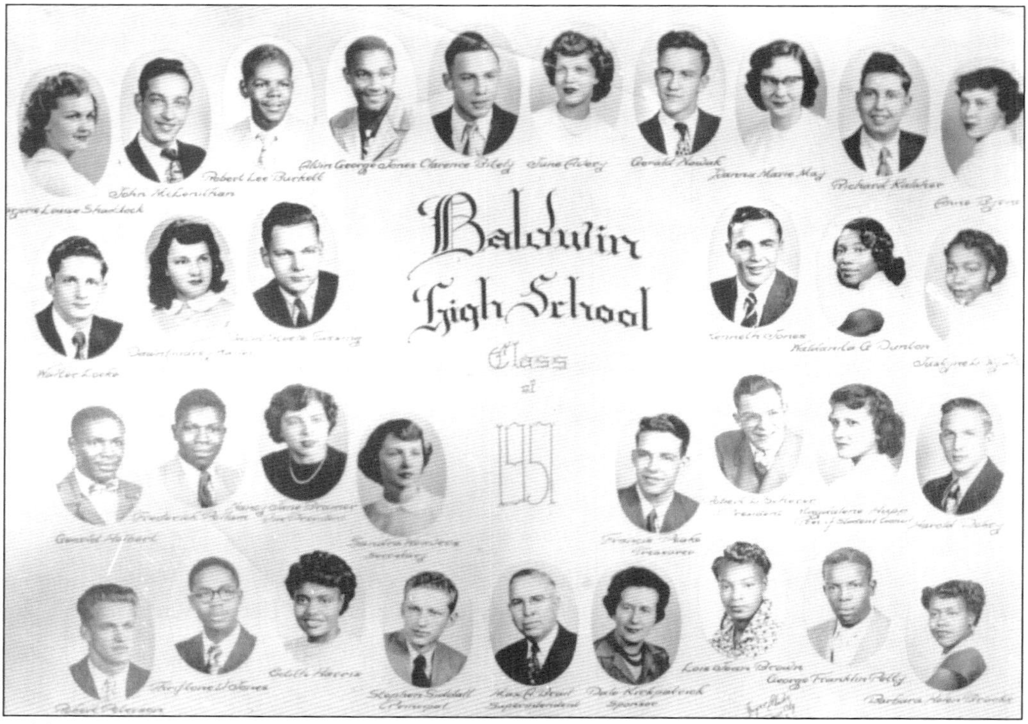

Baldwin schools have had a diverse student base, which can be seen in this photograph. The Baldwin High School class of 1951 was taught by Dale Kirkpatrick, pictured in the bottom row. Kirkpatrick never married and taught school from 1922 to her retirement in 1970. She devoted her entire life to helping children. (Courtesy of Tennis Trucks.)

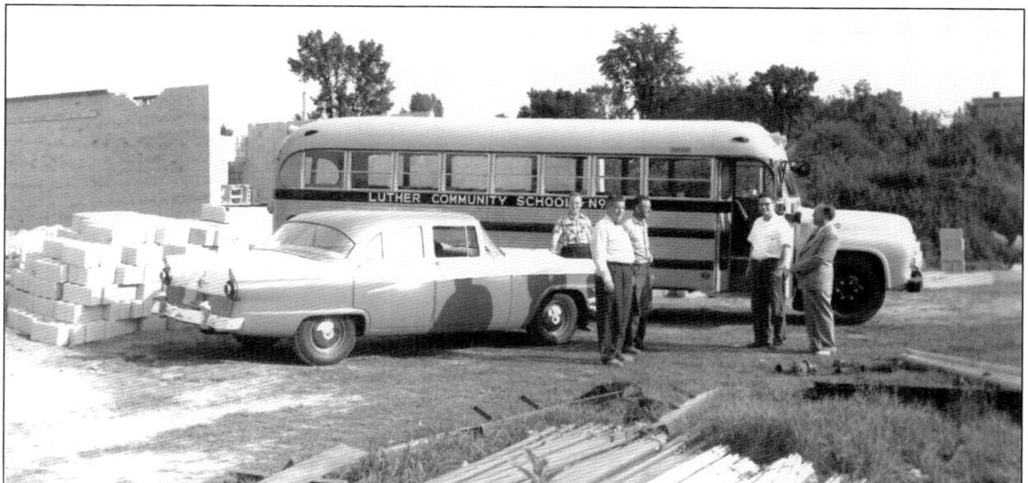

The 1950s marked a change for schools. Luther was building a new concrete block school in 1958 to consolidate several smaller schools. Students living long distances needed school buses for transportation. Gone were the days of walking miles to school in the snow. From left to right are Ed Timm (Ford dealer of Baldwin), Bill Lucas, Fred Lanning, superintendent of Luther Schools Mr. Johnson, and Paul Sutherland. (Courtesy of Tennis Trucks.)

Seven

The Sportsman

By the late 1800s, the county's land was barren. Logging had caused erosion of riverbanks and allowed excessive sunlight on the water. Log drives scarred the spawning grounds, and the fish population plummeted. The native grayling became extinct by 1905. In 1884, a train carrying German brown trout fingerlings to Ludington stopped by chance on a railroad trestle over the Baldwin River and several milk cans of fish were poured into the clean waters of the stream below. Thus the first-ever stocking of a public river with brown trout in America occurred, and with it the beginning of a fishing tradition that has continued for decades. Government stocking programs, and those of conservation groups, continued to supply new life to the rivers. The CCC began planting white pine trees, and in 1938, the Manistee National Forest was established. The waters cooled and the fish population began to increase. Wildlife returned to the forest, and the landscape evolved into what is known today. The county was home to large deer herds, producing trophy bucks when deer season reopened in 1936. Bird and small-game hunting also brought sportsmen to Lake County seeking partridge, woodcock, and rabbits.

Private hunting and fishing clubs were established to provide housing and a social setting for sportsmen traveling from downstate. Kinne Creek Association, Flint Rainbow Club, PM Rod and Gun Club, Fin and Feather Club, and others were formed to serve those wishing to be on the river for "trout opener" or to be in the woods opening day of hunting season. Other sportsmen frequented the Dunrovin Lodge, Pere Marquette Camp, MacDougall's Lodge, Crosby's, and other local cabins and cottages. Rainbow Lodge, Little Red, Lumberjack Lodge, and Trail's End were built along the upper stretches of the Pere Marquette River as personal residences for successful businessmen turned fishing enthusiasts.

Lake County residents fished and hunted throughout the county, and several locals began advertising guide services in the late 1920s at $5 a trip. Ed's Bait Shop opened in the 1940s selling flies, fishing lures, rods, reels, guns, and ammunition. Duffing's Barbershop advertised custom-tied trout flies. Over the years, Lake County developed a successful economy catering to the sportsman year-round.

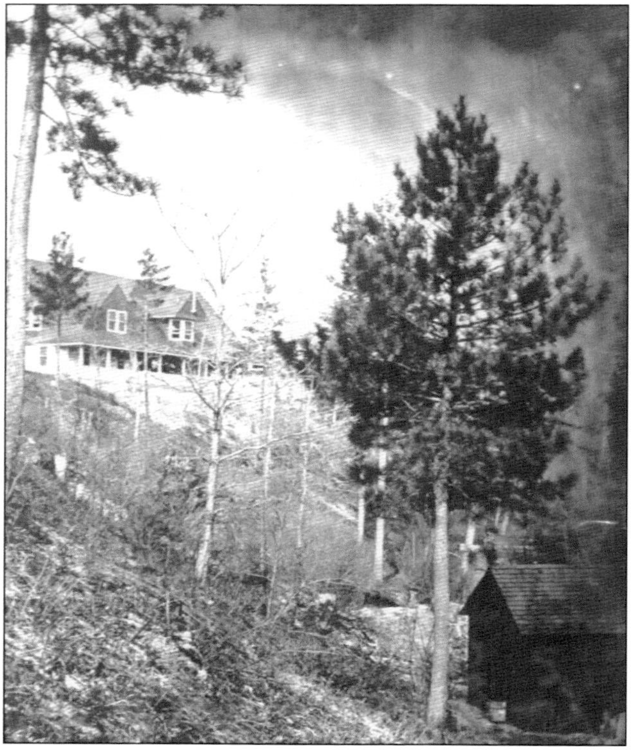

The Kinne Creek Association was founded in 1883 by fishermen from Saginaw and Detroit who traveled to Lake County to fish on the Pere Marquette and Little Manistee Rivers. In 1891, the Pere Marquette Fishing Club, as it was known then, began purchasing land totaling over 1,600 acres. The clubhouse along Nursery Creek, the keeper's cottage, the icehouse, and pump house were constructed in 1898 for $2,700. (Courtesy of the Kinne Creek Association.)

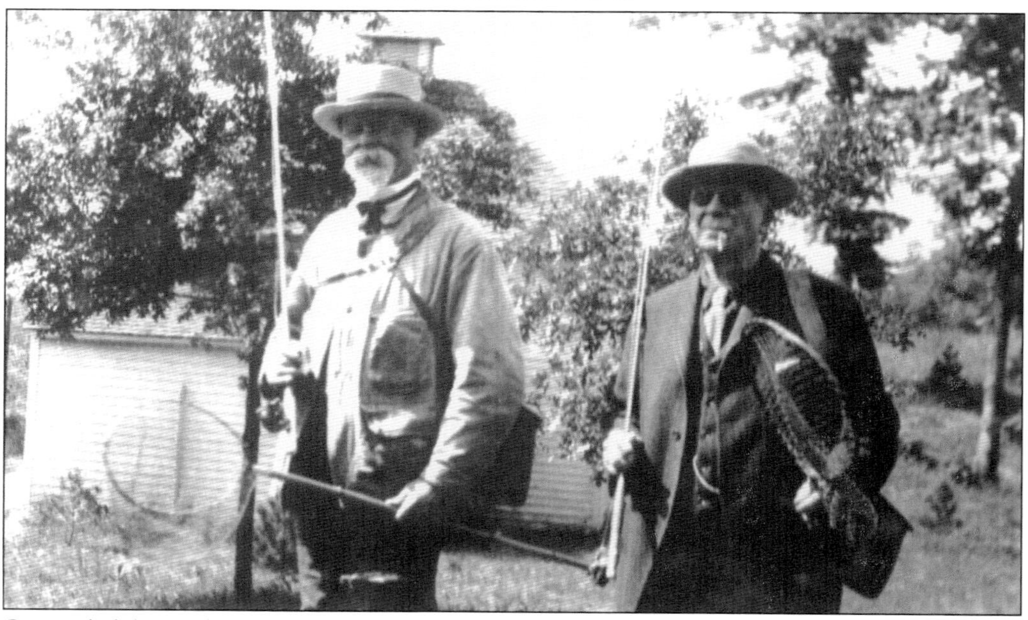

Original club member George M. Brown, with his spinning rod, and guest Maj. Farnham Lyon, with his fly rod, set out to fish the Kinne and Nursery Creeks in May 1904. They, and other Kinne Creek Association members, caught 2,500 fish from Nursery Creek and 1,482 fish from Kinne Creek during that year alone. Lyon's three-piece suit was often the clothing choice of the day. (Courtesy of the Kinne Creek Association.)

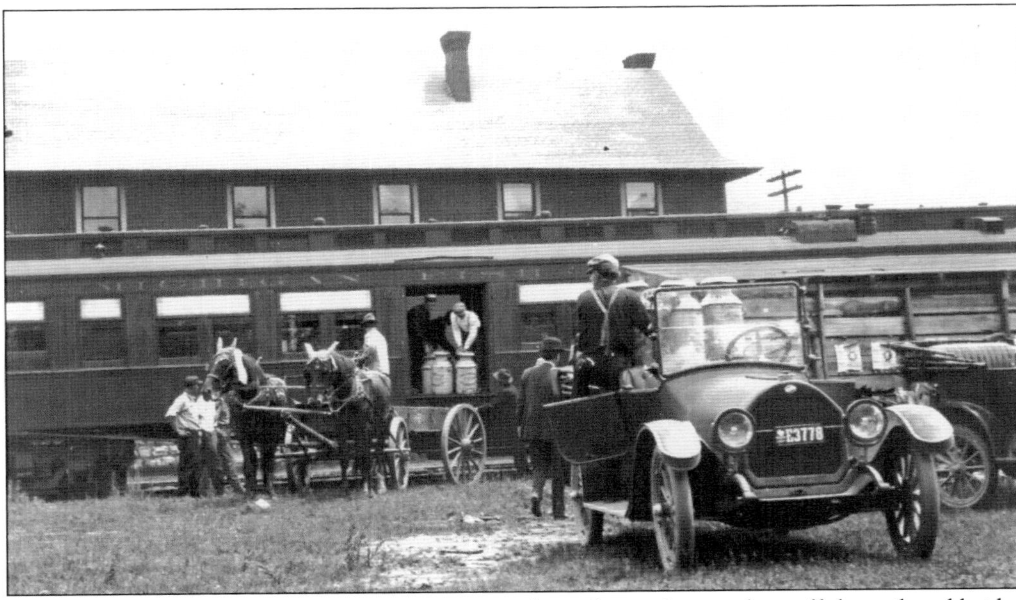

The first German brown trout in America were planted quite by accident off the railroad bridge over the Baldwin River in 1884. The story has come down through the years that the weather was hot, jeopardizing the health of the fish. The milk cans were emptied, and the rest is history. This 1917 photograph illustrates the continued custom of shipping trout in milk cans for fish stocking. (Courtesy of Al George.)

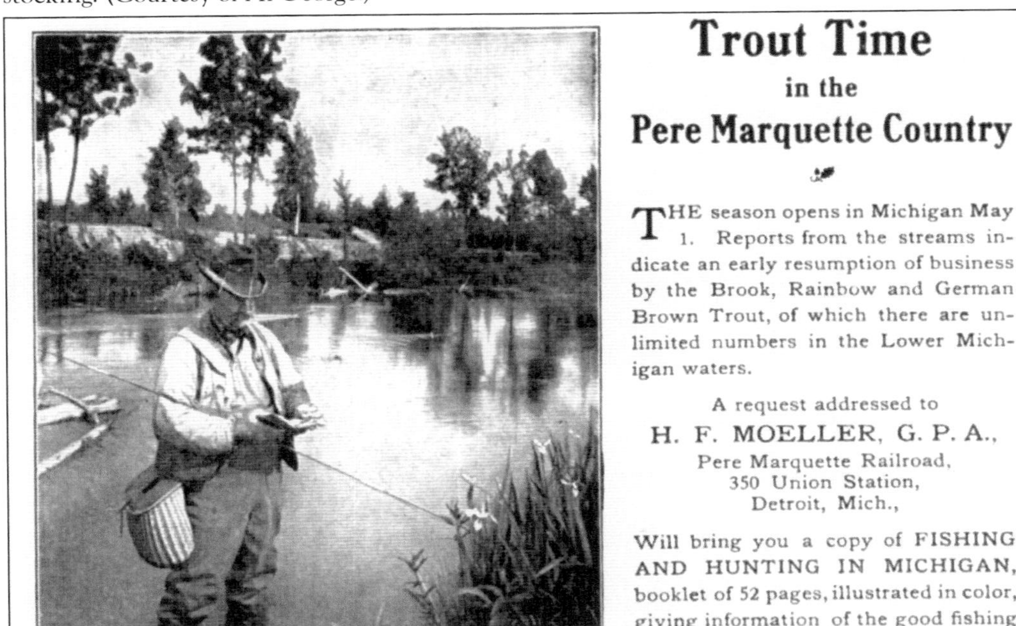

Andrew Bradford, an avid fisherman, moved to Baldwin in 1889, where he started one of the earliest fishing-guide services. In 1904, he was photographed while fishing in the Baldwin River. Appearing in *Field and Stream* with the heading Trouting on the Pere Marquette River, his photograph was also made into this poster, which was distributed to railroad stations across the country. (Courtesy of Michael Oostmeyer.)

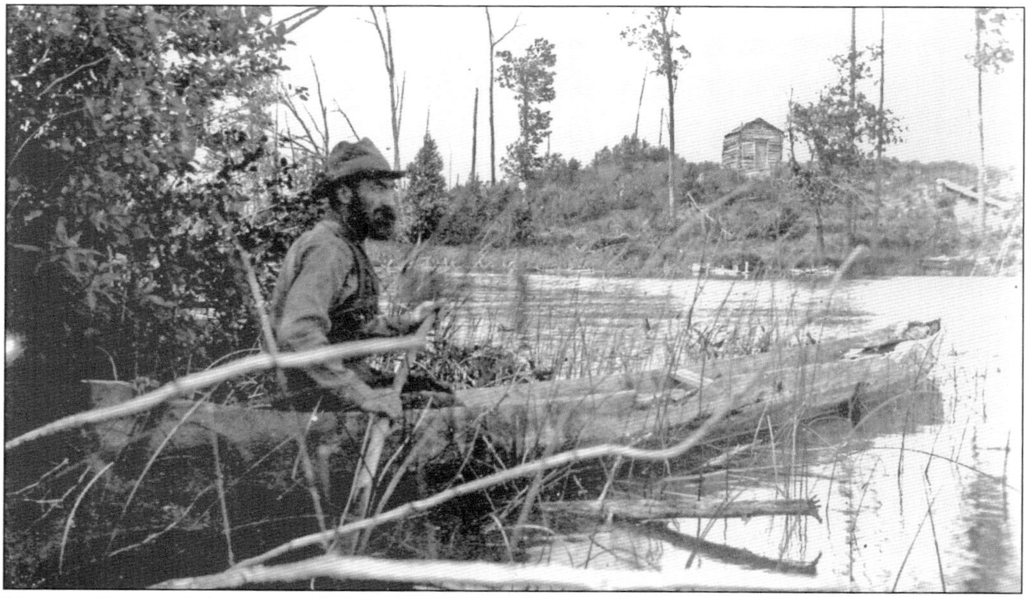

Martin Gustave Johnson settled on Big Bass Lake in 1890, building his first log cabin on the point off the eastern shore. He constructed a dugout canoe from a pine log, gouging out the interior with hand tools. He fished and hunted to keep food on the table and was called by the locals the "Hermit of Big Bass Lake." (Photograph by Martin Johnson, courtesy of the Martin Johnson Heritage Museum.)

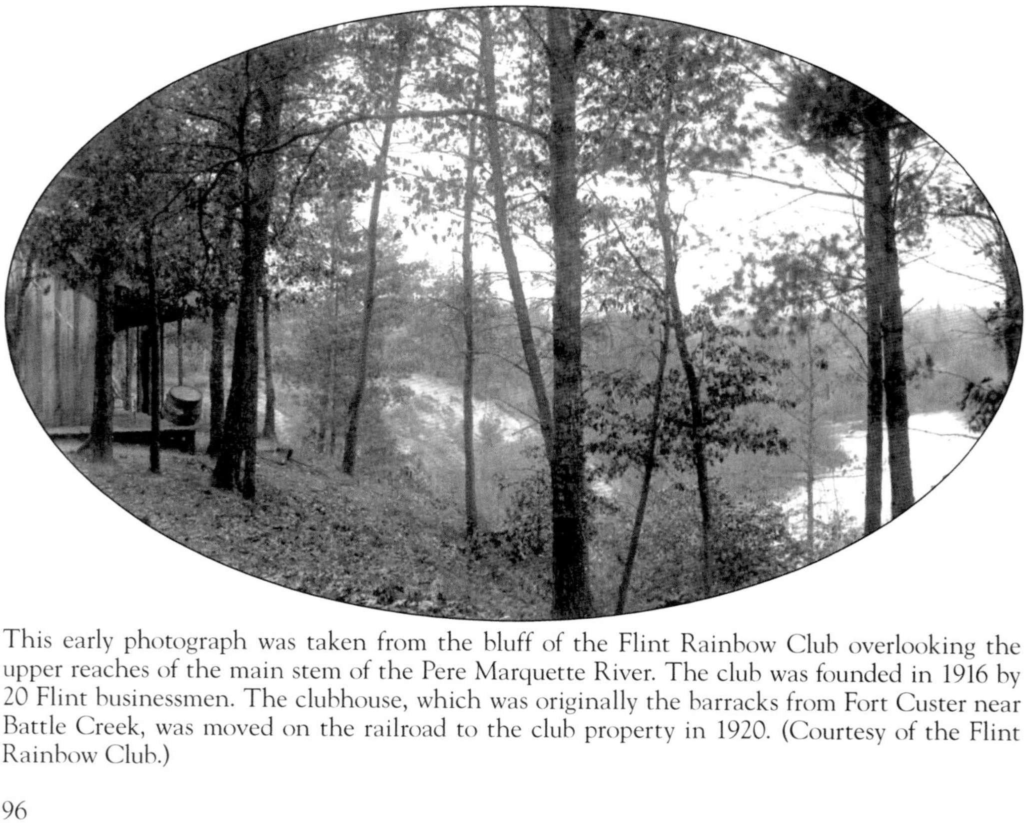

This early photograph was taken from the bluff of the Flint Rainbow Club overlooking the upper reaches of the main stem of the Pere Marquette River. The club was founded in 1916 by 20 Flint businessmen. The clubhouse, which was originally the barracks from Fort Custer near Battle Creek, was moved on the railroad to the club property in 1920. (Courtesy of the Flint Rainbow Club.)

The activities of the Mahoning Camping Club were photographed by member Theodore Kestner. During the months of July and August in 1914, the club camped along Whalen Lake on property owned by Robert Matthews of Baldwin. To supply the cook pot, members trapped turtles in the lake and nearby rivers. (Photograph by Theodore Kestner, courtesy of the Lake County Historical Society.)

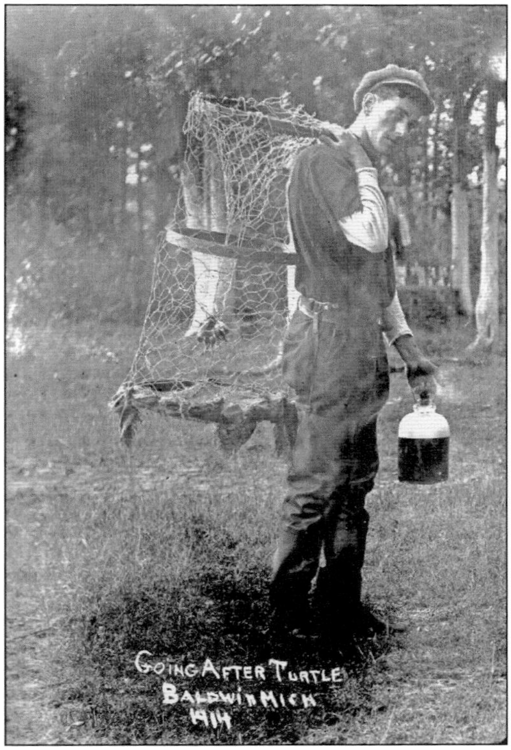

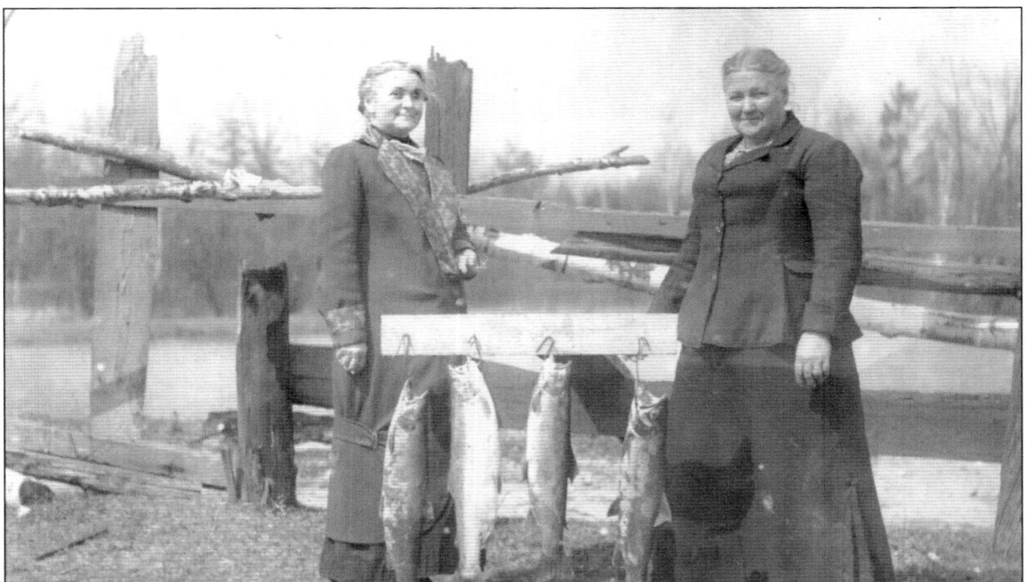

From Niles, Ohio, the members of the Mahoning Camping Club fished in Whalen Lake, L-Lakes, the nearby Baldwin River, and the North and Little South Branches of the Pere Marquette River. The unidentified women were not part of the all-men club, but pose here with four fine steelhead trout taken by club members. (Photograph by Theodore Kestner, courtesy of the Lake County Historical Society.)

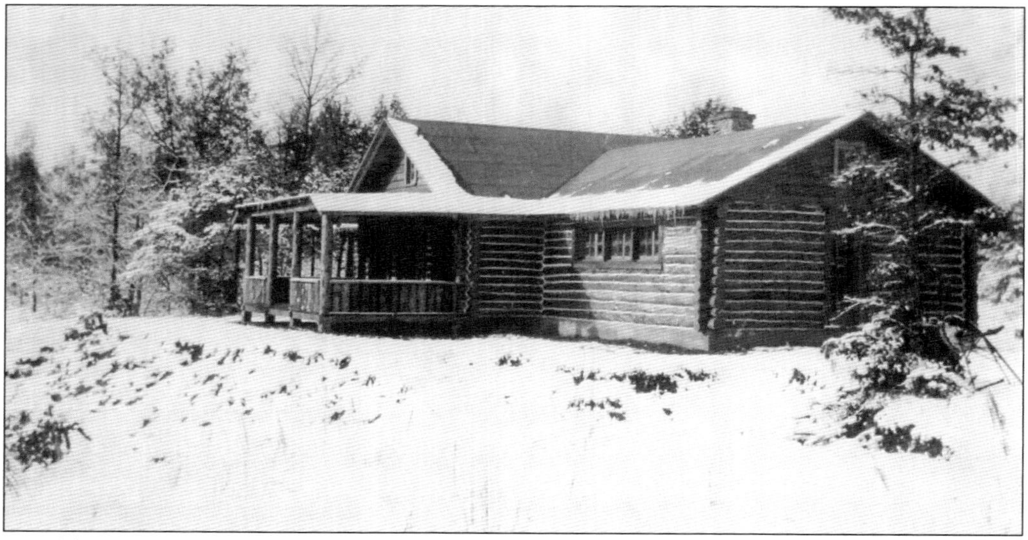

Harold S. Parker and 15 other businessmen from Muskegon purchased 50 acres of land along the Pere Marquette River from Robert J. Smith, the president of the Lake County Bank, and formed the Fin and Feather Club. In 1925, James and Fred Fairburn built the log clubhouse, complete with two sleeping wings, for this private men's sporting club. (Courtesy of the Fin and Feather Club.)

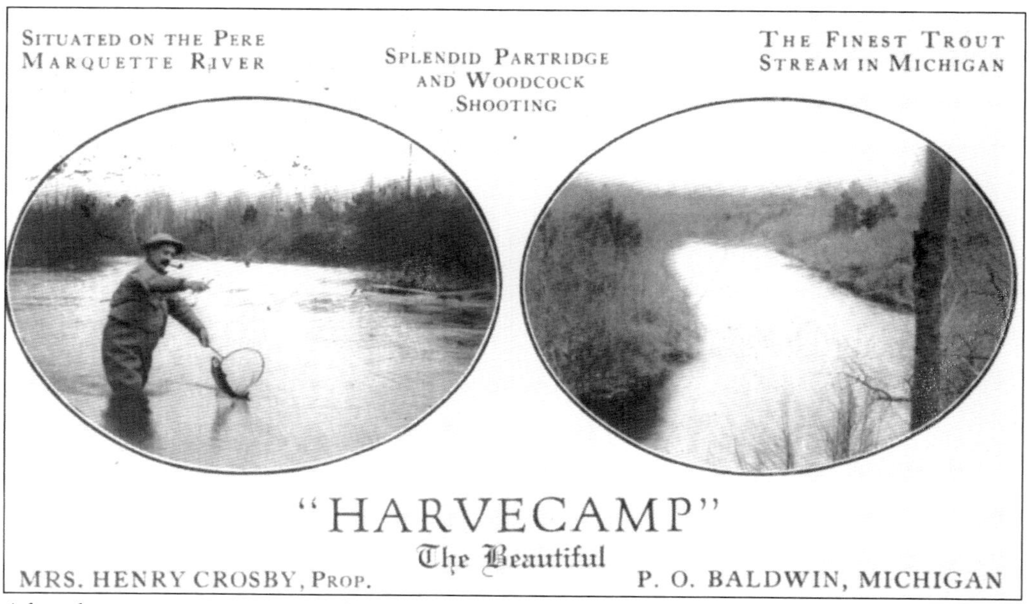

After the trees were cut, many loggers let the ownership of the land revert to the state. Henry Crosby purchased some of this acreage on the Pere Marquette River in 1904. Following his death, his widow, Ida, had the land platted, naming the area Harve Camp. She also turned their home into a hotel. Crosby's was a popular lodge catering to hunters and fishermen. (Courtesy of Jerry Poprawski.)

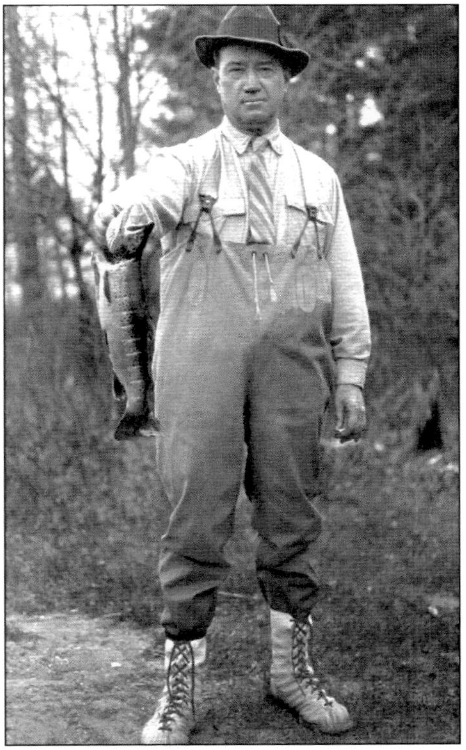

James Duffy, showing off his brown trout, was the president of the Grand Rapids Hardware Company and a member of the Shack—a private men's club on the Pere Marquette. These millionaires made their fortunes during the 1920s booming furniture industry. Ralph Widdicomb of Widdicomb Furniture and John "Jack" Retting of Retting and Sweet Furniture were friends with Duffy and had river lodges in Harve Camp. (Courtesy of Bruno and Jayne Roti.)

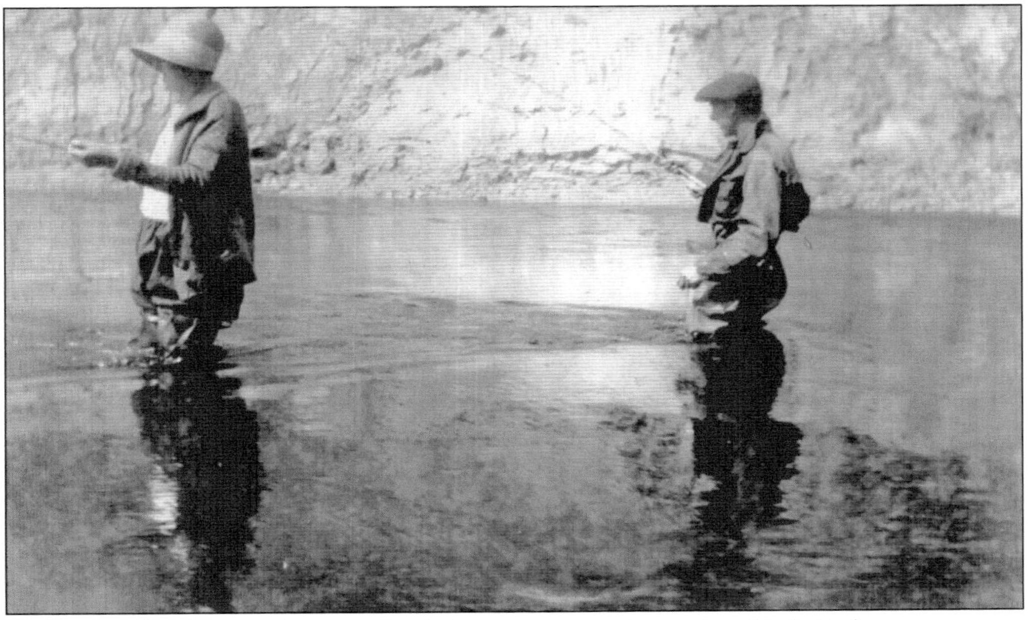

Since 1920, the Clarence Sessions family has returned to their cabin, Little Red, every summer. Located on the south bank of the Pere Marquette River, it was just a step out the door and into the river. James (Jimmy) Fairburn, right, is fly-fishing with the family's cook Alfie, hoping for a fine trout for dinner. Fairburn was a fishing guide on the river for many years. (Courtesy of L. W. Sessions.)

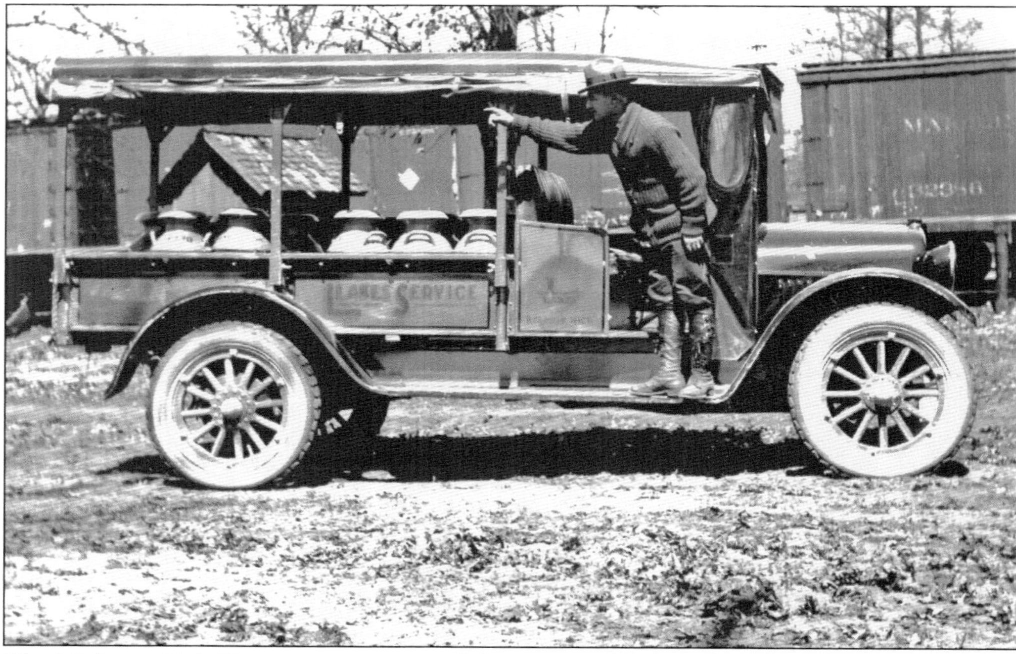

The Michigan Fish Commission continued for years to ship by railroad a variety of fish species to stock the county's rivers and lakes. This late-1920s L-Lakes Service delivery truck is filled with milk cans of black bass slated to be planted in the cottage colony's lakes south of Baldwin. (Courtesy of Tennis Trucks.)

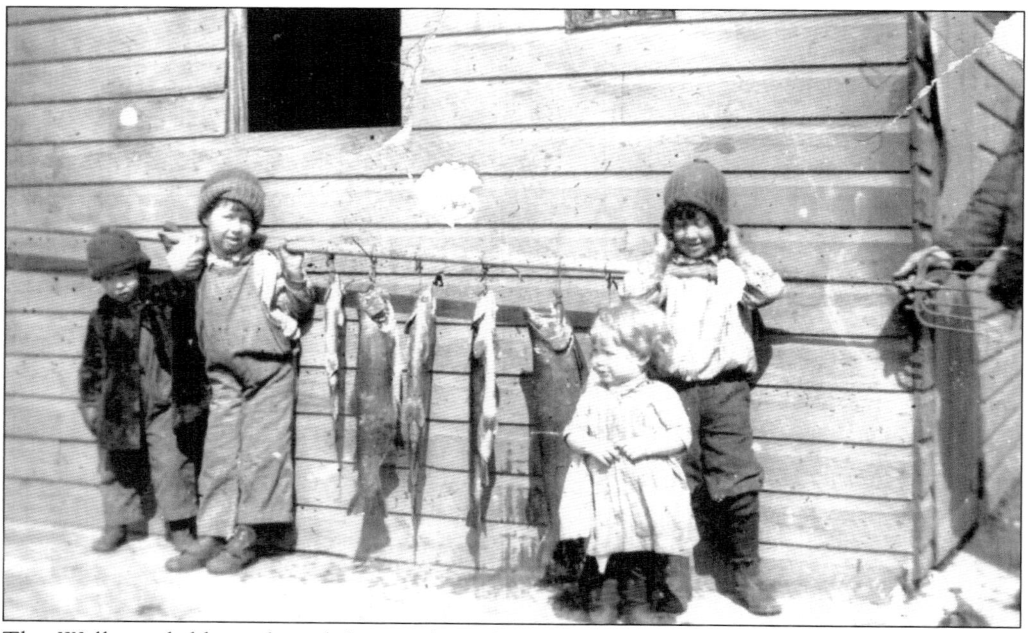

The Wallace children, from left to right, John, Thelma, Art, and Howard, are shown here with their catch of steelhead hung from a fishing spear. The Wallace family often fished at Wagon Wheel on the Pere Marquette River. Spearing was common in the 1920s. (Courtesy of Darci Maldonado.)

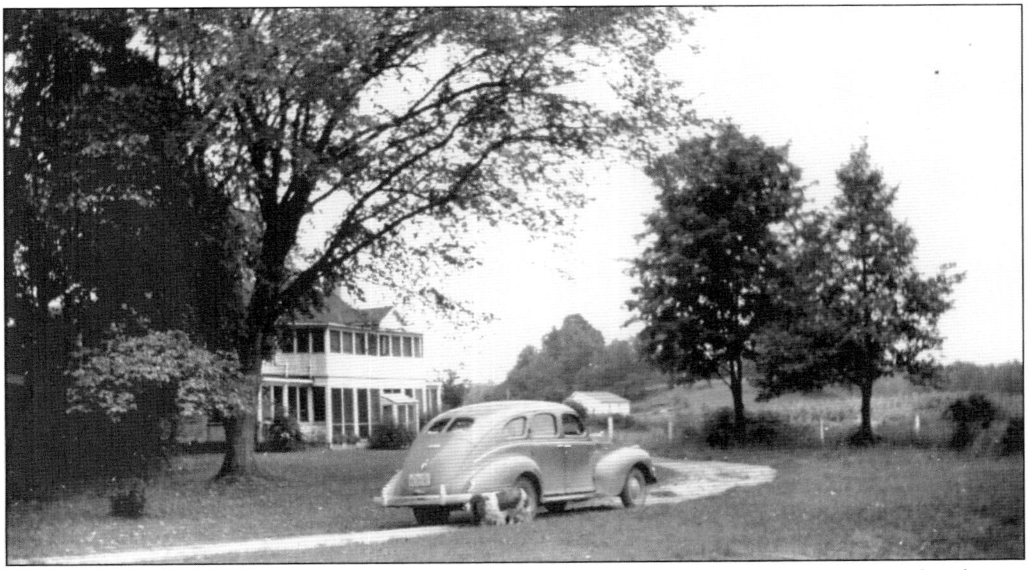

Fred Mans brought his family up from Trenton, Michigan, to stay at MacDougall's Lodge during the summer of 1940. They set up tents on the property, cooked over open fires, and fished every day. Located on the main stem of the Pere Marquette River downstream of Bowman's Bridge, MacDougall's was popular with groups of fishermen from all over the country. (Courtesy of Ellen Mans Kerans.)

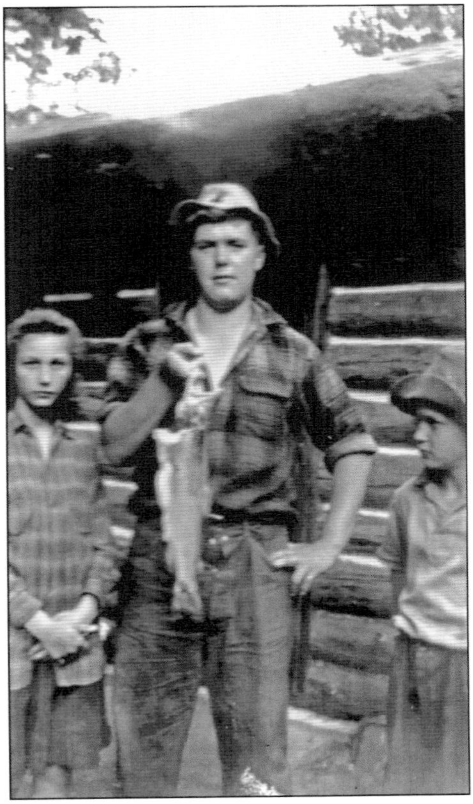

Mary and Bruce are standing with their brother John Bigford, who is showing off a trout he caught during the summer of 1941. Their parents, Harold and Catherine Bigford, had the one-room vacation log cabin at Wolf Lake built in 1933. The cabin and furniture, including a three-high double-sized bunk bed, were all handmade from red pine and slab wood and were constructed for $300. (Courtesy of Paul Bigford.)

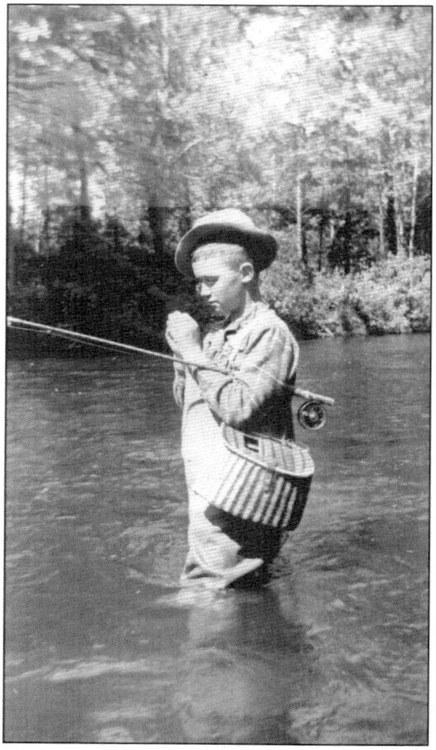

Standing in the Pere Marquette River near Gleason's Landing, 12-year-old Bruce Bigford is tying on a fly getting ready to cast to that elusive trout. This 1943 photograph depicts the epitome of fly fishing of the day: a wicker creel, a bamboo rod and fly reel, and a beautiful day with the river just for a boy and a trout. (Courtesy of Paul Bigford.)

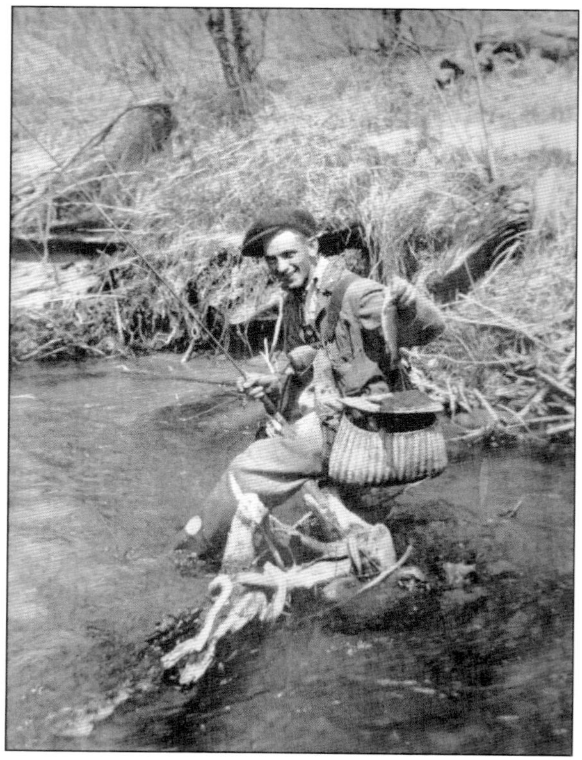

Clarence "Tim" Drilling, a Lake County local, fished as often as possible in the Pere Marquette River. His catch this day was a nice brown trout taken while fishing a nymph along the stream bottom. His tackle was a fly rod and automatic reel, which he could continue to use to reach his 1945 creel limit of 15 fish. (Courtesy of Tennis Trucks.)

Ed and Josephine Sedlecky opened Ed's Sport Shop in Baldwin in the late 1940s. Both were avid fishermen, with Ed shown here creeling a fine brown trout. He was also an excellent skeet shooter and taught classes to many, including guests of Dunrovin Lodge. The shop catered to both locals and tourists and offered every type of sporting goods available. Fishermen would come to the shop after a day on the river or lake and have their photograph taken by local photographer Kurt J. Kahl. The Sedleckys partnered with Merle "Zimmie" Nolph in 1949 to run the first canoe and boat livery on the Pere Marquette River. An outlay of $245 was paid to Mr. Byrne to build six wooden flat riverboats to be used to begin their new venture. (Right, courtesy of Dr. James Bos; below courtesy of Deborah Smith-Olson.)

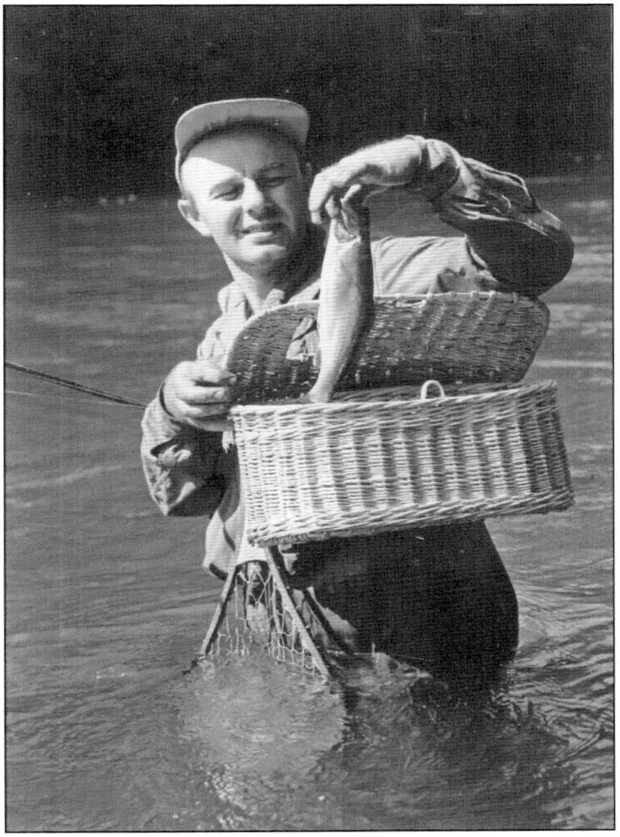

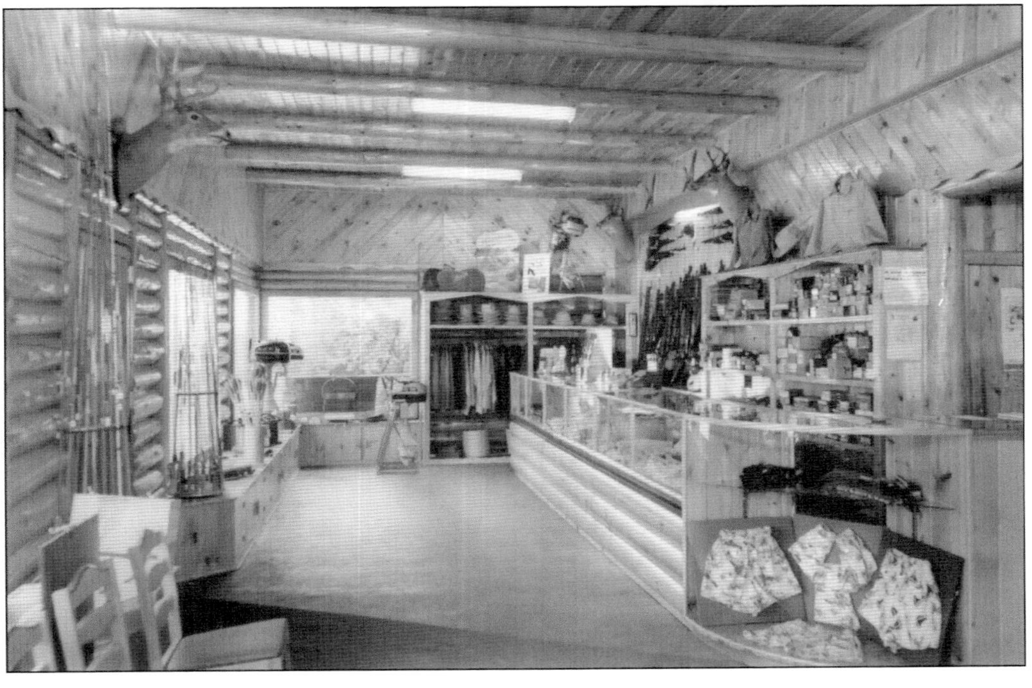

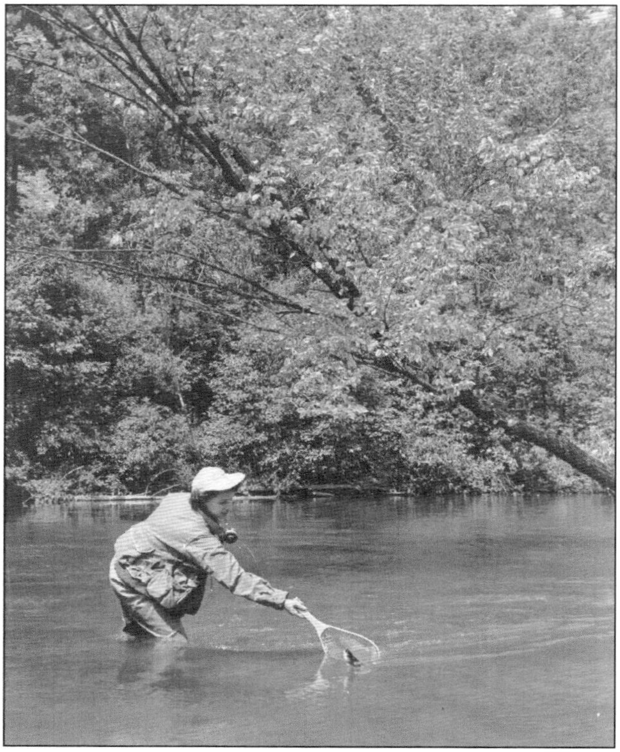

Fishing in the Pere Marquette River, Josephine Sedlecky is netting her catch, which was most likely caught on one of her own custom-tied files. Sedlecky started tying trout flies in her 20s and invented several patterns, such as Tan Fury and Lady Jo Caddis among others. She tied the old-fashioned way, using only one continuous thread and her hands. (Courtesy of Dr. James Bos.)

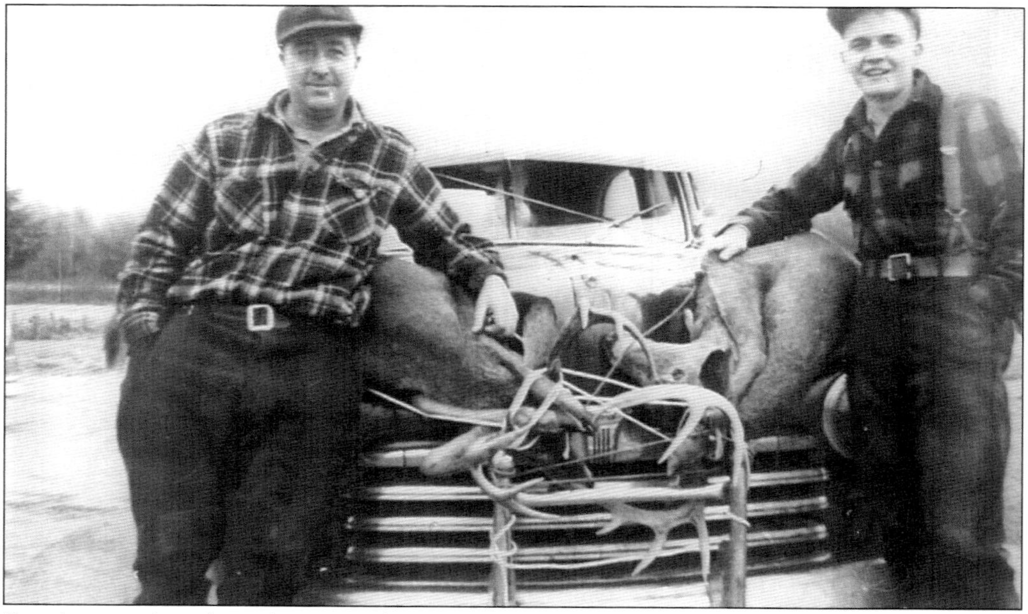

Deer hunting has always been popular in Lake County. A resident license was $1.50 in 1912 and the season ran from October 15 until November 30. The season reopened in 1936 after being closed for two decades due to a depletion of the herds. These trophy bucks, both 10 pointers and weighing 165 and 170 pounds, were taken by Howard Wallace, left, and his cousin Bill Wallace in November 1952. (Courtesy of Darci Maldonado.)

The history of the Dunrovin Lodge can be traced back to Clinton Wittemore, who purchased 110 acres in 1931 and developed a resort on the banks of the Baldwin River. In 1951, Fred and Janice Lewellyn bought the resort. Pictured on the front cover of their brochure, Fred provided their guests guided float trips, lamb-chop shore lunches, hunting trips, and marked trails for hiking. (Courtesy of Dunrovin Conference Center.)

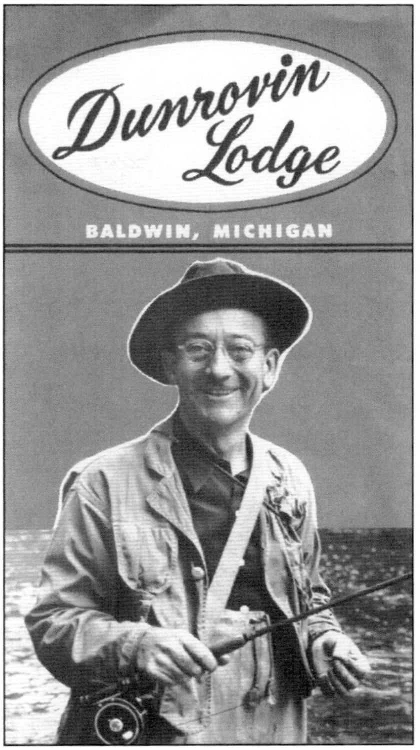

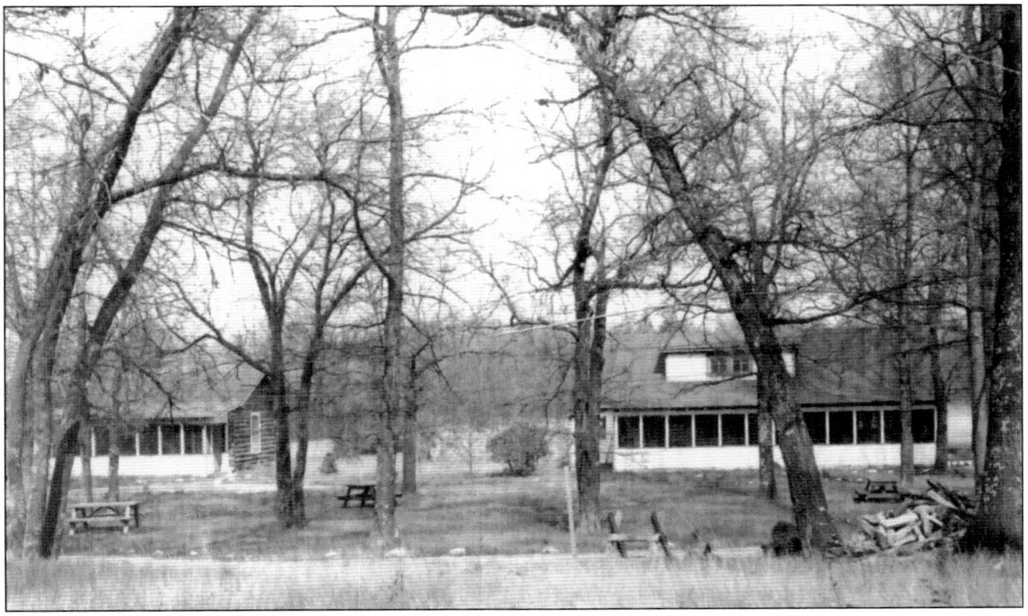

Hank Rouse operated Pere Marquette Camp on M-37 from 1917 to 1955. Rouse's specialty was a floating camp that took fishermen on a 2-to-10-day trip on the Pere Marquette River. Every morning a helper would set up camp downstream from the fishing party, and every night they would meet there for fried rainbow trout, campfire tales, and undisturbed sleep in the quiet wilderness. (Courtesy of Ned Rouse.)

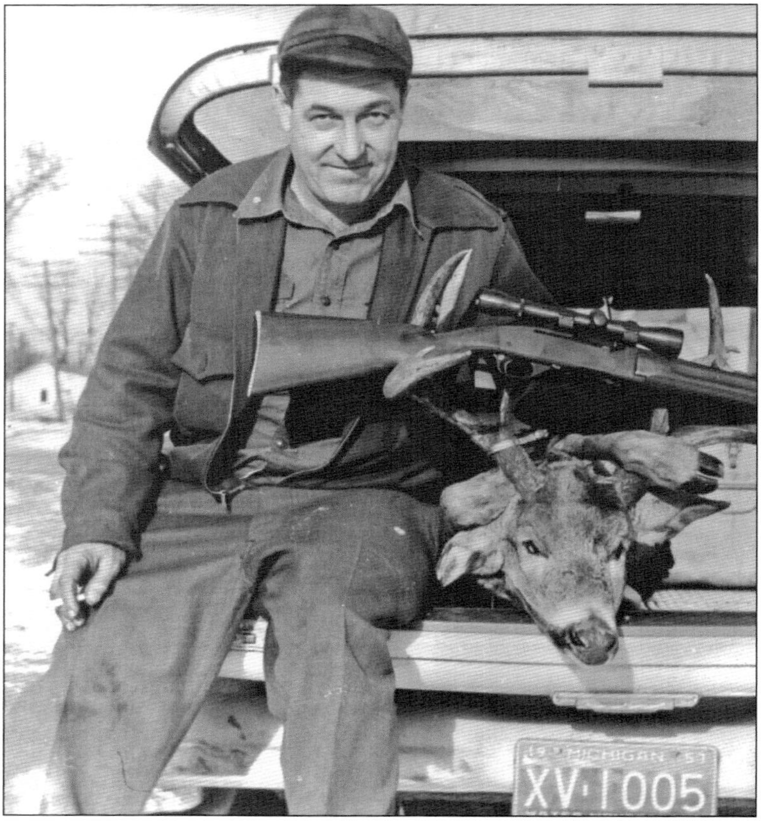

Conservation officer Harold Bonnett worked out of the Baldwin district headquarters of the Michigan Department of Conservation, which was responsible for the Pere Marquette State Forest. He took this buck in the fall of 1957. During the late 1950s, Lawrence Gotchall, also with the department, reintroduced turkeys into Lake County. Against many odds, the flocks succeeded, and the first turkey season opened in 1965. (Photograph by Kurt Kahl, courtesy of Tennis Trucks.)

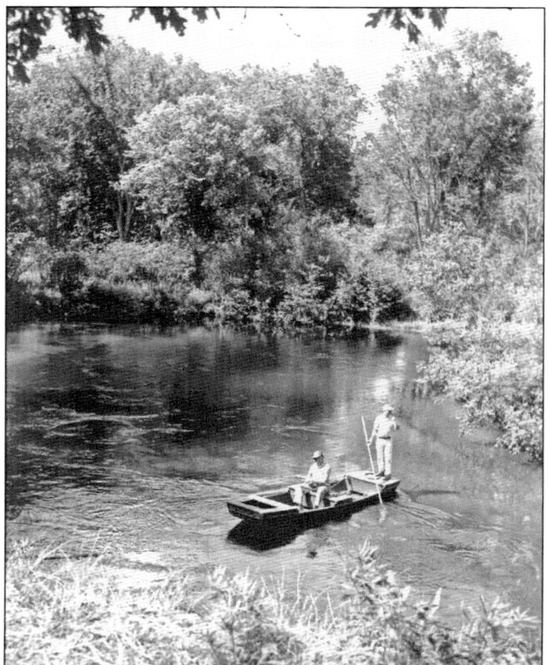

The 15-foot, square-ended boats used on the river were constructed of white pine. Extremely stable, they were steered using a 10-foot maple or ash pole. Merle "Zimmie" Nolph, on the right guiding an unidentified sportsman, was known to many as the "Keeper of the Pere Marquette." He fished the river for over 60 years, understanding it and respecting it like no other sportsman. (Photograph by Kurt Kahl, courtesy of Tennis Trucks.)

Eight

The Seasonal Tourist

Seasonal tourists have been vacationing in Lake County since as early as the late 1800s. Even then, resorts had been built to accommodate the weary travelers, mostly men, journeying north to the county to fish or to hunt. Families followed in a few years, traveling by horse and carriage, railroad, and even early steam-powered automobiles, making their way to the land of rivers and lakes. By the 1930s, the forests, planted by the CCC, were taking hold, and the wildlife returned.

With the improvement of roads and the advent of modern automobile travel, tourism in the county blossomed. Businesses capitalized on this potential new income base and built cabin camps, cottage colonies, resorts, and campgrounds to serve the influx of visitors. The county's lakes, rivers, and forests offered a perfect get-a-way for residents in the cities to the south. On those hot summer days, families would dream of the cool north woods and begin planning their escape. Even the names were enticing: While-A-Way Resort on Big Bass Lake, Isenbarger's Jungle Haven on Sauble Lake, Octagon Castle on the Pere Marquette River, Wood's Rainbow Cabins on the Baldwin River, and Pine Grove Beach Cottages and Blue Horizon Camp on Big Star Lake just to name a few.

White sand beaches, wooded shorelines, lakes and rivers stocked with fish, all with close proximity to shopping, restaurants, mail service, and telegraph, were a draw early on. Children from all over the country attended Camp Martin Johnson, a summer camp built by the Hyde Park YMCA to give city youth a taste of the north woods. The drive-in movie theater, roller rinks, and the many parks provided alternate leisure activities. One could also choose to attend entertainment venues at the famous Idlewild nightclubs or visit the amazing Shrine of the Pines on the Pere Marquette River.

The popularity continues today with each summer bringing families back that have vacationed in Lake County for generations.

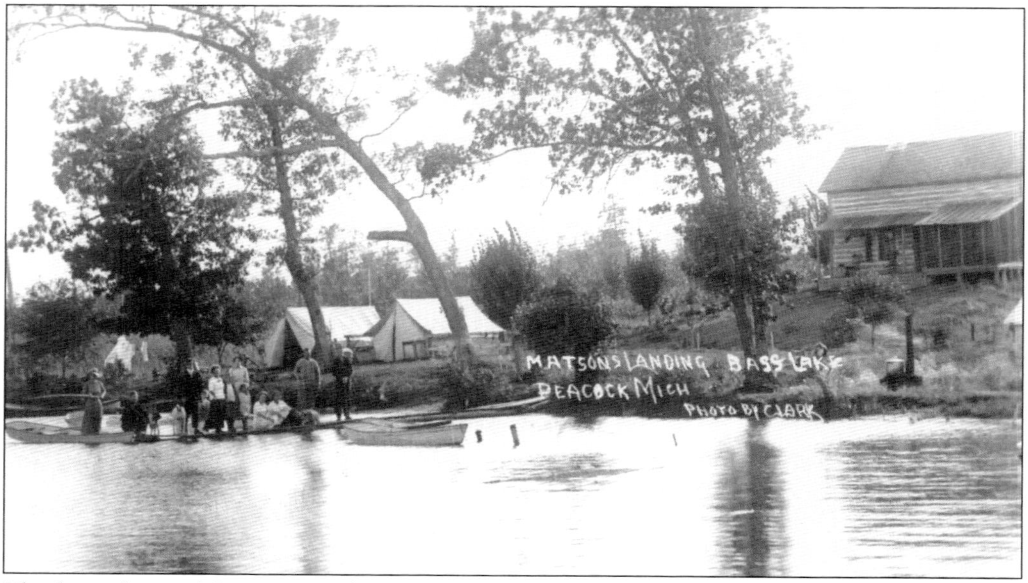

The log cabin at Matson's Landing on Lake Nataka, also seen spelled Natahki, was the first home of Anton and Karen Matson, following their move from Whiting, Indiana, in 1903. The local Native American tribes named the lake, which, when translated, means "lake beautiful." It is known today as Big Bass Lake. Early tourists pitched tents nearby and fished from the wooden boats provided by the Matsons. The Matsons built Big Point Lodge in 1905 to accommodate the increase in men coming to hunt and fish. Sleeping quarters were in small rooms upstairs with meals taken in the first-floor dining room. As the area had only recently been logged, the lakefront was still devoid of trees. The post office address changed from Peacock to Irons by the 1940s. (Above, photograph by Allan Clark, courtesy of Jerry Poprawski; below, courtesy of Jerry Poprawski.)

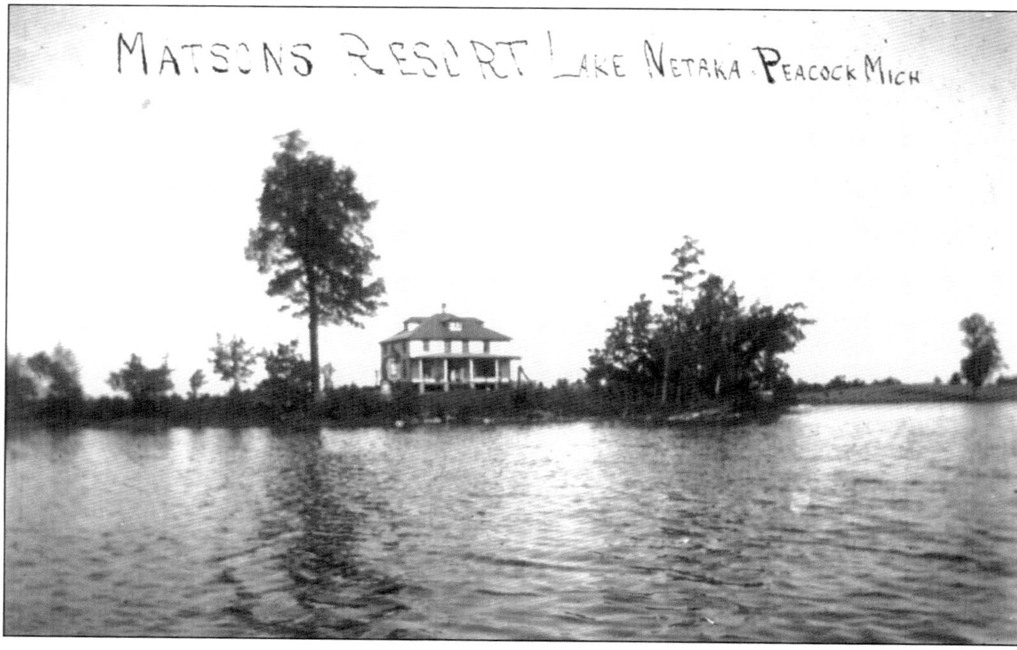

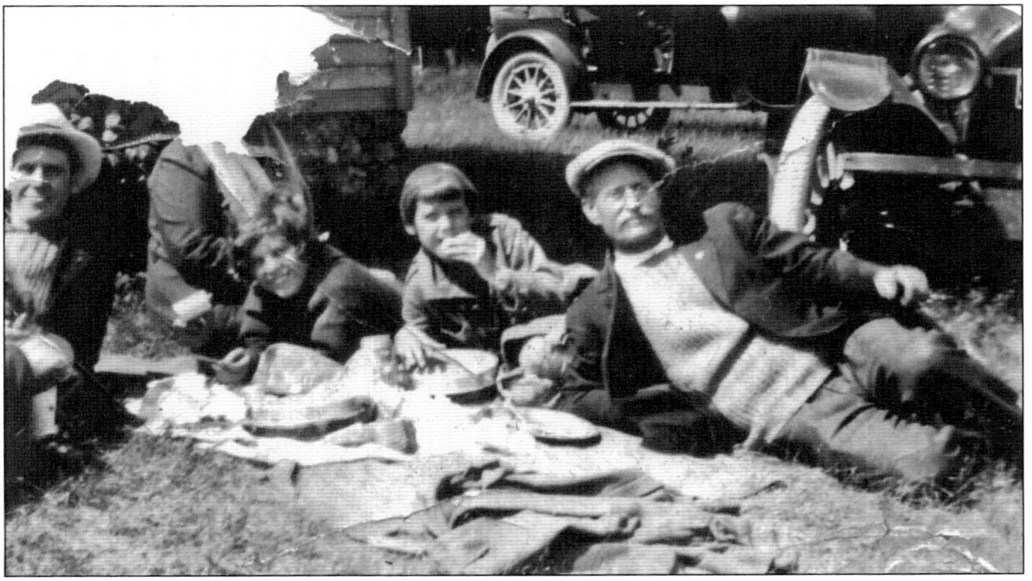

By the mid-1920s families began spending summers at Big Bass Lake. Typical of others, from left to right, John Matson, unidentified, Matson's daughters Donna and Doris, and friend John Welsby, traveled by automobile for three days to reach Big Point Lodge, spending the nights in farmers' fields, sleeping in the car, or in the open air on the ground. The roads were no better than dusty two-tracks from the Indiana-Michigan state line all the way to Lake County. To prepare for the summer guests, Anton Matson cut blocks of ice from the frozen lake, and then transported them on his sled to the icehouse, where they were packed in sawdust to await the hot July days. (Courtesy of Barbara Hart.)

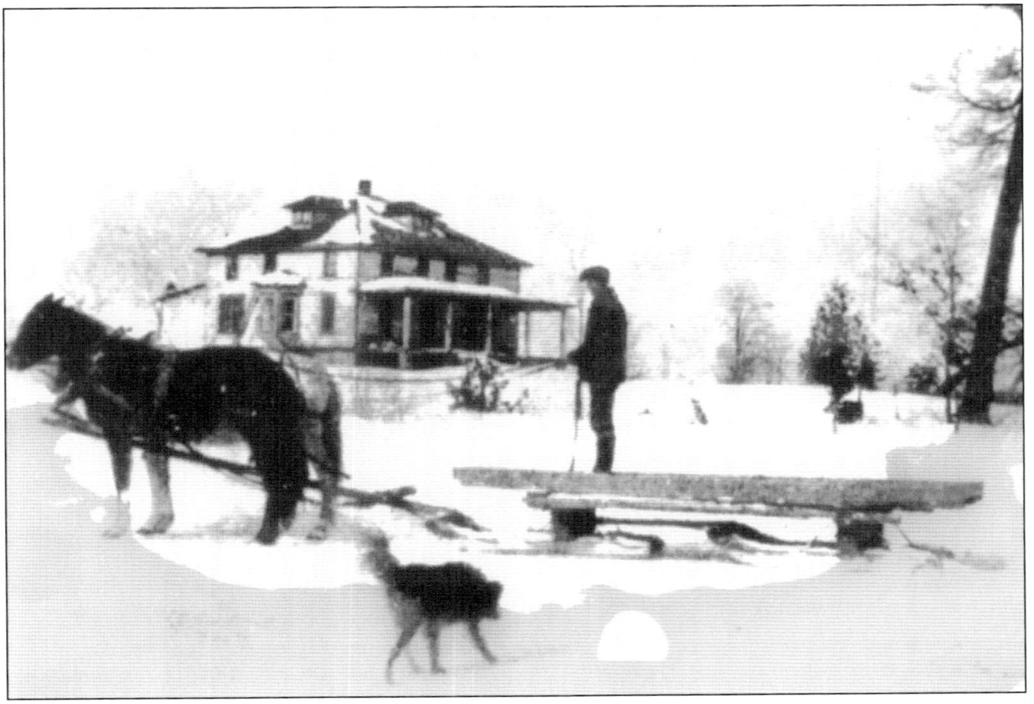

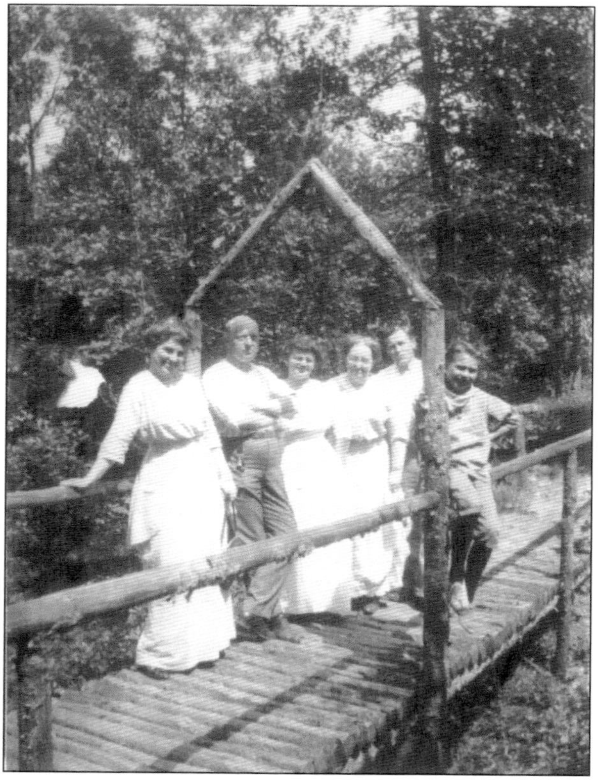

Cottages were also being built to give Grand Rapids businessmen and their families a place to escape from the summer heat of the cities. Louis Cornelius purchased property on the Pere Marquette River in 1913 and built Rainbow Lodge for his family and friends. His wife Sarah (third from left) and son Franklin (far right) are standing with their guests on Kelsey's walkway to the river. (Courtesy of Irma Cornelius.)

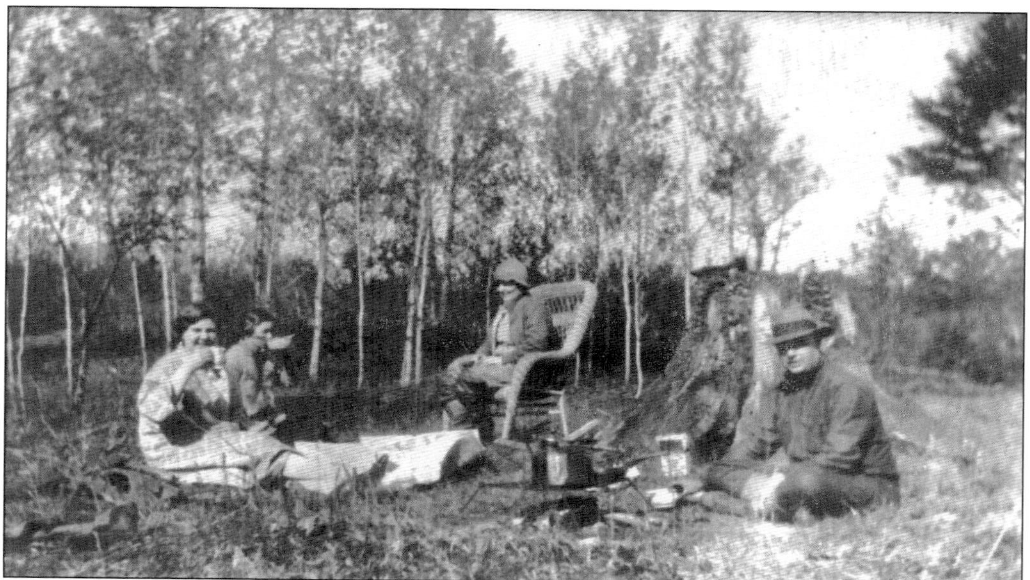

The Sessions family from Muskegon began traveling to the Pere Marquette River sometime prior to 1920. Before their summer cottage was built, they stayed at Mrs. Crosby's—a hotel on the banks of the river. From left to right, the family of Alfie the cook, nurse Ann Brady, Helen Sessions, and husband Clarence enjoyed a picnic in the burned-over woods left from the area's logging industry. (Courtesy of L. W. Sessions.)

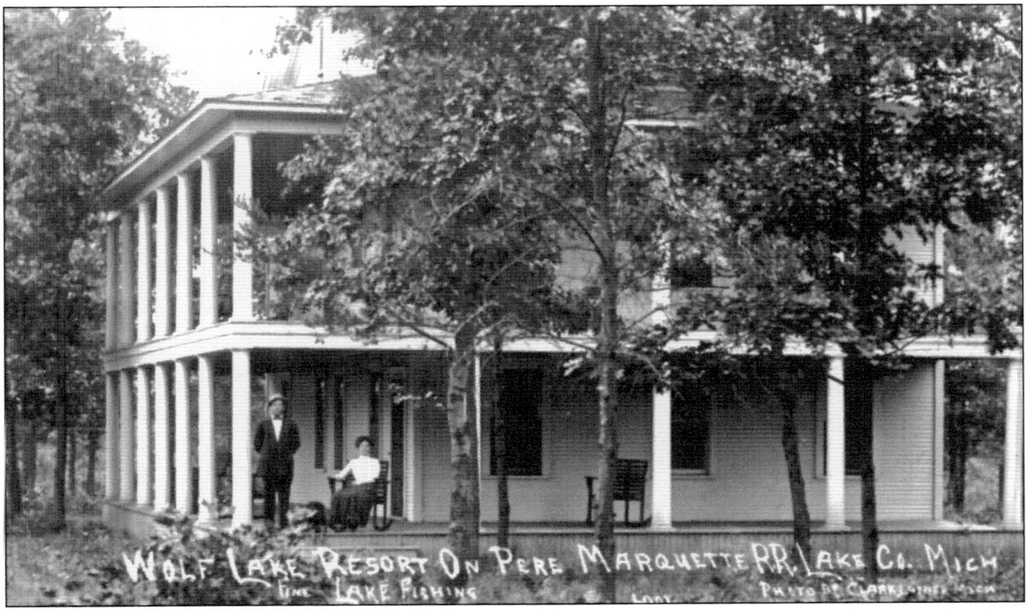

The Wolf Lake Resort, originally known as Wolf Lake Station, was built in 1890 by the Pere Marquette Railroad as a wilderness depot. It served loggers, as well as leading families traveling further north on the railroad. On the return trip, the No. 8 parlor car would stop at the station to pick up passengers on a flag only. Thomas Shook bought the three-story depot in 1942 and opened Wolf Lake Dude Ranch. With the old logging trails surrounding the property, it was well suited to horseback riding. The living room, with its knotty-pine walls, was furnished in the 1950s with rustic hickory rockers set in front of the stone fireplace, providing just the place to cozy up after a long day of riding or lake fishing. (Above, photograph by Allan Clark, courtesy of Paul Bigford; below, courtesy of Jill Engelman.)

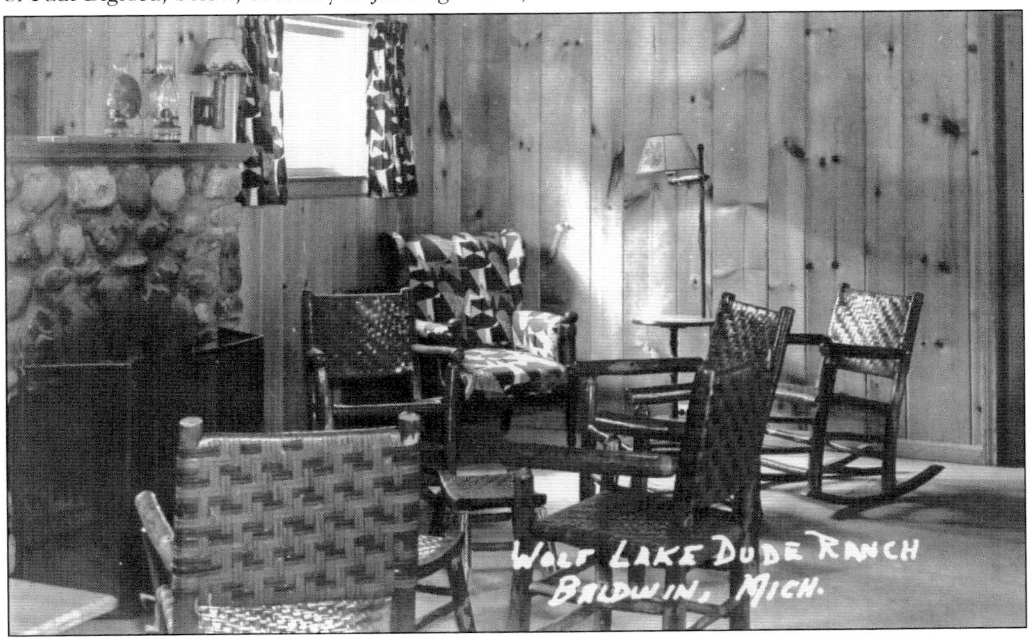

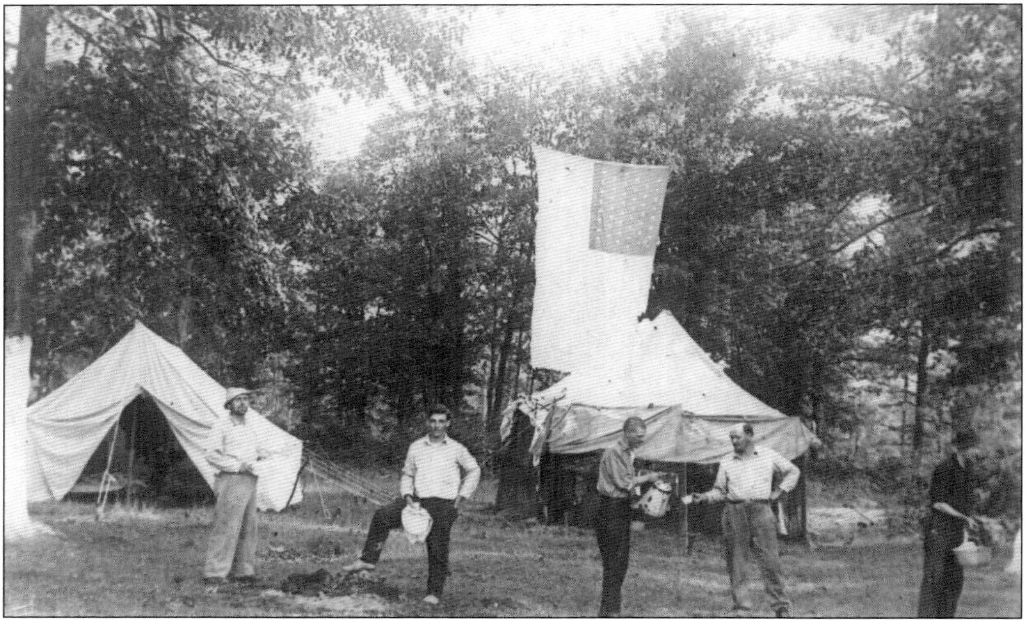

Ten businessmen from Niles, Ohio, joined together and formed the Mahoning Camping Club journeying from Ohio to Whalen Lake to set up their tent camp. Theodore Kestner recorded camp life during the summer of 1914 through his many photographs. The rowdy group not only fished for black bass, swam in the cool lake water, but also partied. They brought dozens of cases of bottled beer from the Grand Rapids Brewing Company, as well as several wooden beer kegs, enough to supply them for their two-month stay. (Photographs by Theodore Kestner, courtesy of the Lake County Historical Society.)

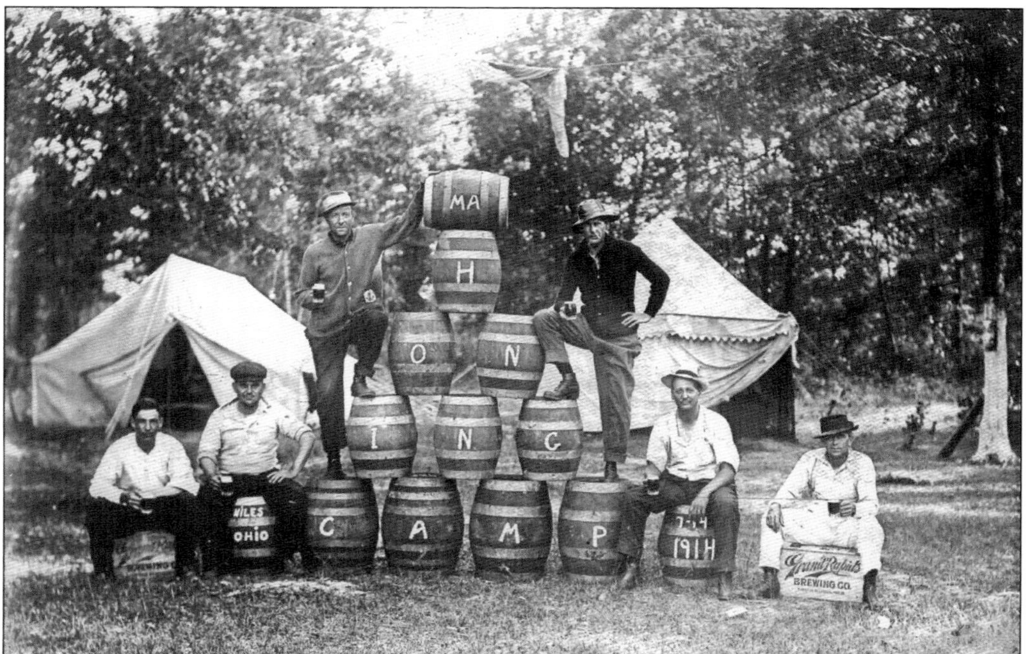

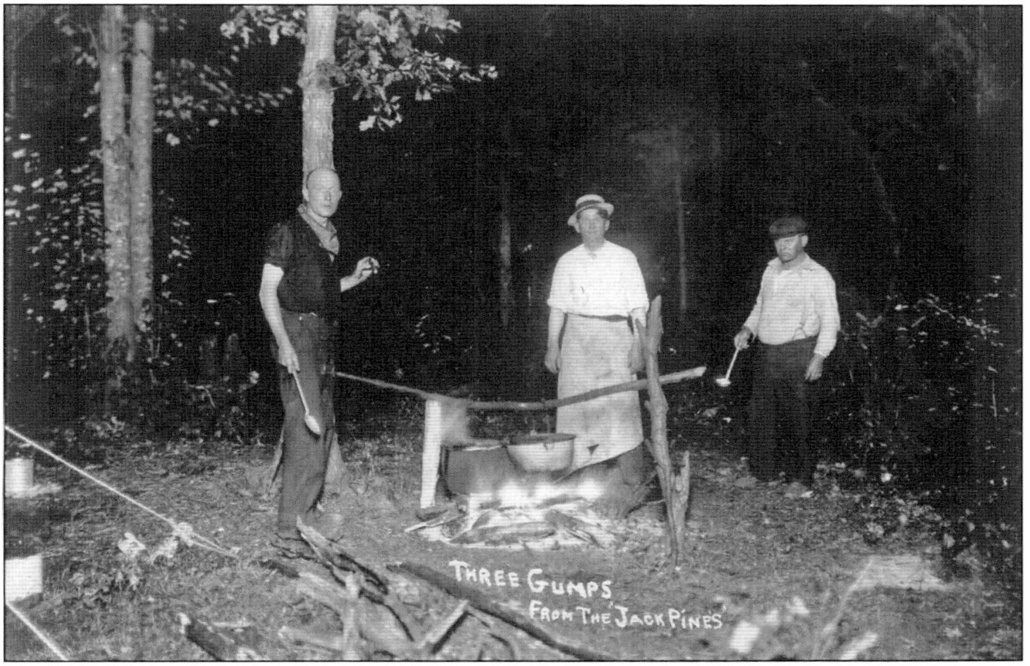

The cooks from the Mahoning Camping Club nicknamed themselves the Three Gumps from the Jack Pines. Stopping in Baldwin prior to their arrival at the lake they stocked up on food stuffs at Mathews Grocery. They supplemented their supplies with fresh fish and turtles caught in nearby rivers as well as in Whalen Lake. Preparing meals over an open fire, they served elaborate fare to the club on slabs of wood set on wooden beer cases. When the occasion arose, they set up an "open air barbershop" to take care of haircuts and shaves to ready themselves for the return trip home. (Photographs by Theodore Kestner, courtesy of Lake County Historical Society.)

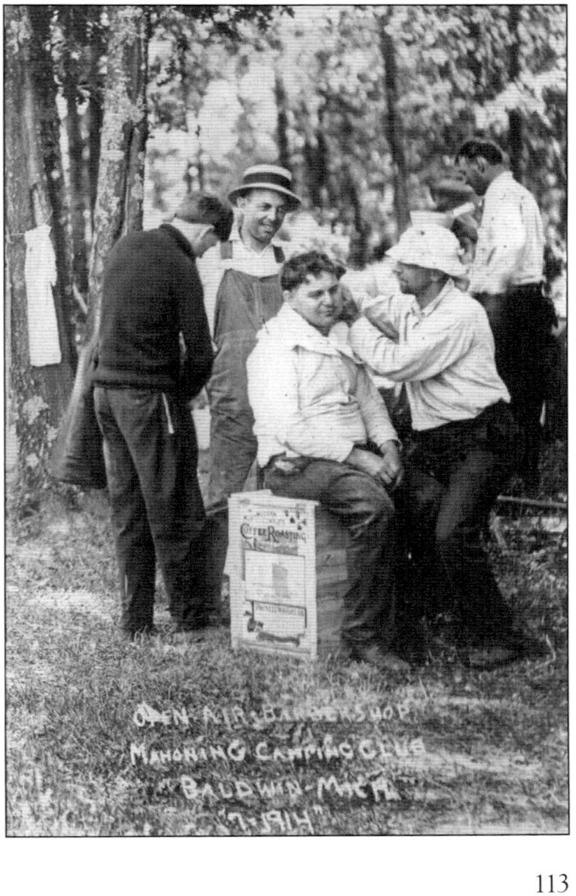

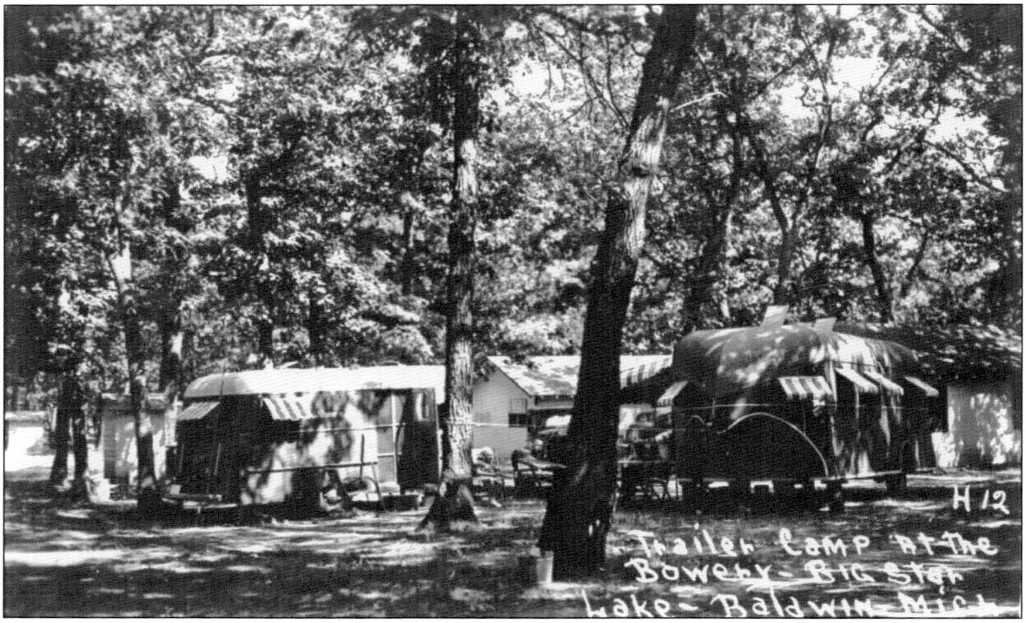

At 912 acres, Big Star Lake is the largest body of water in Lake County. With its white sand beaches, the lake attracted tourists as early as 1916. The Bowery was the first of eight resorts on the lake. Tents were set up and furnished for the vacationers; with the trailer camp, cabins, a restaurant, and a market built a few years later. By 1947, 13 cottages had been added to the resort, although none had electricity or indoor plumbing yet. The store sold beer, groceries, fishing gear, licenses, gasoline, and oil. (Above, courtesy of Jill Engelman; below, courtesy of Gordon Allison.)

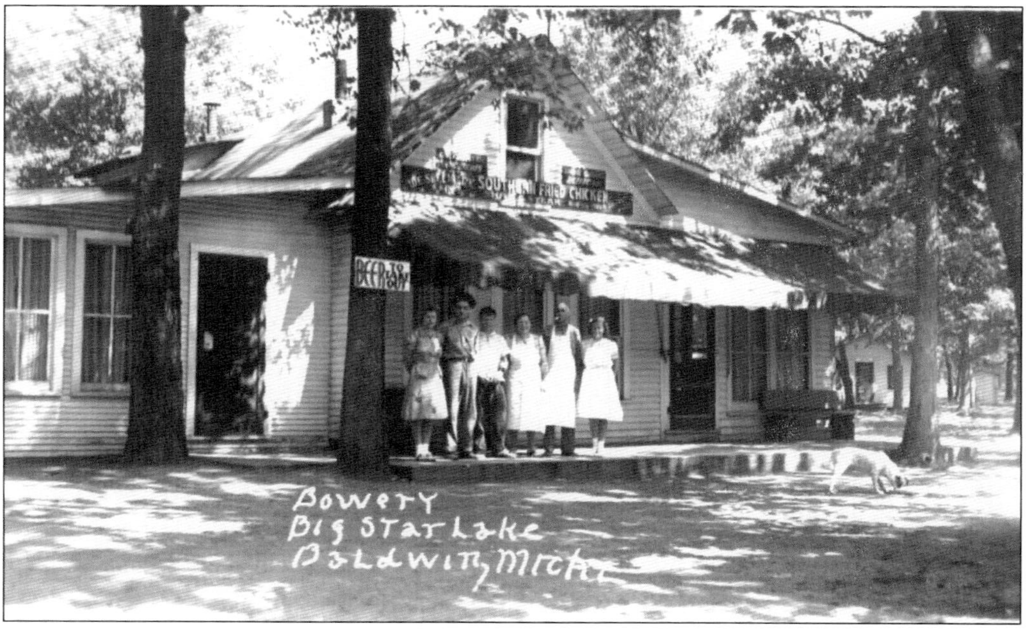

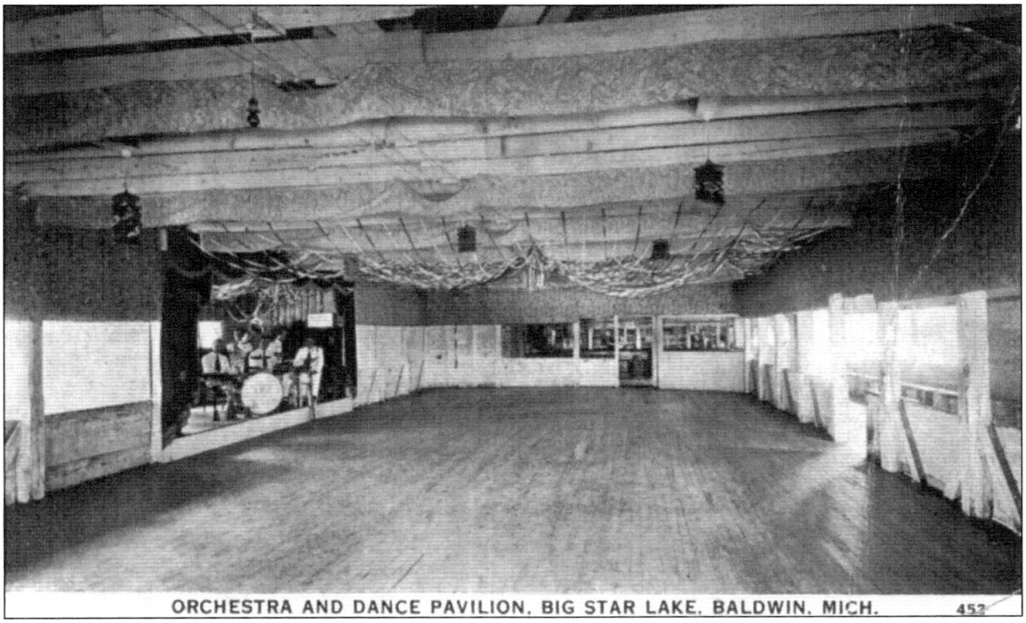

The Bowery Dance Pavilion at Big Star Lake was popular at its inception in 1916. Folks from all over the county traveled to the pavilion, seen in this 1936 postcard, to listen to local talent or traveling bands. By 1940, the pavilion was also a roller-skating hall and beer garden. Teens could skate right into the attached soda parlor. (Courtesy of Gordon Allison.)

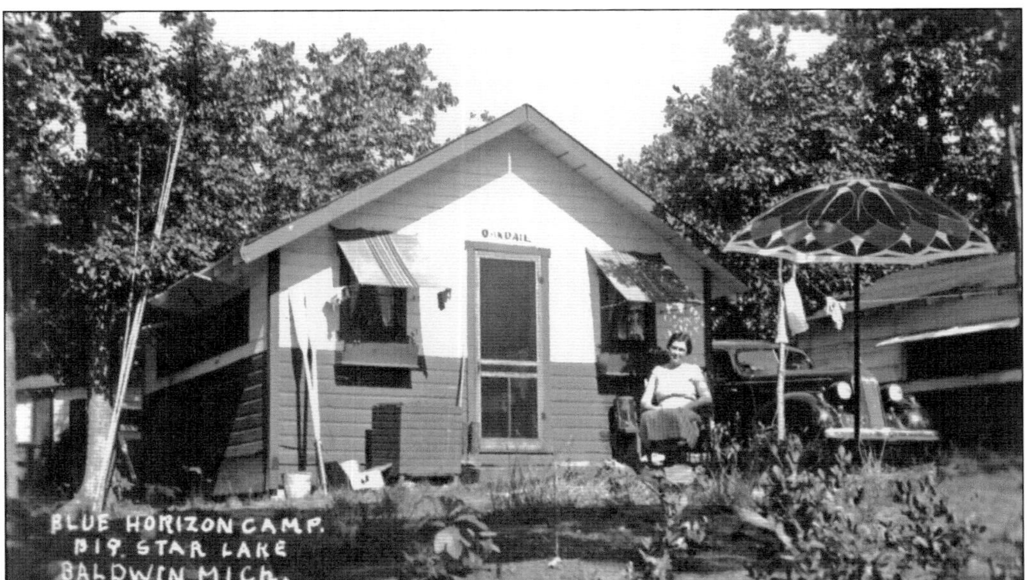

Blue Horizon Camp, another of the resorts, was located on the north shore of Big Star Lake near the Bowery. The camp catered to families and was comprised of several small cottages, including the Oakvale. A grocery store, boasting the only telephone, and a laundry were also on the property. The coin-operated horse in front of the store was a popular stop for children during the 1950s. (Courtesy of Gordon Allison.)

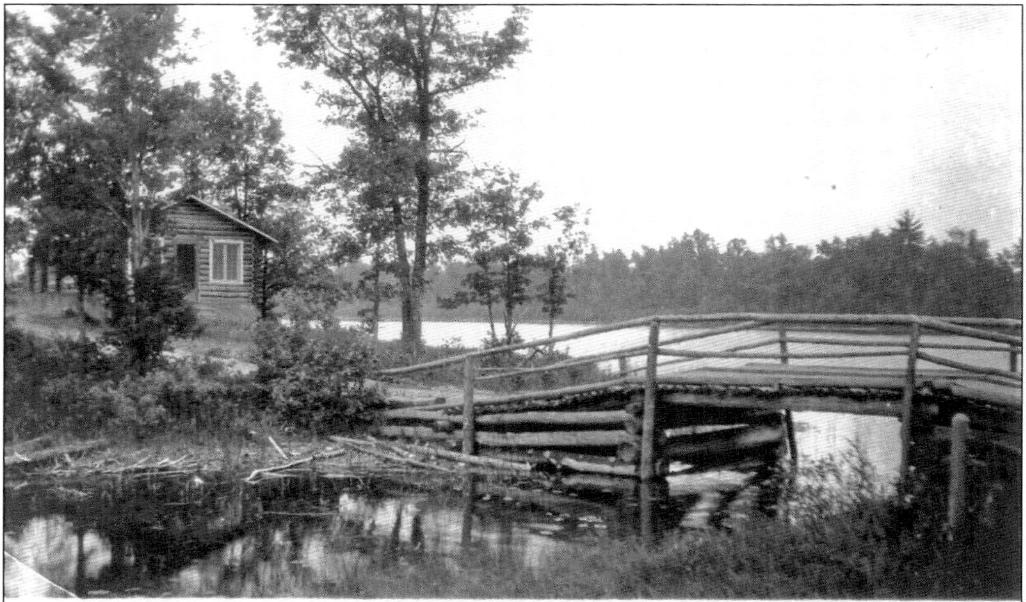

The Bridge, L Lakes, Baldwin, Mich.

L-Lakes was a cottage colony developed in the early 1900s by Ray Trucks. No amusement parks or hotels were included in this community. The 800-acre tract, consisting of the four lakes, was left in its natural state providing a setting for summer homes in harmony with the beauty of their surroundings. Sunken logs, lily pads, and rushes in L-Lakes were left undisturbed providing cover for an abundance of black bass and other game fish. Residents could not only launch a boat on one of the lakes, but could also fish the Little South Branch of the Pere Marquette River, which flowed a few feet from the north arm of Big-L Lake. Within one-half mile were farms providing residents fresh eggs, butter, fowl, and a garden truck. (Above, courtesy of Gordon Allison; below, courtesy of Lake County Historical Society.)

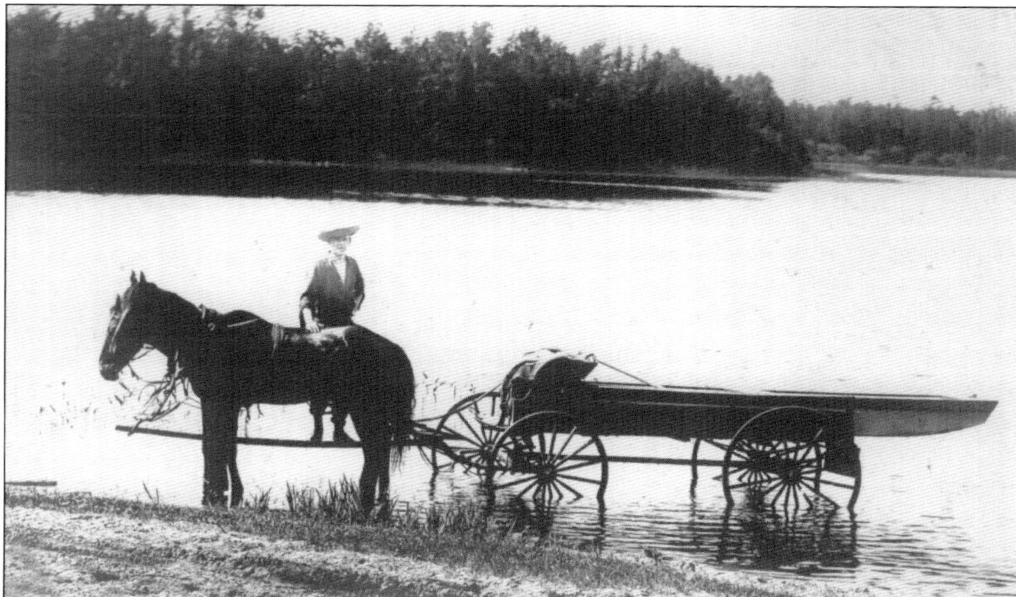

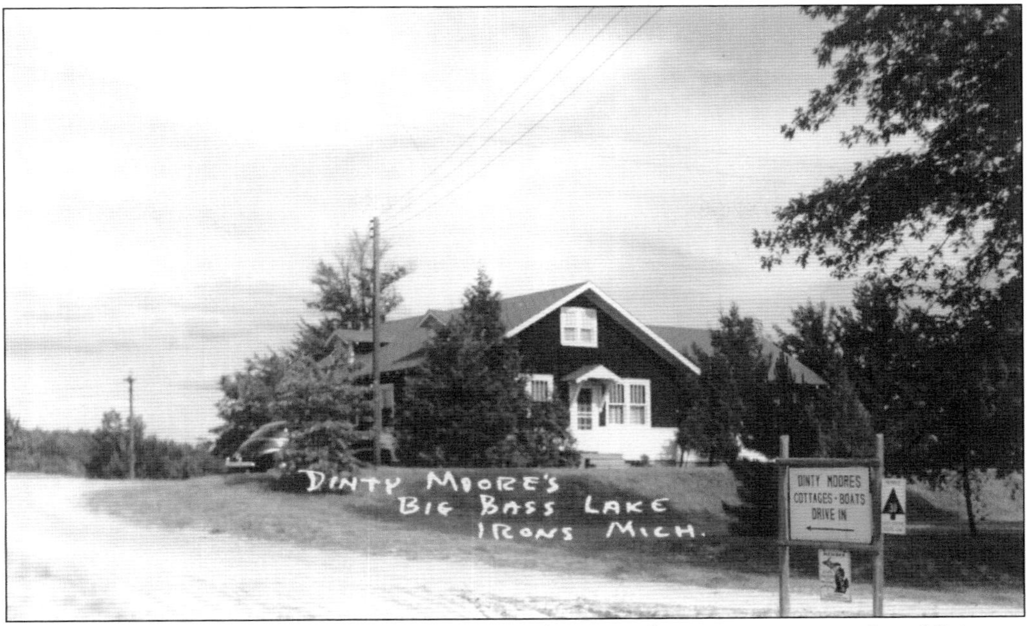

At the northern end of the county, Big Bass Lake sported numerous resorts. In addition to Matson's Big Point Lodge, Wait-A-While Resort, Dinty Moore's Cottages and Boats, Peacock Sun Resort, Woolser's Campground, and W. P. Jones Resort were all home to summer tourists. Most of the resorts had fishing boat rentals as well as fine sandy beaches for swimming. (Courtesy of Martin Johnson Heritage Museum.)

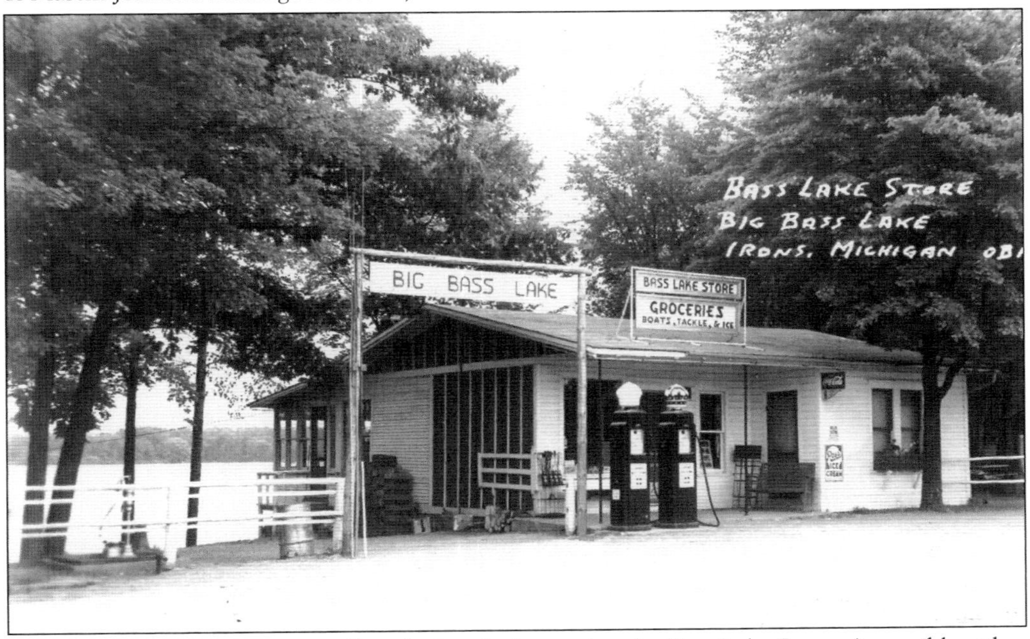

All of the summer tourists as well as the locals shopped at the Bass Lake Store. Accessible either by boat from their dock on Big Bass Lake, or by automobile or walking, the store was popular and one could purchase just about anything. The big coolers along the back wall, with the heavy glass doors, kept the soda pop, milk, and beer cold. (Courtesy of Jerry Poprawski.)

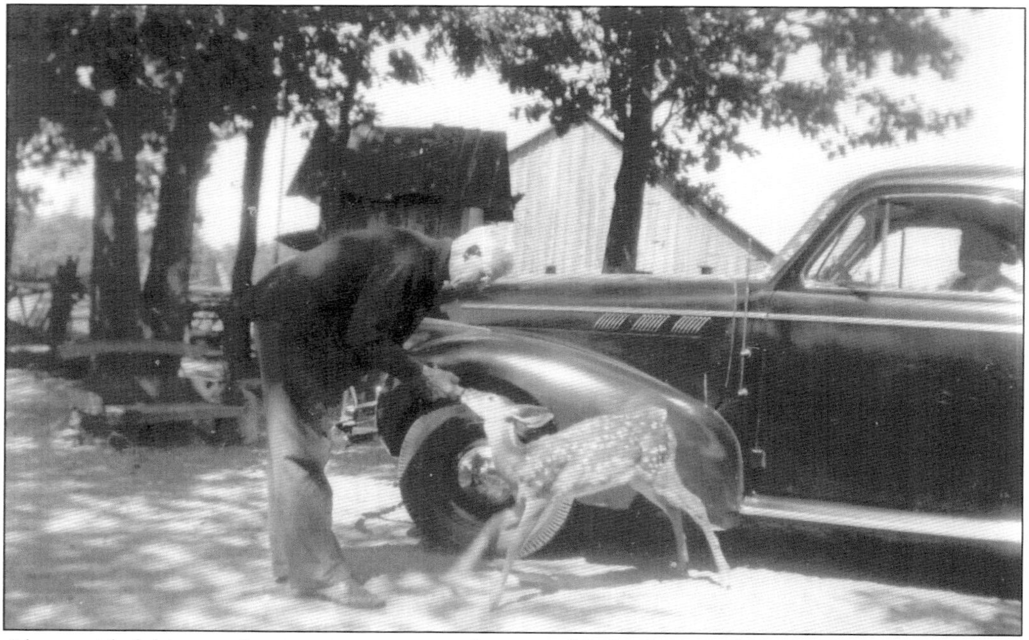

Along with fishing and swimming, tourists also visited Lake County for its wildlife. John Matson is seen here feeding a whitetail fawn with a baby bottle in front of his 1939 Pontiac at Big Bass Lake. In addition to deer, it was not a surprise to see raccoons, porcupine, opossum, beaver, and the occasional river otter or black bear during a stay. (Courtesy of Barbara Hart.)

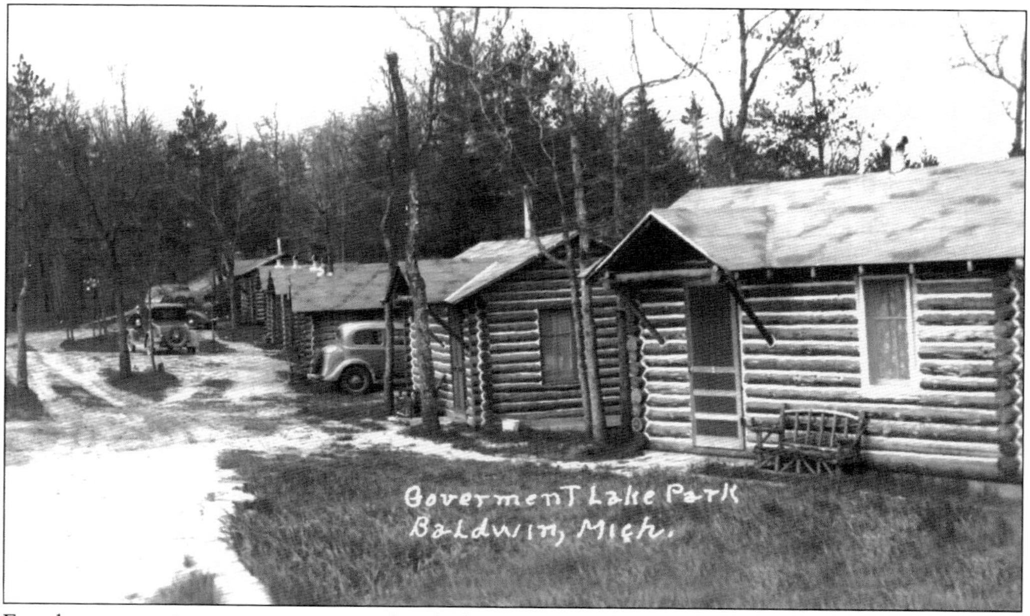

For those vacationers wanting another lodging option, there were the cabins at Government Lake Park. Conveniently located between the lake and M-37 and U.S. 10, the Duffing family built 10 log cabins and an adjacent restaurant that all boasted lake views. The proximity to the highway system made them extremely popular during the 1930s and 1940s. (Courtesy of Bruce Micinski.)

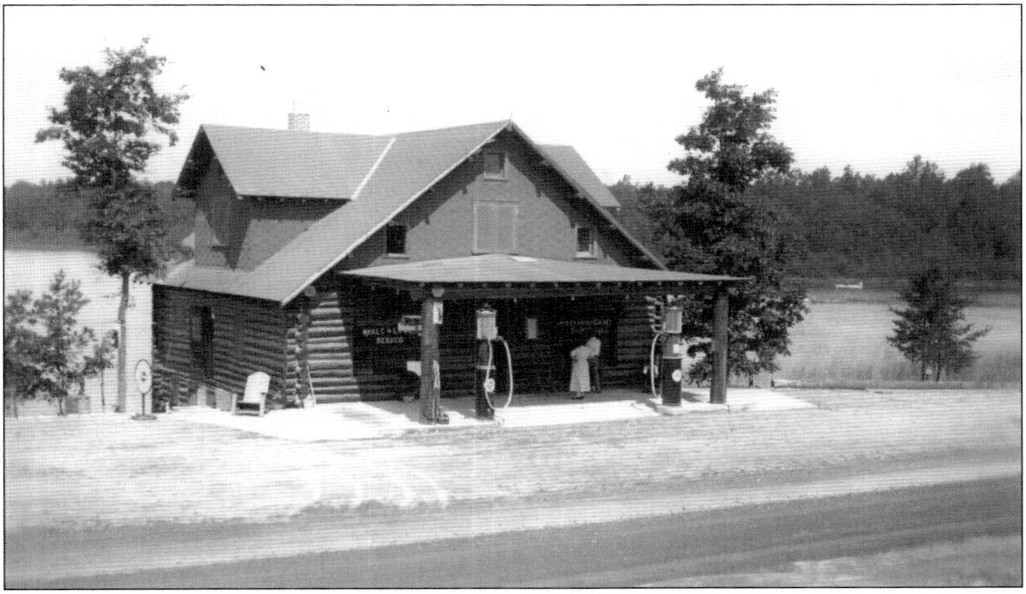

Government Lake Park, known today as Government Lake Lodge, had its beginnings in 1927 and continues to be a popular stop for tourists and locals. In the early years, the restaurant sold gasoline, as well as serving full meals and sandwiches. In the postcard from the 1940s, the chalkboard advertises ice cream, candy, and soda drinks as well as cigars. Waitresses served guests in the dining room with beautiful lake views. Decorated with deer mounts, elk antlers, and fish-themed art, all consistent with the north wood's lifestyle of Lake County, this restaurant was a favorite stop. (Courtesy of Bruce Micinski.)

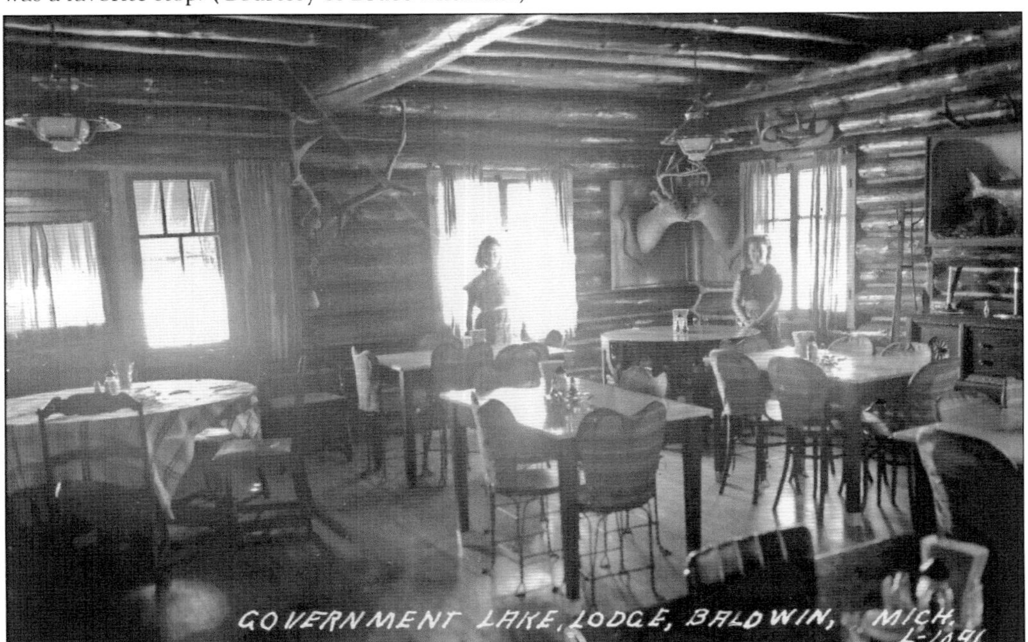

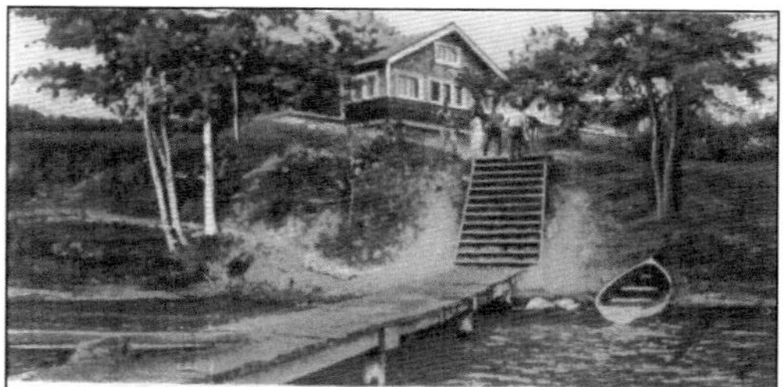

PIER AND MAIN LODGE—CAMP MARTIN JOHNSON.

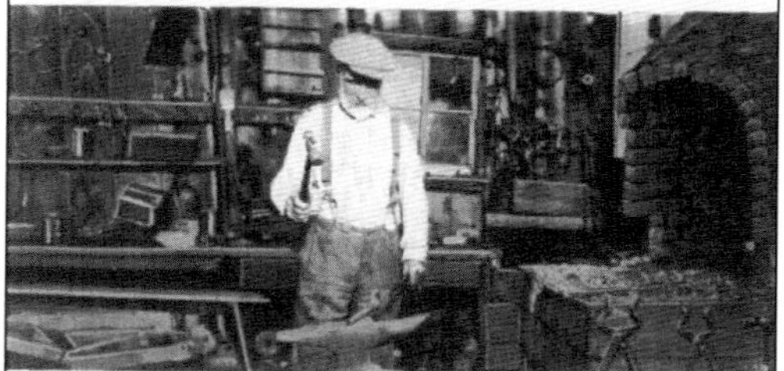

MARTIN JOHNSON IN HIS OWN WORKSHOP.

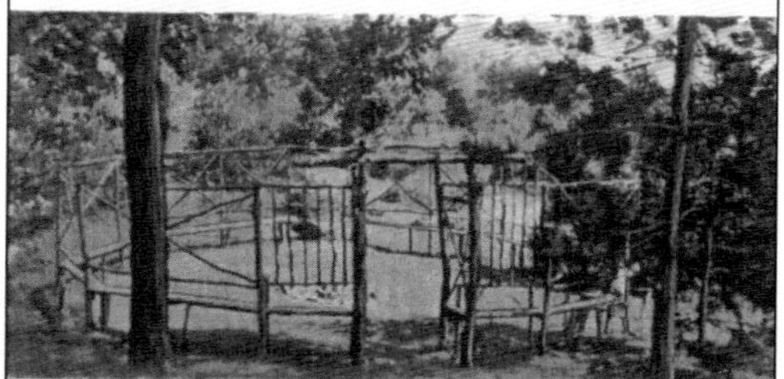

COUNCIL RING—CAMP MARTIN JOHNSON.

Martin Gustave Johnson, an early pioneer on Big Bass Lake, donated 30 acres to the Hyde Park YMCA of Chicago to be used for a boys' camp. Johnson was an artist, naturalist, and philanthropist who made it possible for city youth from 14 to 19 years of age to experience life in the north woods for a few weeks during the summer. Camp Martin Johnson was opened in 1924 and was comprised of the main lodge, council ring where church services were held, and several activity buildings and cabins for the campers and counselors. Sessions lasted four weeks and were advertised in 1932 at $75 each. Transportation from Chicago to Ludington was made on the Manitou ferry, operated by the Michigan Transit Boat Company at $7 round-trip. Girls were admitted to the camp by the late 1950s. (Courtesy of Jill Engelman.)

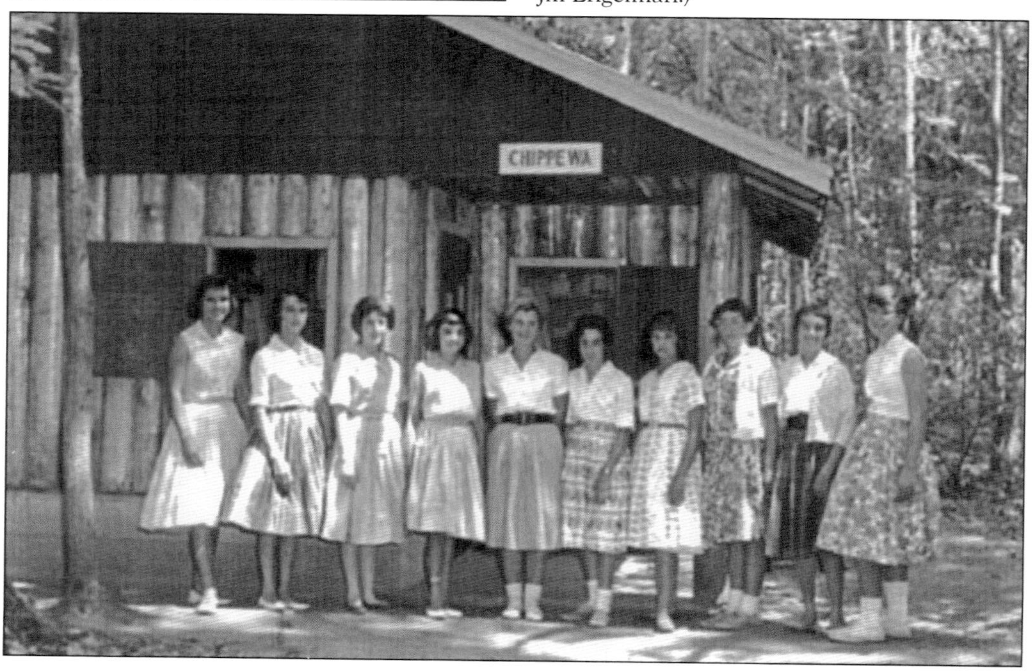

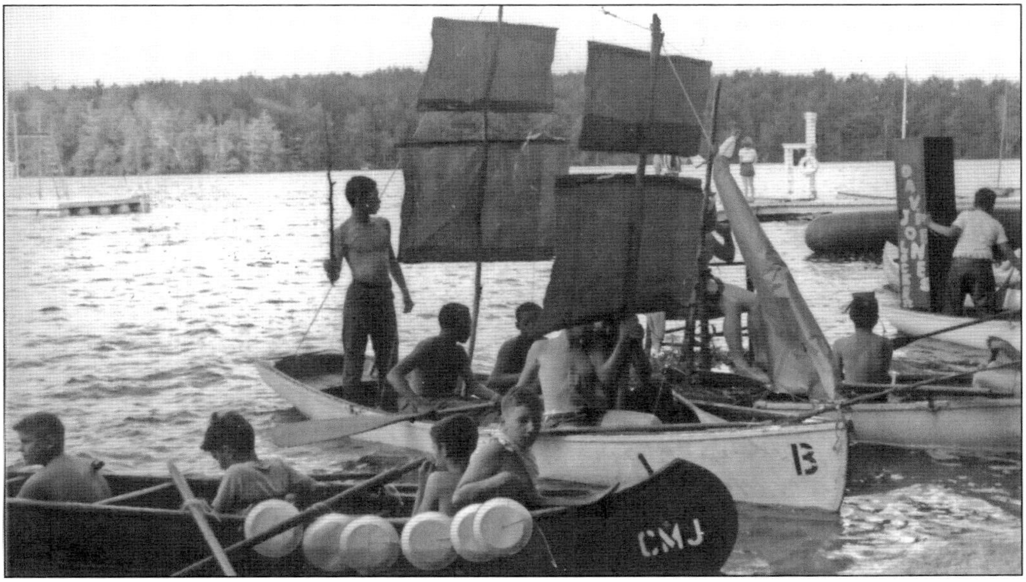

During the early 1950s, camp director Thomas Curtin Sr. organized classes in swimming, canoeing, sailing, rowing and waterskiing on the lake, and horseback riding through the woods. Each camper was required to attend classes in the morning and then could join their cabinmates in nature study, archery, shooting, hiking, shuffleboard, or handcrafts in the afternoon. Covered wagon campouts were a highlight for most campers. By the mid-1950s, Camp Martin Johnson provided cabins in five different "villages" on the property. The oldest girls stayed at Four Winds on the island, while the youngest girls were housed in cabins in the Indian Village. The boys were separated by age into the Frontier Village and the Voyager Village. The 26 cabins provided housing for over 250 campers and counselors each four-week period. (Courtesy of Thomas Curtin Jr.)

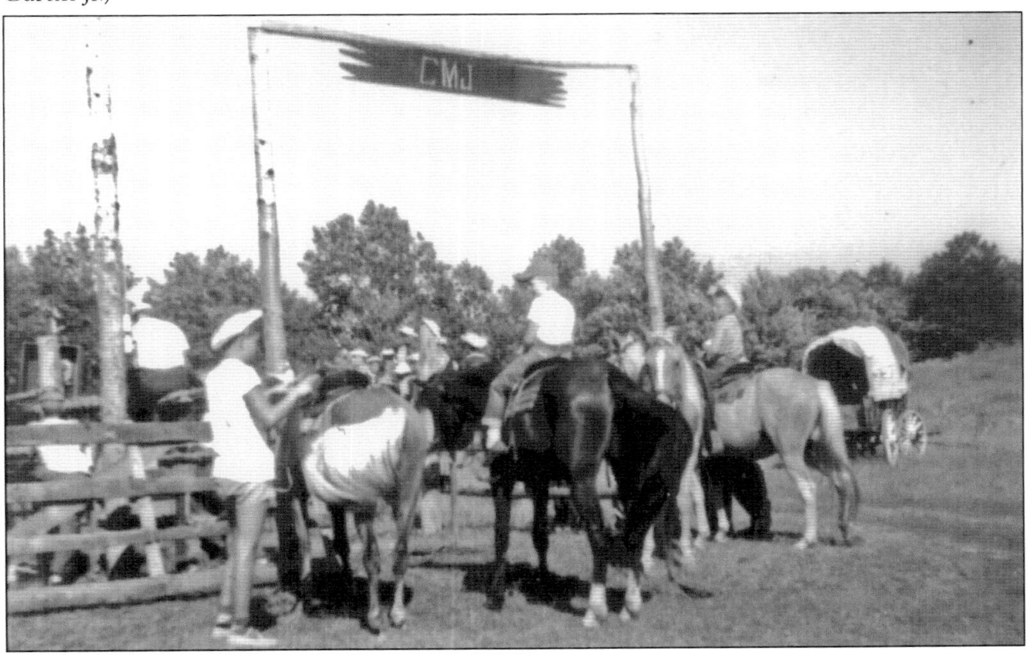

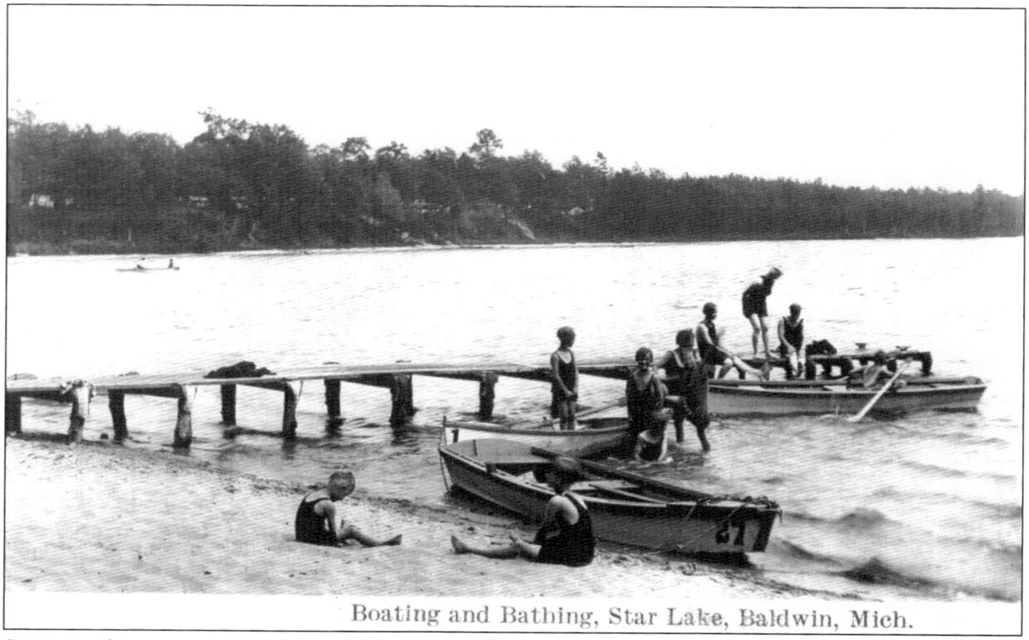

Summer fun was always the objective. Whether it was in a boat on the water, swimming, or fishing, tourists have enjoyed leisurely days on Lake County's 156 lakes. The children at the public pier on Big Star Lake in the 1940s are seen enjoying the day in the water. Seen below, Thomas Curtin Sr., left, and son Thomas Jr. are spending some family time in the summer of 1953 on Big Bass Lake. Toddler Paul Bigford, with his hand on the throttle, is motoring down Wolf Lake in August 1952. (Above, courtesy of Bruce Micinski; below, courtesy of Lake County Historical Society.)

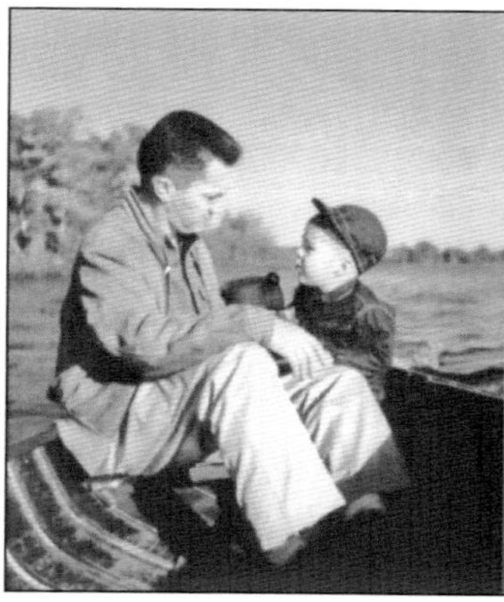

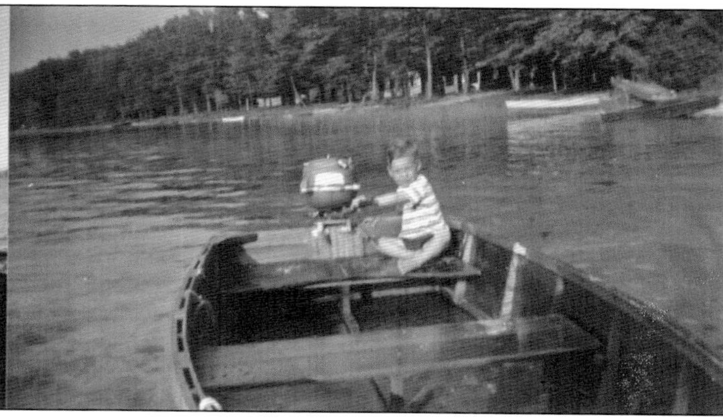

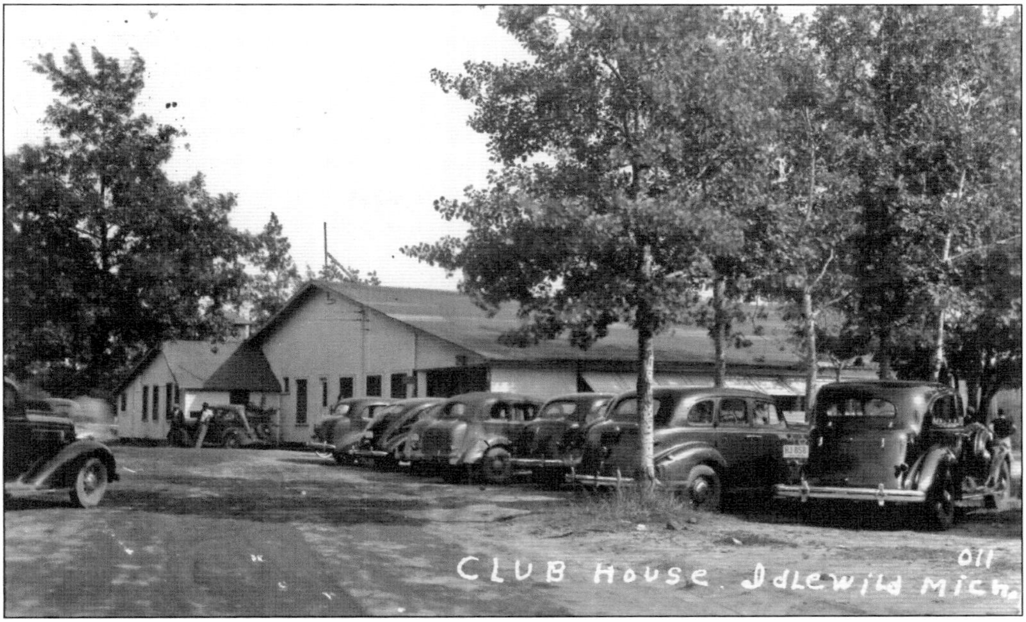

Adelbert Branch, Erastus Branch, Wilbur Lemon, and Alvin Wright founded the Idlewild Resort Company in 1912 to provide the African American population a place without prejudice. Idlewild, known as the black Eden of Michigan, was described in a 1919 pamphlet as the hunter's paradise as well as having pure springwater and an abundance of game fish in Lake Idlewild. Families, driving their 1930s automobiles up from Detroit, Toledo, and Chicago, as seen in the above postcard, stayed the summer months on the lake, some purchasing land for permanent homes. The Idlewild Club, accessed by a roadway to the island, was the center of activity for the community. The Purple Palace Nightclub and Paradise Club provided entertainment during the early years. Following World War II, Idlewild evolved into an entertainment mecca. (Above, courtesy of Jerry Poprawski; below, courtesy of Bruce Micinski.)

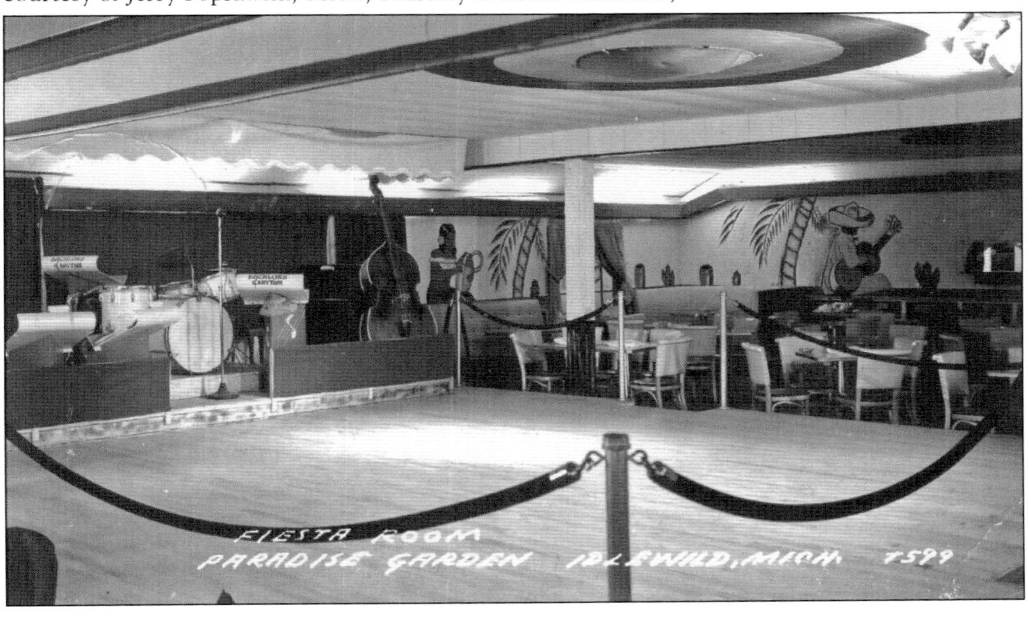

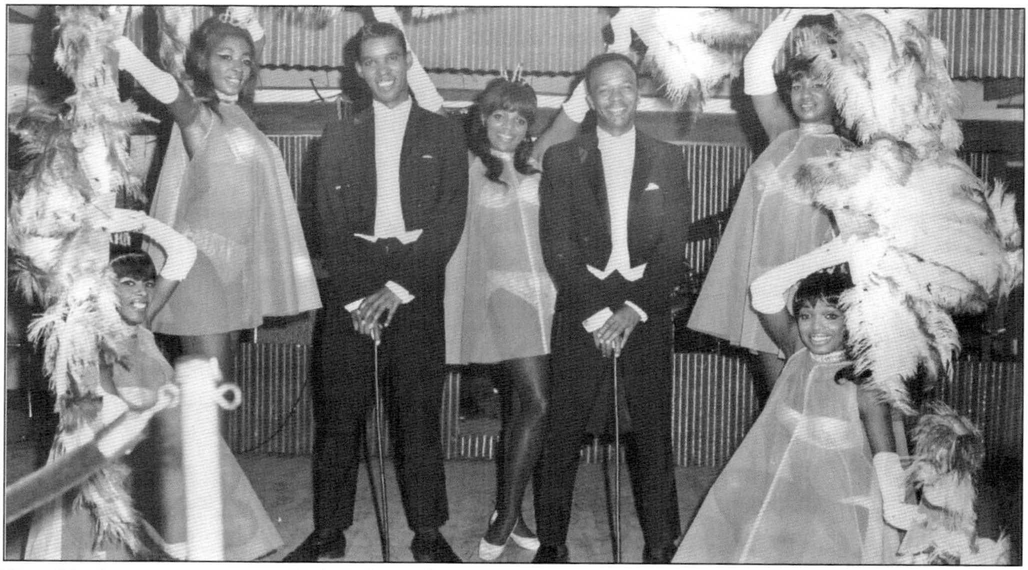

Two black entrepreneurs, Phil Giles, who opened the Flamingo Bar, and Arthur Braggs, who leased and managed the Paradise Nightclub, completed renovations to meet the increased demand for entertainment in Idlewild. Giles added a 500-seat room, creating the Flamingo Nightclub in 1955. These men hired famous talent for their classy shows such as T-Bone Walker, the Four Tops, and Jackie Wilson. In the above photograph, Poly Gore is pictured second from the left dancing with a group entertaining in the Flamingo Club. By the late 1950s, whites attended the clubs. Seen below, seated third and fourth from the left are Dotty and Edward Kreidler, with a group of unidentified friends, enjoying a show at the Flamingo Club. (Above, courtesy of Terri Jamison; below, courtesy of Diana Hipshier.)

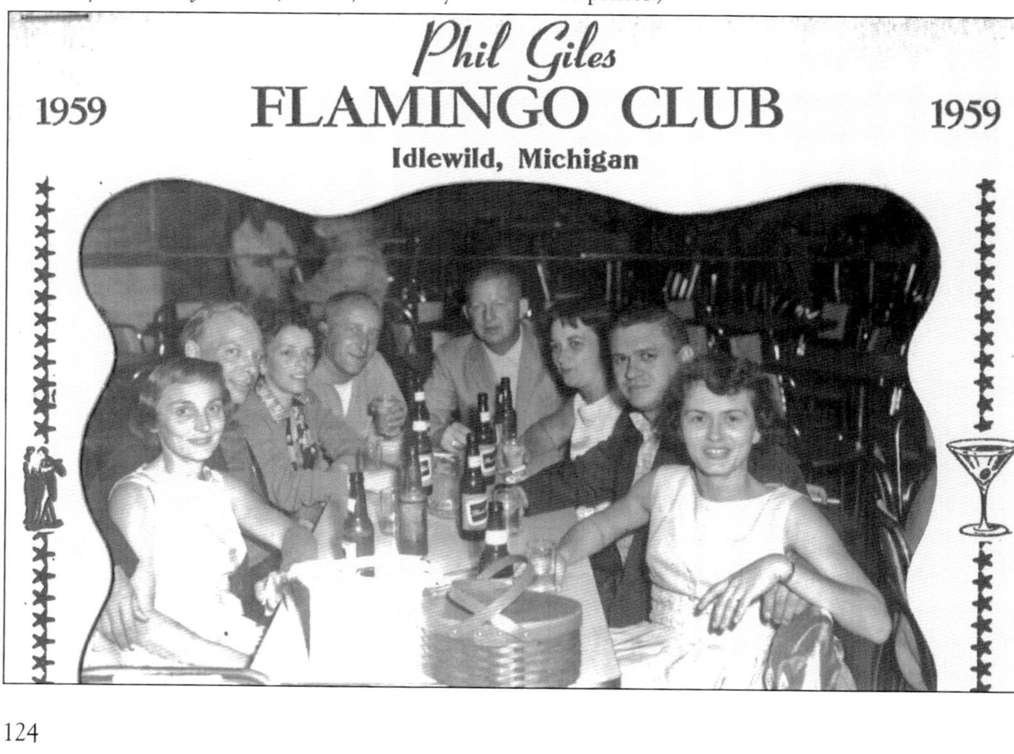

Raymond "Bud" Overholzer was a hunting and fishing guide, taxidermist, and woodworker who moved to Lake County from Ohio in 1920. In the late 1930s, he purchased property along the Pere Marquette River. In the next decade he began building a wildlife museum he envisioned as a lodge for 12 imaginary hunters, thus Shrine of the Pines began. The lodge was built using white pine, except for the floorboards, which were of red pine, and the original roof, which was thatch. The logs were notched and fitted by hand. Two free-form plate glass windows overlook the river and were cut to the natural contour of the roots that frame them. (Right, courtesy of Tennis Trucks; below, courtesy of Jill Engelman.)

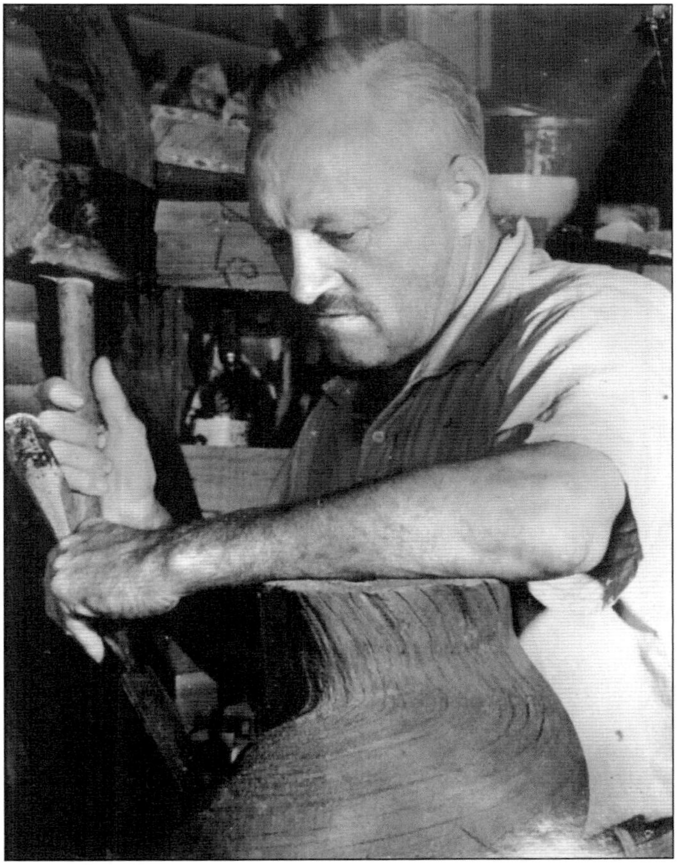

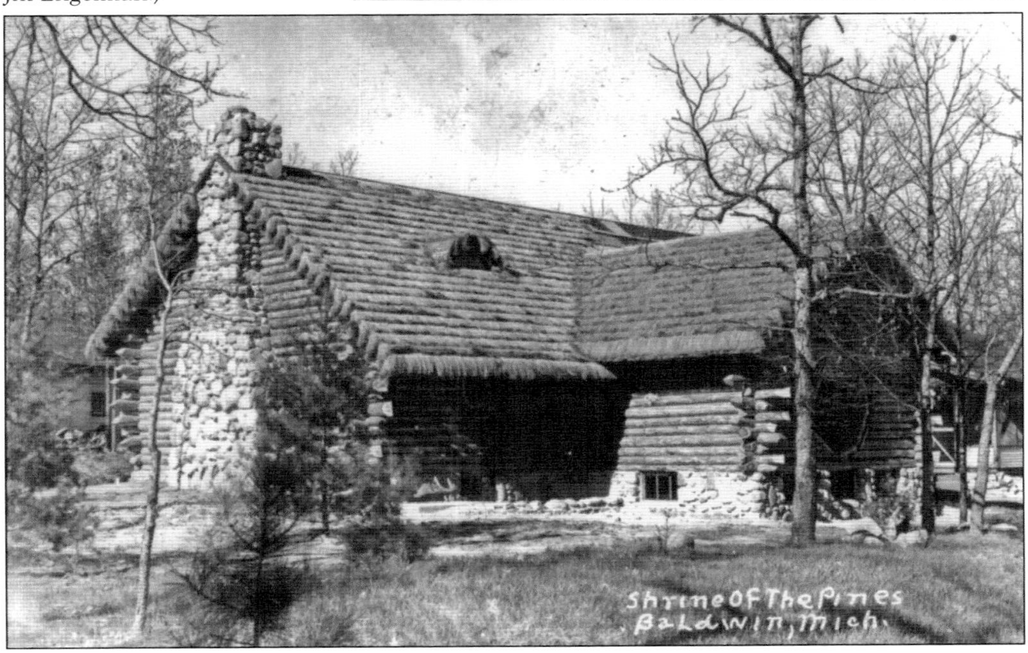

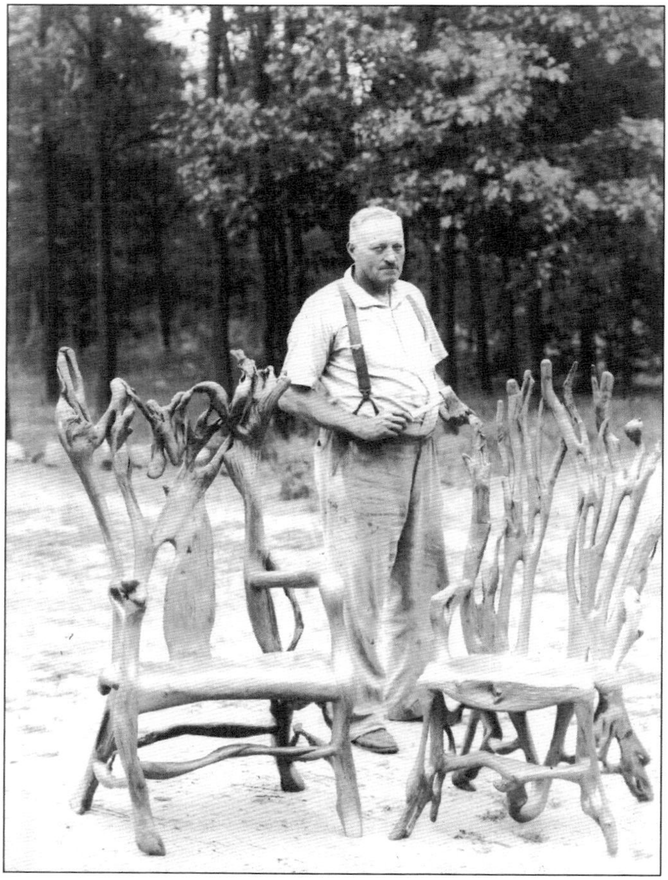

Each piece of furniture Raymond Overholzer fashioned for his lodge had to meet three criteria: each piece had to cost nothing, be made from white pine, and had to be useful. Much of the furniture was made using stumps and root structures that he found in the river and woods. He constructed a dining room table from a 700-pound stump. He also made 12 chairs, a poker table with a special seat guaranteeing a winning hand, and a bootlegger table with a secret drawer. Overholzer made a rocking chair for his wife, plus an assortment of side tables, fireplace chairs, beds, and a Shrine of the Pines sign, which he installed over an interior archway. (Left, courtesy of Paul Bigford; below, courtesy of Jill Engelman.)

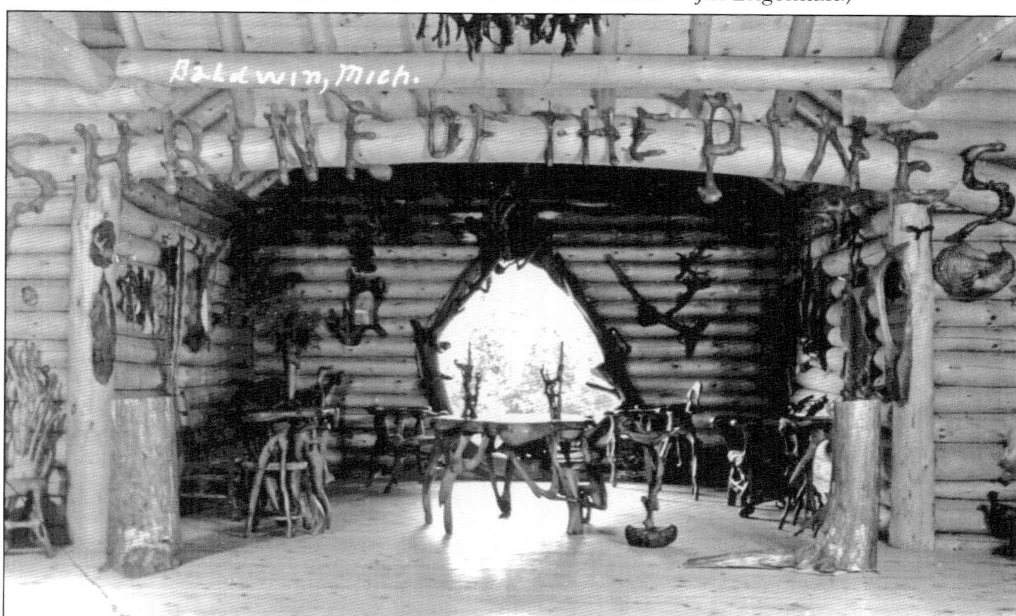

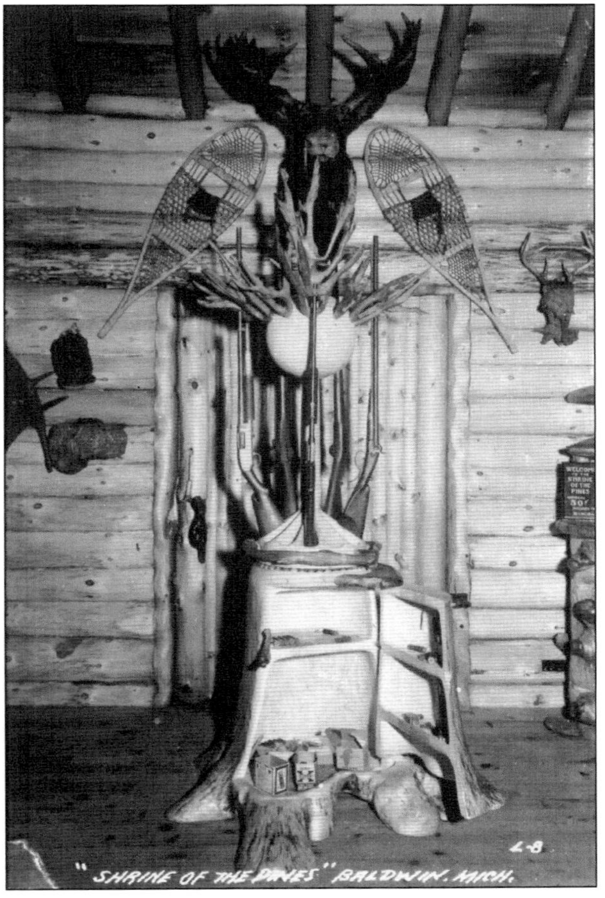

Raymond Overholzer did not like to go hunting with fewer than 11 other men, thus he built his gun rack to hold 12 guns. It was made of a white pine stump. The turret turns on 39 ball bearings, whittled and worked by hand. The ball at the top is solid pine. The door is a section of the stump, swinging on a floating hinge which leads to storage for ammunition. Overholzer used no wax, stain, or varnish on any of his furniture. Instead he used pine oil, deer hides, and maple sticks combined with elbow grease to rub the pine till it shone. Each piece of furniture is remarkable for its craftsmanship. Shrine of the Pines was opened to the public following Overholzer's death in 1952. It remains a Lake County gem. (Courtesy of Jill Engelman.)

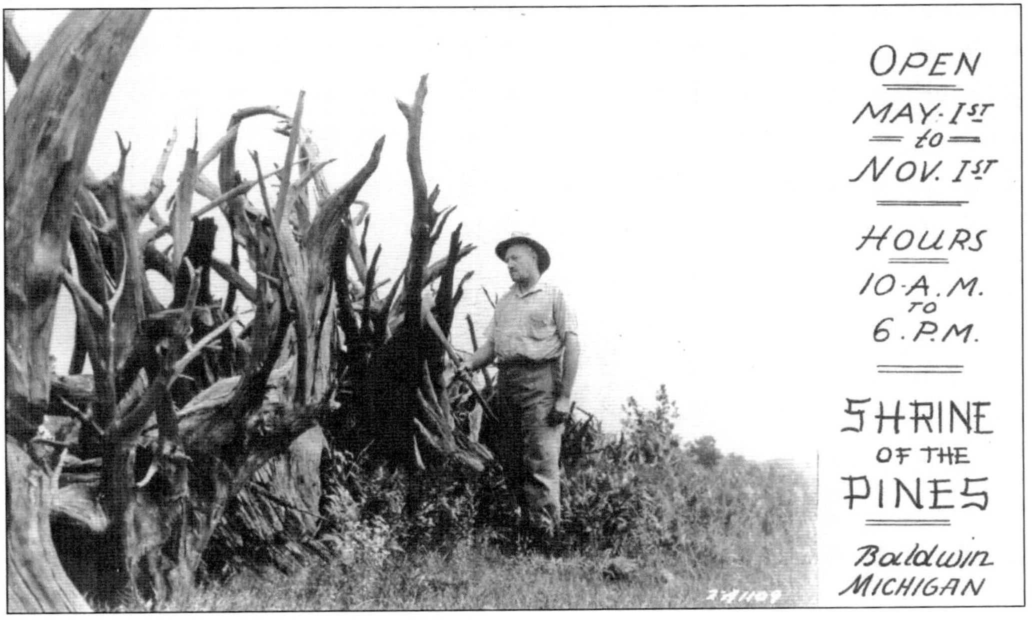

Consistent with our mission to preserve history on a local level, this book was printed in South Carolina on American-made paper and manufactured entirely in the United States. Products carrying the accredited Forest Stewardship Council (FSC) label are printed on 100 percent FSC-certified paper.